I.S.A.M. Monographs: Number 13

Richard Franko Goldman

Selected Essays and Reviews 1948-1968

EDITED BY DOROTHY KLOTZMAN

I.S.A.M. Monographs: Number 13

Richard Franko Goldman

Selected Essays and Reviews 1948-1968

EDITED BY DOROTHY KLOTZMAN

Institute for Studies in American Music
Department of Music
School of Performing Arts
Brooklyn College
of The City University of New York

Grateful acknowledgment is made to the following for use of articles reprinted in this collection. Complete citations will be found at the beginning of each article.

The American Scholar, for articles in Volume 35, Number 3, Copyright © 1966; Volume 36, Number 1, Copyright © 1967; by the United Chapters of Phi Beta Kappa. By permission of the publishers.

The Juilliard School, for articles in *The Juilliard Review,* Volume I, Number 1 (January 1954), Volume II, Number 3 (Fall 1955), and Volume VIII, Number 1 (Winter 1960-61).

The Musical Quarterly, for articles and reviews in Volume XXXIV, Number 4 (October 1948), to Volume LIV, Number 1 (January 1968).

Perspectives of New Music, for the article in Volume 4, Number 2 (Spring-Summer 1966).

Stereo Review, for articles in Volume 19, Number 1 (July 1967), and Volume 20, Number 4 (April 1968).

Further acknowledgments are made with gratitude to *The Musical Quarterly,* for granting permission to reprint photographically the music examples in articles from that journal, and to the publishers of the music, whose permission to reprint will be found in footnotes accompanying the examples.

Published by Institute for Studies in American Music
Department of Music, School of Performing Arts,
Brooklyn College of the City University of New York
Brooklyn, New York 11210

CONTENTS

Richard Goldman died in Baltimore on 19 January 1980, a few days after copy for this book was delivered to the printer. He had assisted in its preparation at every stage and was looking forward to its publication with keen anticipation. Mr. Carter's foreword was to have been a post-publication surprise for him, as was Professor Klotzman's preface. However, on learning the gravity of his illness, editor and publisher sent both foreword and preface to Mr. Goldman, ostensibly for proofreading. Thus not only did he write the book; he read with surprised pleasure its front-matter, which now must be viewed as not only celebratory but valedictory.

H. Wiley Hitchcock, Director
I. S. A. M.

FOREWORD

What a remarkable musical figure on the American scene is Richard Franko Goldman, conducting, as he has, New York City's finest outdoor concert band for many years, while making very important contributions to what some consider its opposite—"serious" music —as president of the Peabody Institute in Baltimore, as teacher at the Juilliard School, as writer, and as composer.

Taking over his father's famous band many years ago, he has been remarkably successful at maintaining its high standards of performance and of popularity, conducting brilliant free concerts in New York's parks and adding to the lively repertory of Sousa and Gold-man (father) marches and operetta overtures new works, commissioned from young Americans, which have given the popular audience a taste of the new. This progressive attitude is seen in his book *Harmony in Western Music,* in his renovations of the music teaching curriculum, in his general commitment to artistic excellence in the entire field of music, "light" or "serious," old or new (as expressed in the writings collected in this volume), and in his compositions—as well as the beautifully turned, apt English phrases of his translations of the short stories of the great Portuguese novelist, Eça de Queiroz. His impatience with, and even contempt for, the culture industry, which he saw—long ago—as a genuine threat to artistic excellence, is revealed in his polemic, "The Wonderful World of Culture *or: A Strictly Highbrow and Artistic Subject,*" attacking the point of view expressed in *The Performing Arts: Problems and Prospects—Rockefeller Panel Report on the future of theatre, dance, music in America* (1965).[†] In looking back on Goldman's strictures now, one realizes that his kind of protest has been so completely by-passed, so disregarded, that no one even questions that, as he remarks bitterly,

> . . . art and culture are [considered] special varieties of consumer goods, foods that are "enriched," to be marketed in conventional ways, "with all the resources of advertising and public relations." The spectacular difference is that it is morally virtuous to sell these goods, *because they are good for the consumer.* One merely has to persuade more consumers that this is so. . . .

[†]See pp. 245-49 of this volume.

. . . The *Report's* doctrine of equal talent: "As talent is needed to create and perform a work of art, so equal talent—though of a different sort—is needed to create and govern the institutions that provide the settings for these arts." There are—or are there?—perhaps just a few concerned with the arts who will not accept this equation of the talent of a Beethoven with the talent of a Board member, however carefully auditioned the Board member may have been.

The same no-nonsense attitude informs his book *Harmony in Western Music* and his extensive contribution toward the formulation of the "Literature and Materials" program of the Juilliard School. His approach enlivened musical education for Americans by deriving the study of musical techniques directly from the important works of musical literature rather than by doing the routined exercises formulated by musical theorists, which by the '20s and '30s had begun to seem irrelevant to the actual practices of composers of the past and even more so of those of the twentieth century. The return to sources in education was, of course, widespread then in America, where Great Books programs were taught from the original texts instead of from commentaries on them, and where practice in speaking and reading languages took precedence over memorizing conjugations and declensions. It took the bold, original thinking of musicians like Dick Goldman to apply this new point of view to the study of music, and once put into effect it affected American musicians in all fields and gave them a special native outlook.

Clarity, intellectual penetration, logic, and artistic awareness combined with a highly varied experience with, and an extensive knowledge of, music history were obviously necessary for the working out of such a project. These same qualities inform Dick's writings, which, for the most part, deal with contemporary music. It is these which make them such absorbing reading. To be a critic of the New York concert scene for the twenty years between 1948 and 1968 for *The Musical Quarterly,* during its editorship by the musicologist and journalist Paul Henry Lang, meant for Richard Goldman, as it did not for most of its other authors who wrote on new music, to adhere to the high standards characteristic of the best articles on older music that were the main concern of the periodical. During part of this time, Dick also founded, edited, and wrote for *The Juilliard Review* in order to give wider expression to his views. In these contexts his criticism had to appeal to readers accustomed to paying strict attention and able to reason logically, who expected intelligent, well-supported, informative, and thoughtful writing such as could not be found in most newspapers. Nowhere else, especially after the demise of *Modern Music,* could a reader expect to find new music so seriously dealt with during those years.

It is true that his views occasionally reflect opinions of the times, perhaps because of a lack of sufficient opportunity to hear and see certain new scores. For instance, there is his denigration of twelve-tone music *per se,* while admitting that the Viennese managed to make important use of the method; or his condemnation of Stravinsky's heterogeneity of styles in a work like *Perséphone,* while praising his work in general and pointing out in one essay the many excellences of the *Mass.* There is by and large much justice in what he has written and much useful clarification of musical principles, and a great sense of dedication to music that was and still is trenchantly important. One wonders how much of what is being written at present will stand up so well in ten or twenty years.

Indeed—to pursue such an elegiac thought—what has happened to those scores—like Riegger's *Third Symphony* and *First String Quartet,* or Dallapiccola's works—that once provoked such praise in these pages and elsewhere? Do we now have so many good scores that we can forget those so easily?

Elliott Carter

PREFACE

Richard Franko Goldman was born and educated in New York City, where, until he went to Baltimore as president of the Peabody Institute, he spent most of his long and distinguished career as a composer, conductor, author, and educator. His writing, which is an absolute joy to read, displays the richness of mind of the supreme intellectual whose grasp of the artistic and cultural issues of the time transcends the individual works, composers, and performances of which he speaks.

It is this extraordinary quality that has prompted the Institute for Studies in American Music to publish this collection of Goldman's essays and reviews on music that were written during the years 1948-68. The volume opens with an essay that Goldman wrote for the inaugural issue of *The Juilliard Review,* which he founded. In it, he sets the tone philosophically for everything that follows, from his major essays on the composers Wallingford Riegger, Percy Grainger, Elliott Carter, Henry Cowell, and John Philip Sousa, through his many articles from the Current Chronicle and Reviews of Records sections of *The Musical Quarterly,* to his last devastating indictment of the culture industry in "The Wonderful World of Culture *or: A Strictly Highbrow and Artistic Subject*" from *The American Scholar.*

For the most part, the articles appear in the order in which they were originally published. Three essays from *The Juilliard Review* are followed by writings from *The Musical Quarterly, Perspectives of New Music, Hi-Fi/Stereo Review,* and *The American Scholar.* Those from *The Musical Quarterly* have been placed into three sections: major essays, Current Chronicle articles, and Reviews of Records. Within each of these categories the work is presented in chronological order. While most of the recordings that were reviewed are no longer in print, the importance of the ideas that Goldman expresses about musical values demanded the reviews' inclusion. Only the most particular references to individual performances and to the technical quality of the recordings have been deleted.

The penultimate article, "Place An X to the Left of the Writer" from *The American Scholar,* was written after the final essay and is not strictly about music per se. Yet its message, written with the greatest good humor, is significant and fits so well with the values that concern Goldman in the rest of the volume that it had to be included here.

It is my belief that this collection of work by Richard Franko Goldman will provide the rich nourishment for the spirit that is essential for all serious musicians, scholars, and amateurs.

To my colleagues in the Institute, H. Wiley Hitchcock and Rita H. Mead, for their assistance, encouragement, and enthusiasm in this project, I owe my thanks; also to Frances Solomon, IBM Composer operator, who typed the camera-ready copy.

Dorothy Klotzman

The Juilliard Review

The Juilliard Review I/1 (January 1954)

Each age has intellectual and artistic battles that are in some ways peculiar to itself but that are, in other ways, permanent. It is worth noting that these are never won; however resolved, they give way to new aspects of old problems. But it is also worth remembering that the battle itself is the only real manifestation of cultural life and continuity. When struggle ceases, the Barbarians and Philistines will descend still further.

In many respects, nothing much has changed since Schumann's day, or Matthew Arnold's. The mediocre and the witless are always with us. A serious idea of art, and even a serious view of education, are pre-occupations of a buffeted minority. Seriousness is not the same as earnestness, of which there is plenty; the relation is the same as that of jargon to idea. An idea, to quote Ortega y Gasset's brilliant dictum, is putting a truth in checkmate; jargon is the counterfeit of idea, and the moral stigma affects equally those who accept and those who issue it.

Our own age, however, is in some ways radically different from any that has gone before, and presents us with a crisis in which seriousness itself, and the possibility of having or circulating ideas, require active defense. "The minority now is made conscious, not merely of an uncongenial, but of a hostile environment." This is F. R. Leavis' summation, in his penetrating essay "Mass Civilization and Minority Culture." The machine, and particularly the machines of mass communication, have made a difference so great that only a few can find strength to face the implications for things in which they believe.

Belief must be strong: belief in seriousness, belief that the greatest achievements of the human imagination are represented by the Mozart Symphony in itself and not by a High-Fidelity technique for reproducing it. The Mozart Symphony exists, continues, and represents what is best in human experience; it is this that is serious, this that symbolizes our values. It is this idea and this thing that matter and that would continue to matter even if all electronics were to disappear from man's knowledge.

Not that the machine does not have positive uses, or that it does not, though not invariably, convey benefits. It is not to be supposed that the 20th century, with the machine, is less fortunate than the 10th, without it. But Matthew Arnold read well the present and the future; and "Culture and Anarchy" bears re-reading. One cannot be confident that the future will take care of itself, and that the machine will serve us. "Teaching the democracy to put its trust in achievements of this kind is merely training them to be Philistines to take the place of the Philistines whom they are superseding; and they too . . . will be encouraged to sit down at the banquet of the future without a wedding garment, and nothing excellent can then come from them."

We cannot be indifferent; we have some responsibility for the future if there are any values that are still meaningful to us. And we cannot disguise from ourselves the implication that an age of machines, of rapid change, of quantitative values, an age of levelling, an age of inattention, makes the maintenance of these values both more difficult and more necessary. "To keep open our lines of communication with the future" was Arnold's faith in the early days of industrialism and cultural anarchy; how much more needful this faith is today seems evident.

The case of music is not divorced from the condition of other arts, nor from the state of language, nor from attitudes toward learning. In the abundance of distraction, the belief in quantity, the levelling for mass consumption of the great and the trivial, the task of acquiring discrimination, of maintaining a sense of that which expresses the finest consciousness of man, has become much more difficult. The machines—radio, film, and phonograph—seem to make art accessible and easy; they affect music in a special way, and reduce it, in a sense, to a species of useful noise. It would be false to say that music does not have a place in society today: it exists, if for nothing else, to feed these machines, and to prevent silence. For these machines the great and the trivial serve equally as fuel; but who would say that Beethoven does not deserve somewhat better than to be heard as an accompaniment to conversation, or as a salesman for vermouth?

The machines, in short, tend to make of art a vacuous entertainment—worse, a time-filling commodity aimed at the passive diversion of great numbers of people. And the machine, again to quote Leavis, "tends to make active recreation, especially active use of the mind, more difficult." There is no atmosphere in which a serious view of music as an art could find it harder to exist. It is true that we have "more music"; but we have no reason to believe that this is good for any except the salesmen. One is shocked, in this connection, to read recently the complacent pronouncement of the president of one of our leading universities hailing the fact that today there is *more education,* in terms of enrollment and number of degrees, than there has ever been before. One cannot argue with the mind that believes that addition or multiplication equals "progress"; there is no ground on which inquiry and sheer acquisitiveness can meet. Education can, like music, become a trade; we see evidence that both are, and that occasionally they can even be usefully so. But they are both more than trades; both involve the noble idea that "Excellence dwells among high and steep rocks, and can only be reached by those who sweat blood to reach her."

High art is excellence; it is not "the deliberate exploitation of the cheap response," nor is it to be perceived without effort. Our age is not alone in its preference for the second rate, in its easy encouragement of the talentless. It is alone in its second-handedness, in its increasing inattentiveness, and in its deep scorn for the "high-brow," a term of contempt for anything that has even the appearance of excellence in art, in language, or in manners. Its second-handedness demands that art be not made, in Cyril Connolly's phrase, "by the alone for the alone," but by "competent craftsmen" for the common man, with commentators, annotators, and explainers in attendance to make sure that neither the intellect nor the spirit is taxed. Its inattentiveness is natural; in an age of inescapable noise, of unprecedented assaults on all of his senses, man finds concentration difficult; the meanings of experience are, at the extreme, no longer felt directly, but must be explained if they are felt at all.

This is not the atmosphere for music, an art which exists at its highest in the minds, ears, eyes, and hands of those who are devoted to it. It requires both concentration and a favorable climate. That the art remains is due to devotion and conviction, but these are not enough. Conviction requires defense and counter-attack. Never have the uses of art been so debased as they are now; never has its status as a legitimate pursuit of man been so threatened. The support given music today is in part a false one that can be withdrawn in a second, and it is a support almost totally lacking in discrimination. In this last sense, it is more damaging than no support at all, for it reduces art to a question of purchase price and establishes this status in the minds of most people as the normal one. Music's support today is designed in many cases to impress the donors of money with a sense of having fulfilled their cultural obligations. Prince Esterhazy at least listened to Haydn's music and, from what we are told, appeared to enjoy it. He did not, it may also be noted, feel obliged to share his enjoyment with those who could not hear, or to convince the entire population of Hungary that listening outside the windows would make them "cultured."

For that is what the "audience" has perhaps become: a crowd of listeners outside the windows, somewhat removed from the scene, and listening for some reason that is entirely secondary, if, indeed, it is any reason at all. A state of music, or of art and life in general, is vigorous and meaningful when it depends on participation, and when there are countless devoted amateurs whose pursuit of an esthetic, a spiritual, or an intellectual satisfaction implies effort and patience. We may question that this amateur is still much with us, but our need of him is indeed desperate.

Percy Grainger's "Free Music"

The Juilliard Review II/3 (Fall 1955)

Nearly everyone, musical or not, knows *Country Gardens;* and it is probable that most people associate the name of Percy Grainger with that appealing piece. Grainger has a world-wide reputation, rather like that of Sousa or of Johann Strauss: each is a genial composer of pleasant music in a specialized vein. To have such a reputation is, undeniably, no sad fate, but in Grainger's case it is so partial a recognition of artistic accomplishment that one is forced to reflect on the obscurity created by the wrong kind of fame. Grainger has suffered in many respects through his own phenomenal success both as pianist and composer. Even musical people, at least those over the age of thirty, who remember Grainger as one of the great piano virtuosi, have a tendency to associate him more or less exclusively with the Grieg Concerto, of which he was almost the "official" interpreter, forgetting that Grainger's piano repertoire was vast and unorthodox, and that he was a superb performer of Bach, Chopin, and Debussy as well as of Grieg, Tchaikovsky, and Franck.

Grainger's last piano recitals in major cities took place some years ago, and he has thus to a degree been out of the public eye. His compositions, except for the perennially popular folk settings, have received little attention. There are no consequential Grainger recordings, which is greatly to be regretted, as to both piano playing and composition. Grainger, now seventy-three, has been living quietly, almost in retirement, for some time, working out a number of radical musical ideas about which he has been thinking for over half a century. It is the radical and experimental aspect of Grainger's musical activity that remains generally unknown, and it is precisely this that provides the key to understanding one of the most original and stimulating musical personalities of our time.

The interest now apparent in the experimental work of such composers as Harry Partch, Cage, Carter, Varèse, Boulez, Messiaen, Stockhausen, Nancarrow, and the many others engaged in problems of scale, rhythm, electronic resources, and so on has been created only in the past few years. The achievement of Charles Ives, too, is only now being recognized and evaluated. Grainger's work, which has something in common with that of these men, actually antedates all of them. Rhythmic problems attacked by Ives occupied Grainger at about the same time, or somewhat earlier, as did the concept of completely independent polyphonies. It may be said, without stretching fact, that Grainger and Ives had more than a little in common, both working in an atmosphere as close to willful independence as possible, and both anticipating later practices to a degree that amounted, in its time and place, to eccentricity. Grainger's thinking and experimenting were, however, combined with a virtuoso professionalism, embracing not only the art of piano playing but an immense and practical knowledge of almost every variety of sound-producing instrument, including the human voice, and a wide-ranging acquaintance with the music of the entire world. Where Ives was provincial, and an amateur, Grainger is neither; and on the whole, I should not hesitate to say that Grainger is quite simply the more musical.

To understand what Grainger has done, it is necessary to go back fifty-six years, and to retrace the relevant steps of his musical evolution. In 1899, when Grainger was seventeen, he first formulated clearly his thoughts about the limitations, in terms of pitch and rhythm, of traditional Western music. His first experiments with "beatless music" took place in that year. "Beatless music" he defined as "music in which no standard duration of beat occurs, but in which all rhythms are free, without beat-cohesion between the various polyphonic parts." He was convinced at this early date that the problems of rhythm and rhythmic notation in Western music required intensive thought, and that new resources could be introduced into common practice. Much of his time from 1899 to the present has been devoted to developing these ideas, and to studying the allied problems of mechanics and techniques that they engender, including "non-harmony," "gliding tones," and absolute independence of voices.

A split has always been evident in Grainger's activity, and it was already clearly marked in the compositions of his early years. The best known works are four-square, diatonic, rather Handelian in harmony and texture, but while these works were captivating audiences, Grainger was also sketching compositions of an intentionally impractical complexity, using a polyphony of twelve to twenty parts, with as much rhythmic freedom as conventional notation would allow. Because of the difficulties of both notation and performance, most of these have never been completed or performed, but many sketches have been preserved. They are the forerunners of Grainger's "free music" for which the means of execution has now been devised. At the same time—that is, beginning in 1899—Grainger began seeking a solution in irregular barring of the type that is now commonplace, but which was quite radical at the time. The *Love Verses from The Song of Solomon,* composed in 1899 for voices and chamber orchestra,[1] contain passages in which the meter shifts in such patterns as: 2/4, 2 1/2-4, 3/4, 2 1/2-4, 3/8, 2/4, 2 1/2-4, 3/4, 4/4. Grainger makes a distinction between 2 1/2-4 and 5/8, and between 1 1/2-4 and 3/8 (as in the *Hill Song* of 1901). The impetus for *The Song of Solomon* setting came, Grainger recalls, from his asking friends to recite the verses aloud. Noting the speech rhythms accurately, he attempted to give the melodic declamation the same rhythmic elasticity as the recitation.

---

[1] Like most of Grainger's compositions, the *Love Verses* were scored and published for a variety of alternative combinations. From his earliest years he has made remarkably effective use of conventional instruments in odd groupings as well as of unconventional

Much of what Grainger was writing in the first decade of the 20th century was in advance of its time in the way that Ives's music also was. We have it on the authority of Cyril Scott that Grainger, while still in his 'teens, began to "show a harmonic modernism which was astounding . . . and at times excruciating to our pre-Debussyan ears." Scott also notes that Grainger used the whole-tone scale before he was aware of Debussy, and independently arrived at much of Scriabin's vocabulary. One of his very early projects (not carried out) was to go to China in order to acquire first-hand knowledge of Chinese music. (He later acquired extensive knowledge of much non-Western music, and was one of the earliest to make recordings of "primitive" music.) His interest in complex polyphony led him naturally to an anticipation of polytonality, which he described, with his flair for anglicizing, as "double-chording" or the passage of unrelated chord groups through and around one another without regard for harmonic clash or tonal resolution.

Grainger's chief preoccupation at this time, and indeed continuously up to the present, was, however, with what he calls "free music," and most of his experiments with such techniques as irregular barrings and polychordal combinations led him away from, rather than towards, his goal. "Free music," in Grainger's definition, is free not only rhythmically, but free from the bondage of scales and fixed intervals. It is in this crucial respect that Grainger's thought differs from that of Busoni (who toyed with the idea of an 18-note scale) or that of Partch, with his 43-note scale. Although Grainger studied with Busoni, he did not become involved in theoretical speculation with him. "Free music" implies no scale, and *all intervals* from the tiniest micro-interval to the widest leap, but *not* arranged in a predetermined or necessarily related manner. It is, in a manner of description, a music of ideal curvilinear freedom and flexibility, lacking bar accents as well as tonal restriction.

If Grainger, at an early date, rejected the idea of new scales, *ragas,* or modes based on various subdivisions, he concentrated on the idea of melodic line, singly or in combination as polyphonic texture, as found in any or all existing modes. Those who know his music— and one must include even the simpler folk settings—are aware of the fine feeling for line that is everywhere evident. This sense of line characterizes Grainger's piano playing, as well as his conducting. The senses of line and texture, both innate, Grainger continued to develop over the years not only through his study of folk music—he claims that his instinct for melody was developed by the beauty and variety of "pure line" in English folk song— but also of Bach, the composer he most reveres, and eventually also of Renaissance and medieval music. Since 1933, he has been associated with Dom Anselm Hughes in a study of Gothic music. Grainger has edited and arranged works of Dowland, Jenkins, Josquin, Willaert, and others, for various instrumental and vocal combinations, always in his pursuit

instruments of all origins. His sense of timbre and sonority is remarkable, and he should be recognized as one of the most original and gifted "orchestrators" of our time.

of interesting polyphonic textures and rhythmic usages that lie out of the "harmonic" period. This has led to continued interest in so-called "primitive" and "exotic" music. Grainger is quoted by D. C. Parker as saying that the modern composer has as much to learn from Chinese or Zulu music as from Scarlatti or Schoenberg. It is worthwhile to note in passing that Grainger was aware of Schoenberg's work in the first decade of the century. He was one of the earliest admirers of the *Five Orchestral Pieces,* and expresses today, as he did over forty years ago, the greatest sympathy with Schoenberg's work.

From this brief outline of Grainger's formative studies and ideas, it should be apparent that he has ranged far and wide and that the seriousness of his interests and convictions is of very great force. His musical point of view can embrace Grieg and Schoenberg, Delius and Machaut, Chopin and Monteverdi, Scriabin and Stravinsky.[2] He is thus, in perhaps the truest and most meaningful sense of the word, a *modern*: his historical consciousness is highly developed and forms the basis for his explorations of techniques and materials. The restless spirit, searching past and present, reintegrating experience both interpretatively and creatively, is one of the distinguishing marks of the artist of our times.

II

Grainger's views, which he formulated as a youth and has steadily maintained, may be summed up as a conviction that the path of future musical development lies along the three lines of freer rhythms, gliding intervals (including, by definition, all gradations of the micro-interval), and greater dissonance. This conviction, with the possible exception of Grainger's advocacy of gliding intervals, is rather widely shared today, but one must credit Grainger with having formulated it more than fifty years ago. A study of some of Grainger's early and little-known scores will reveal experiments covering both the first and third aspects of development. For the exploitation of closer intervals, there has been (at least until recently) the limitation of Western notation and performing traditions. In his composing, however, Grainger's lines develop with increasingly sinuous chromaticism, to the point at which one is aware that the intervals between the half-tones must eventually become points of focus as well as points of passage. For that reason, Grainger became increasingly dissatisfied with the piano, and it was inevitable that his attention should be drawn to instruments capable of both true *glissando* and accurate control. In 1912, he became enthused over the possibilities of an instrument devised by a Dutch inventor, but he was never able to obtain the instrument for his own use. Grainger describes the instrument as a fore-runner of the Theremin, an instrument with which he later experimented. In 1937, he wrote out some of his own compositions for this instrument, but felt that it

[2]I am happy to record the fact that I was first directed to the works of both Schoenberg (*Five Orchestral Pieces*) and Stravinsky (*Piano Concerto*) by Mr. Grainger in the 1920's,

offered only a very partial solution, since it could satisfy pitch requirements of gliding intervals, but added no resources for the solution of rhythmic problems.

The rhythmic problems have come in for much attention on the part of American composers, including notably Ives, Cowell, Carter, and Brant. Cowell worked with Schillinger on the development of the Rhythmicon, an experimental instrument for producing complex polyrhythms. This worked, however, without pitch, and offered only the suggestion, if that, of a practical solution. Carter's work is discussed by William Glock in a recent issue of *The Score* (No. 12, June 1955); in the same issue Carter himself writes on *The Rhythmic Basis of American Music,* with particular attention to Ives and to Conlon Nancarrow. Nancarrow's work, as Carter points out, is hardly known. It exploits the possibilities of composing directly, by patient measuring and perforation, on player-piano rolls. It is curious that this should now be brought to our attention, for Grainger also discovered this method, at a time when Nancarrow was still a child. Needless to say, Grainger's and Nancarrow's results and aims are not identical, yet they are strangely parallel. This parallel exists also between Grainger on the one hand, and Ives and Brant on the other, in the area of unrelated or uncoordinated rhythm.

Since no known human performers can at present cope successfully with the envisaged complexities and intricacies of possible polyrhythmic or uncoordinated rhythmic combinations, especially when these are further combined with small or gliding intervals, most experimenters have turned to mechanical means. (It is of course possible that live performers will eventually acquire the necessary techniques; but this is not likely in the immediate future.) In about 1944, Grainger joined forces with a young scientist named Burnett Cross, and together Cross and Grainger have developed an apparatus that will produce the gliding intervals and desired rhythms of "free music." The apparatus is essentially a "composing instrument," and it is important to make this distinction in order to differentiate its principle from those of the Theremin or the Ondes Martenot, which are performing instruments. The Cross-Grainger instrument will "read" what is written by the composer and fed to it by him. Since, at least in its present stage, it is too cumbersome to transport, it may best be used in conjunction with tape or disc recordings; that is, the "free music" ("free" but *composed*) may be recorded in permanent form, to be used either with or without other instruments or performers.

Composing "free music" with this instrument is mechanically simple, but there is no bound to the imaginative and aural ingenuity that may, or perhaps must, be employed. One can, at least in theory, "write" out a simple four-part chorale; or one can write out a piece using gliding intervals, in which the voices have completely free and uncoordinated rhythms. In practice, someone completely unschooled might produce "free music" experimentally,

---

when I was a young student. Grainger wanted very much at the time to perform the Stravinsky *Concerto* with a major orchestra.

or by accident, without even attempting to imagine in advance what the resulting sound might be like: the purest kind of paper music is possible. But of course, any end may also be accomplished by design, provided that the composer can really hear micro-intervals, and can think in free rhythms.[3]

The machine consists of two parts, the first of which is basically a set of oscillators, each of which is set to produce a range of pitch covering about three octaves. The pitch is varied by the elevation of a control rod which follows a moving track. Volume is controlled similarly, but independently; thus each voice has two controls: pitch and volume. The music is written in graph form, in rising and falling curves of varying depth and grade. (See accompanying sketches, made by Grainger in 1952.) On the present scale of operation, Grainger and Cross are using large sheets of brown paper, with one-half inch representing a half-tone. This gives ample scope for minute measurements of "drawing" and hence of pitch control: 1/16 inch equals 1/16 tone for example; decimal or other measurements may of course also be used. Thus:

The reader will see that rhythm can be easily calculated and controlled by horizontal measurements, and that any *duration* of sound, or combination of durations in various voices, can be achieved by simple linear measurements from left to right. Rests can be produced by the use of contact-breakers. The *speed* of playing is at present controlled manually, but Grainger concedes that for a finished composition it would be well to have the machine run by a mechanism that would ensure absolute evenness of performance at the speed designed by the composer. All voices are of course fed simultaneously. At the present stage, the instrument will accommodate four independent voices.

The greatest difficulty so far has been the production of skips without *glissando*. A minute break in continuity is necessary for almost any skip, even of a half-tone; for small intervals this can be made relatively imperceptible, but it is noticeable for large ones. To take care of this difficulty, the inventors have devised a supplementary mechanism, which can be can be used in conjunction with the oscillators or separately. This consists of what is basically a large reed-box, or giant harmonica, with reeds tuned in eighth-tones, and with air-power provided (at this experimental stage) by a vacuum cleaner. Over this box is rotated paper with accurately measured perforations; the principle is exactly that of the

---

[3]There have been other experiments in "drawing" music which is translated directly into sound, notably those of Norman McLaren in composing music directly on sound film.

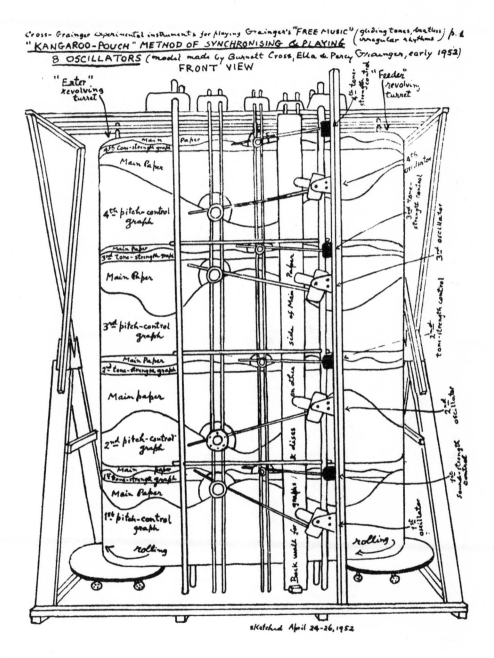

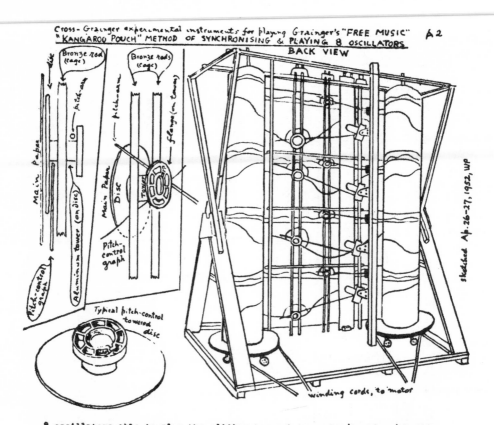

Sketched Ap. 26-27, 1952, WP

Bronze rod (cage)

Bronze rods (cage)

Main Paper

Pitch-control tower (on disc)

Aluminium tower

Aluminum tower

Platinum

Flange (on tower)

Main Paper Disc

Tower

Pitch-control graph

Pitch-control graph

Typical pitch-control towered disc

winding cords, to motor

8 oscillators, able to play the gliding tones & irregular(beatless)rhythms of Grainger's FREE MUSIC(first thought of around 1892),are manipulated by paper graphs,towered discs & metal arms. A sheet of light brown wrapping paper, 80 inches high(called "Main Paper"),is rolled continuously from the "Feeder" revolving turret onto the "Eater" revolving turret,passing thru a metal cage on its way(the cage keeps the Main Paper,the graphs & the discs in place).

Each of the 8 oscillators has its own special pitch-control graph & sound-strength-control graph. To the front of the Main Paper are attached 4 pitch-control graphs(mauve & greenish paper)& 4 tone-strength-control graphs(pinkish paper),their top edges cut into "hills & dales" in accordance with the inter-vals,glides & tone-strengths desired. These graphs operate oscillators 1,2, 3,4. To the back of the Main Paper are attached 4 addtional pitch-control graphs & 4 additional tone-strength-control graphs,operating oscillators 5,6, 7,8. The bottoms of these 16 graphs are sewn onto the Main Paper at various heights,but the top of each graph is left unattached. Into each pouch thus formed(between the Main Paper & the graph paper)is inserted a towered disc,the tower riding upon the top edge of its graph & following its up & down movements. These movements are passed on to the axle & tone-strength-control box of each oscillator by means of metal arms,causing whatever changes in pitch & volume are intended. The blue-&-white discs controlling tone-strengths are smaller than the variously colored discs controlling pitch. In the above sketches the connecting electric wires are not shown.

player-piano roll composition with which Grainger experimented much earlier. With this reed-box, limitless voices are added to the potential, and skips may be executed easily.

Grainger emphasizes that his whole concept of "free music" is evolutionary, and that it has a direct connection with existing music, which it is intended to supplement and extend. To illustrate his thesis, he is at present writing graphs for selected passages from Wagner (opening of *Tristan*), Grieg, Scriabin, and other composers. Among the graphs are also excerpts from Cyril Scott's *Quintet,* which employs gliding chords, and Arthur Fickenscher's *From the Seventh Realm.* [4] Of his own compositions, Grainger has so far graphed only a few experimental sketches. These have been heard only by a few friends, but it is hoped that the instrument will be sufficiently perfected, and the "repertoire" sufficiently demonstrable before very long, so that it can be seen and heard by interested musicians. Grainger feels that all of this is still very much in the stage of development, and he is not impatient. He insists also that this electronic realization of his very early hopes is not an end in itself; it is a possible adjunct to note-composition and live performance, but not a substitute. The advent of the Electronic Synthesizer, developed by Dr. Olson and his associates at RCA's Princeton laboratories (see *The Sound and Music of The RCA Electronic Music Synthesizer.* RCA-Victor: LM-1922 Experimental) suggests such a vision on the part of engineers, but it is hardly one to be shared enthusiastically by musicians. At any rate, Grainger's point of view about his "free music" is a musical one, in which the technique by which it is to be achieved is secondary. With technicians, and even occasionally with musicians, the means tend to become the end. Grainger's interest is not the machine itself, but the possibility of realizing in actual sound the complex "beatless" or completely free-rhythmed polyphony that he has heard in his mind's ear without ever having been able to notate or perform it with conventional techniques. With the interest in micro-intervallic music and complex rhythmic problems evident today, it is a fairly safe assumption that further development, both musical and technical, will continue. How great Grainger's contribution in this field will eventually be, remains to be seen; but we have in the first practical demonstrations of "free music" a challenging accomplishment by one of the great musicians of our time.

---

[4] Arthur Fickenscher (1871-1954) was an American composer of experimental tendencies who invented an instrument which he called the "Polytone." He was for many years head of the music department of the University of Virginia.

The Copland Festival
Juilliard Review VIII/1 (Winter 1960-61)

Aaron Copland's sixtieth birthday was altogether a heart-warming occasion. In an age
which seems to seek pretexts for celebrations, festivals, holidays, commemorations, and
every other variety of public activity, it was pleasant to have an occasion that really meant
something to everyone. The most striking aspect of the Copland birthday was not so much
that the composer was honored, as that he was honored with sincerity and with affection.
There seemed to be nothing perfunctory, nothing grudging, nothing of the merely dutiful
about the expressions, both public and private, that the occasion brought forth.

Juilliard could have done nothing more fitting (and, I should think, nothing more gratifying to all associated with the School) than to present the two concerts of Copland's
music on November 14th (the composer's birthday) and the following evening. For a composer is first of all his music: in some cases, where the personality of the composer is unknown, or unpleasant, it is easy to remember this. But with a composer whose activities
have been as varied as Copland's, and whose image as a public figure is as vivid, we need
to be reminded that the essential creative activity gives meaning to everything else. Not
that the "everything else" in Copland's case is unimportant. We should all be the poorer
without his teaching, his criticism, his efforts on behalf of contemporary music, of American composers, without the kind of moral leadership he has exerted for over thirty years.
But we should be poorer still without the essential Copland that exists only in a wide range
of scores.

When Aaron Copland emerged, in the early Twenties, as a young composer of promise,
there was only "modern music" itself as a cause, or a conviction, or a way of life. Today,
we have a rather large variety of modern musics. But I do not think that anyone, however
committed to a modern music developing along lines quite different from Copland's, would
deny that he has been, and is, our most important, our most representative, American composer up to now. He is in many ways still the most original, and has surely been, in matters
of style and idiom, our most influential voice.

To speak of matters of style in Copland's case may seem to involve an element of contra-
diction, for the superficial sounds of Copland are several. *The Tender Land* does not have
the same idiom as the *Piano Fantasy,* nor does the Sextet much resemble *Appalachian
Spring.* There is a "severe" Copland, and an amiable one; one might even say there is a
Western Copland and an Eastern one. But all of these works speak authentically and

individually; they are related by a habit of musical thought, a conciseness of utterance, a spareness of sound, a lack of grandiloquence and a real originality of melodic and harmonic material. What may appear to be two, three, or even four Coplands are really one.

The two Juilliard concerts were particularly successful in making this evident. A wide range of Copland's music, representing all aspects of his work except the jazz pieces (Piano Concerto; *Music for the Theater*), gave us all a happy occasion to review a musical contribution which is in effect the basis of any "American school" that may be said to exist. This is obvious in the cases of "American" works such as *Rodeo*, the stage music in general and *Music for the Theater*; but listening again to a work like the Piano Variations, written thirty years ago, one realizes also how immensely powerful a shaping force it was, how vivid an impression it made when first we heard it, and how vivid that impression has remained. This work, just as surely as *Appalachian Spring*, and perhaps in a larger way, is a real landmark in American music.

The two concerts allowed us to hear again some works not often presented: the score for the documentary film *The City*, the Sextet, and *In the Beginning*. One wonders how *The City* appeared, socially, cinematically, and musically, to the young in the audience. Films are perhaps the least durable of period pieces; but how many better film scores have ever been composed than this one? And how unmistakable its sound, and that of the Sextet! From the first bar one knows that this is Copland, and no one else.

But this is true of all the works heard on the two programs. It is interesting to reflect, at this point in time, on the corruption our ears have experienced through the many varieties of imitation Copland that have been presented to us, and on the unmistakable distinction of the real thing. In this way again, the unity of Copland's work becomes more apparent, for the personal quality is as clear in the Piano Fantasy or the Sonata as it is in *The City* or in *In the Beginning*. And one can take pleasure also in noting how well all of these works stand the passage of time. The Fantasy seemed, especially in the brilliant performance by William Masselos, an even stronger and greater piece than it did when first heard at Juilliard three years ago. The Variations remain, after a much longer career, among the great keyboard works of our time.

The entire second concert, devoted to Copland's major piano works, was a fascinating and memorable event: the thanks of all are again to be tendered to Paul Fromm and the Fromm Foundation, who sponsored the evening jointly with the School.

The birthday greetings are now in the past; the celebration was a happy one for all, and most of all, one hopes, for the composer, to whom we are all indebted in so many ways. Most of his music, fortunately, is firmly established in the current repertoire; and we all look forward to the works still to be written. No composer among us has made his mark as widely among the diverse publics of our time; none has written as effectively in every medium from "advanced" chamber music to accessible works for high-school performance; none has succeeded so well in the little hall and on the large stage. And none has added the weight of his influence as teacher and author more successfully to the sum of his activities as composer.

Copland's new book, entitled simply *Copland on Music,* was published by Doubleday and Company on the composer's birthday. The volume contains an assortment of essays, lectures, and random jottings covering a period of many years. Most of these have not previously appeared in collected form. It is a pleasant and instructive book to read; the pleasure and the instruction are afforded equally to the musician and the member of the audience. Copland has always had a certain serenity, a result of an attitude of what may be called impassioned tolerance, and this quality illuminates all of his writing on music. He is deeply committed, truly *serious*; but he remains open-minded and charitable. His accounts of himself, his estimates of other composers, his opinions in many areas of musical esthetics and technique, are all informed by honesty, modesty, and sound knowledge. Furthermore, although he would be the first to deny it, Copland is a real writer; his book, like his music, has style.

At the beginning of an essay written in 1949, Copland declares that he always instinctively thought of himself as part of a "school" of composers. This seems in many ways to be a curious statement. Although Copland clearly and sincerely believes in a *community* of music and musicians, it is the mark of his importance as a composer, and of his importance to us, that he appears today with an identity easily distinguishable from all others of his generation. If there is a school, it can be indeed only the one of which he is the undisputed leader.

The Music of Wallingford Riegger
Musical Quarterly XXXVI/1 (January 1950)

Wallingford Riegger's music has never been widely popular or often performed, nor has it had the critical recognition it plainly deserves.[1] His position as a leading figure among active American composers has, it appears, been acknowledged by inattention or, in some quarters, granted with an uncomfortable reluctance. To compose music is apparently not enough: in the helter-skelter of organizations, pronouncements, publicity, popularization, and glamorizing that characterizes musical life in a modern world, it is often necessary to have been favored by an aggressive nature or an aggressive sponsorship to arrive decisively; and it seems particularly necessary to have written a few exaggerated works for perform-ance by the loudest orchestras or on the most fashionable stages. Riegger is a quiet man in a noisy world; he has enunciated no principles, demanded no "rights," made no claims, and written nothing that substitutes size for content. His energy has flowed into the cre-ation of music which is unlike that of anyone else, which has an extraordinary quality at-tained by invention and discipline, and which owes nothing to fashion or the desire to reach an audience by means of shock or false simplicity. Riegger's music, striking in its vigorous individuality, has clarity without naïveté, force without bombast, resourceful-ness without pedantry, independence without rootlessness, and vitality without boyish-ness. This shy man, ill at ease in the society that career necessitates, lacks only jargon and grandiloquence.

For many years, however, Riegger's music has commanded the respect of a number of people who know it in score or performance. The Pan American Association of Compos-ers, founded by Varèse, Chávez, and Cowell in 1927, included Riegger in its group of im-portant radicals, and he has been closely associated with the *New Music Quarterly*. Re-cently, the circle of admirers has grown, and a certain measure, not quite of popularity, but certainly of awareness of his unique quality, has been granted him. His music early attracted attention in Europe, where he still, perhaps, receives more of his due than he does at home. Lately, in the United States, his admirers have been largely among the young, and, not unimportantly, among music students, who have discovered in him a sig-nificance, an integrity, and a mastery worthy of study. If Riegger's name is known at all to the larger musical public in the United States, it is probably because his Third Symphony

---

[1]Published material on Riegger is scant: an autobiographical piece in the *Magazine of Art* (1939); an excellent article by Henry Cowell in *Musical America*, Dec. 1, 1948; scattered reviews and mentions in books and periodicals. No magazine has given him the attention usually accorded composers who have "arrived."

received the New York Critics Circle award in 1948. From the standpoint of publicity (which is surely the goal of some creative effort) this award is doubtless worth a number of performances; and one may hope so indeed, since the Symphony, except for its pre-mière at the Columbia University Festival, has not received a single performance by a major American orchestra or conductor.[2]

One must face a fact in musical life: that composers are able to succeed with effects rather than substance and often yield to the temptation to do so. Bad-boy music (it being symptomatically "progressive" at times to say dirty words in public) attracts attention; slickness draws applause; and chauvinism applied to musical composition, whether it be oratorical or simply folksy, is supposed to rouse the common audience. One need not consider these means debasing, but one must observe that Riegger has never utilized them as a way of establishing contact. Perhaps because his music is written for adults, the real-ization of his stature continues to grow slowly. But it grows surely, none the less, and per-haps more enduringly for the lack of expedient extraneities in his music. It is time that his position among his contemporaries be recognized as a significant one.

"My advent as a composer," Riegger once wrote, "could hardly be described as meteoric." He appeared, as a matter of record, at the late age of thirty-five, as the sound, conservative, and unremarkable composer of a Trio in B minor for piano, violin, and 'cello, excellently styled in a late Romantic idiom and entirely appropriate for performance at genteel gath-erings. This work won the conservative Paderewski Prize in 1921 and the benediction of publication by the Society for the Publication of American Music. It is hard to imagine a less meteoric advent. There are, however, two noteworthy things about the Trio: it is the work of a man not lately come to composing, but with sufficient conscience not to take his student efforts as worth the world's attention, and it is a work clearly professional in craftsmanship, which says what it has to say with great sureness: instead of trying to be something, it *is* something.

Riegger was raised in that 19th-century German atmosphere which recent history has quite successfully obscured. Discipline, work, and duty, both practical and moral, were at the core of a family life in which love of music and literature was also central; so that in the best sense communication with high ideas existed independently of geographical accident, which happened, at the time of Riegger's birth, on April 29, 1885, to be Albany, in the state of Georgia. Constantin Riegger, the father, was at heart a musician, although he

---

[2] Hermann Scherchen, however, has done it a number of times in Europe; it was also one of the most impressively praised works performed at Palermo during the dodecaphonic congress.

owned a lumber mill; he played the violin and had an idea of the world to which it gave access. The family moved to Indianapolis when the son was three. There his father directed the choir of the Second Presbyterian Church and Riegger, at the age of eight, began to study the violin with an old pupil of Spohr. There was always music in the house, with the whole family participating, for the mother (*née* Ida Wallingford) was an accomplished pianist and the sons received encouragement as well as instruction. The musical atmosphere of the home was wholly orthodox as to taste, but decidedly unaffected; that its level of accomplishment was not mediocre may perhaps be gathered from the future composer's surprise when he learned that not everyone has absolute pitch.

When the Riegger family moved to New York in 1900, Wallingford took up the 'cello so that the family could have its own string quartet. Sunday afternoons were devoted to rehearsals of Haydn, Mozart, and Beethoven; but the family always remained attached to the idea of music as an end rather than a means of life, and it was planned that Wallingford should enter his father's business upon completion of high school. However, he won a scholarship to Cornell, where he spent one year before finally determining to make music his profession. Entering the Institute of Musical Art as a 'cello student in 1905, he was graduated with the first class two years later. His first lessons in composition were received at that time from Percy Goetschius, of whom Riegger still speaks with admiration.[3] The following year saw the beginning of Riegger's real *Lehrjahre* in Germany, where he became a 'cello student of Robert Hausmann at the Hochschule in Berlin, and acquired orchestral routine as a player in numerous ensembles. Conducting as well as composition attracted the student, who worked hard at counterpoint, memorized scores, and carefully observed Nikisch and Richard Strauss in action.

Some years ago, Riegger wrote an engaging paragraph of retrospect on that period. Viewing his five hours a day devoted to the 'cello, and the one hour each to piano and counterpoint, he discussed his emergence from provincialism through avid reading of the German classics, haunting of museums in all spare moments, through the endeavor to acquire languages and to pursue poetry and philosophy. With all this, he felt that he wanted to compose; and he wrote:[4]

---

[3] "And let me warn you, most earnestly," Goetschius wrote Riegger in 1907, "to avoid the teachings of the ultra-modern school. If you will build your foundation on the principles of the *classic* ideals, you will (if diligent) one day attain the master's rank."

[4] In *The Magazine of Art,* August, 1939.

What I was doing all along was basically an act of evasion. To compose, to create, requires a degree of integration which I did not then possess. A passion for perfection made me ultra-critical of every note; besides which, I had not resolved the conflict between the old and the new. In my childhood experiments at the keyboard I had invented whole-tone chords (literally invented, not having been exposed to any) and yet the home influence and all my training had been along orthodox lines. The Hochschule had made me a confirmed Brahmsite; I revelled in the works of the classic and for that matter the romantic period, and falsely construed them in the light of norms in my own creative undertakings—or to put it bluntly, I blushingly admit to having upheld at that time the good old academic tradition, so much so that at the first Berlin performance of Scriabin's *Poème de l'extase* I hissed exactly in the same manner as did the Philadelphia boxholders twenty years later when Stokowski gave my own *Study in Sonority*.

Riegger gradually was drawn more and more to conducting, and made his professional début in 1910 with the Blüthner Orchestra of Berlin, conducting the Tchaikovsky Sixth and the Brahms Third, and accompanying Anton Hekking, then his teacher, in the Concerto for 'Cello of Saint-Saëns. After an interlude in the United States, Riegger returned to Germany in 1914 to conduct opera at Würzburg and Königsberg; for the season of 1916-17 he was engaged as one of the regular conductors of the Blüthner Orchestra, but the war terminated all these activities. Riegger returned to the United States, found no possibility of an engagement as conductor (except for a guest appearance with the San Francisco Symphony in October 1917, which gained an excellent press), and accepted a position as head of the theory and 'cello departments at Drake University in Des Moines, Iowa, where he also conducted the school orchestra.

II

All of this was background for a musician who had neither embraced nor abandoned the career of composing. While in Berlin, he had studied with Max Bruch and with Edgar Stillman Kelley, and had written an *Elegie* for 'cello and orchestra, performed by Hekking, and a few small pieces, to which he rightly attached no importance. It was at Drake University in 1919-20 that Riegger made his first sustained creative effort, the B minor Trio, Opus 1. Riegger admits that this was not easily written; that it was, in fact, written and re-written with many doubts, trials, and pains. He wondered "why I should wish on myself the most difficult task in the world," and was possibly inhibited by a half-conscious feeling that the world had no need of another Trio which would, perhaps, delight only Goetschius. In any case, the recognition given the work encouraged its composer, who came East in 1922,[5] to write more; and in 1923 his setting of Keats's *La belle dame sans merci,* for four voices and chamber orchestra, received the Elizabeth Sprague Coolidge Prize for chamber music. It was the first work by an American to be so honored.

Immediately after this period, Riegger undertook a reconsideration of his musical beliefs, with decisive results. From 1923 to 1926 he completed no new work. His "early period" had already come to an end, with four works to show and none likely to embarrass him; two of them, moreover, had won important prizes. Of the others, the *American Polonaise* (1922) had received a respectable première at the Lewisohn Stadium concerts; *Whimsy* (1920) was in the catalogue of an eminently conservative publisher. It is possible that Riegger was about to become a composer with a relatively straight path to popularity and rewards. But he preferred to develop himself rather than his career. In three years a good deal happened inwardly; except for a piano piece (*Blue Voyage,* oddly impressionistic), the first works to appear at the end of that period were the atonal *Rhapsody* (one of Riegger's few works for large orchestra) and the radical *Study in Sonority* for ten violins or any multiple of ten.

It is evident that much thought and much self-questioning had preceded the composition of the *Study,* in which Riegger's personal style is not merely announced, but thoroughly realized. It is the key to his later work, the features of style remaining characteristic. Riegger relied on a purely arbitrary invention, tested only in his ear, of dissonant harmonies of motion and repose ("dominant" and "tonic" in function), and sought in the discovery of new tonalities and textures, both harmonic and contrapuntal, unexplored possibilities of formal structure. One notes in the *Study* an alternation of unison melody with harmonies of thick texture and extreme dissonance; the frequent occurrence of augmented melodic intervals, and of major and minor harmonic seconds; an insistent and hammering rhythm, often of repeated notes or chords, setting off melodic curves of much grace. Lastly, one remarks a virtuoso knowledge of strings that never ignores the practical aspects of performance, but produces sonorities of exquisite freshness.

The *Study* opens, as do many of Riegger's later works, with the unison presentation of a motif, contrasted with a chordal pattern, both melodic and harmonic elements clearly

---

[5]Riegger taught for a time at The Institute of Musical Art, and later at the Ithaca Conservatory.

announcing the basic material of the entire work.[6]

Ex. 1

The "dominant" harmony may be analyzed as two interlocking seventh chords, on B and
B♭ respectively,[7] suggesting a polytonality which, at the same interval, appears later:

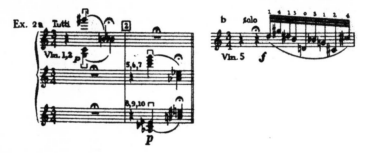

Ex. 2a

This polytonality of course produces, or is the result of, the seconds that figure so prom-
inently in Riegger's harmonic thought.

The *Study* was first misnamed "Caprice for Ten Violins," and still lacks a satisfactory
title; while Riegger may have felt that it was the fruit of exploration or study, there is
nothing either capricious or tentative about it. It is brilliantly logical in its development,
economical of material, stunning in sound. If it is a "Study," it is a study in more than
sonority, and it is a study successfully completed, the work of a composer who has solved,
rather than merely posed, his problem. It appears to be (but is not) the work of a man
who has spent three years in a thoughtful, and by no means parasitical, study of Schoen-

---

[6]The examples from the *Study in Sonority* are copyrighted by G. Schirmer, Inc. Used by
permission.

[7]Another possible analysis is that of three triads with roots a major second and an augmented fourth apart (D-E-B♭). These are intervals much exploited by Riegger. In atonal
music the spelling of sharps and flats sometimes provides a complication for the eye.

berg. Riegger's acquaintance with Schoenberg's theories was in fact limited at this time to general notions derived from casual readings and to conversations with Adolph Weiss. His approach to atonality, and this is crucial in the discussion of Riegger's work, was entirely his own. The *Study* is plainly not a twelve-tone piece, although passages such as:

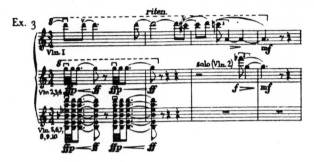

suggest the *texture* at least of Viennese dodecaphony.

The Suite for Flute Alone, Riegger's next work (1929), again suggests his interest in (but at the same time his independence of) this approach. The ten-note subject of the first movement suggests a tone-row, but is not employed as such; the fourth movement actually presents a twelve-note series:[8]

This row, however, is not followed in the remainder of the movement; it states motifs that are developed in traditional ways. The movement ends with the *tour de force* of a thirty-six-note row, using all practical notes of the flute's compass without repetition (Ex. 4c). This procedure assumes that notes in different octave levels are, in effect, different notes, whereas orthodox twelve-tone theory stands firmly on the identity of C, c, c′, c″ etc. for purposes of row construction. The idea suggested in the Suite for Flute has never been methodically exploited by Riegger, nor has he theorized about it; but it is a suggestion that may merit thought.

---

[8]The excerpts from the Suite for Flute are printed here by permission of New Music Edition, copyright owners.

In other works of this period, the Canons for Woodwinds (1931) and the Fantasy and Fugue for orchestra and organ (1930-31), imagination of the same sort is discerned. There is clearly an influence of twelve-tone technique on a composer with an already vigorous and independent atonal idiom. It was at this time that Riegger naturally enough became identified with the "radical" or advanced groups active in New York. The Pan American Association of Composers presented the *Study in Sonority* here and abroad, and the Canons were done by the League of Composers. The Fantasy and Fugue, calling for larger resources, has yet to be performed anywhere. Stokowski, to his great credit, had the courage to present the *Study* to a subscription audience. This work had a sensationally abusive reception. Riegger's earlier admirers, who had acclaimed the Trio and *La belle dame,* may understandably have felt despondent.

Dichotomy (1931-32) climaxes this period in Riegger's work. Here the composer consciously uses the device of the tone-row, and although his liberties with the orthodoxies of the twelve-tone system must be horrifying to the literal-minded, the work illustrates the superiority of art to theory. *Dichotomy* uses two "rows" (the opposition giving rise to the title); the first has eleven tones, the second ten, with three recurring notes:[9]

The music is developed with all the resources of twelve-tone technique, but it has a *brio* not usually associated with dodecaphony, which tends towards the intellectualized. Riegger at this time appears to have determined how to make use of the technique for his own purposes. All of his twelve-tone works, even when they are stricter in terms of conventional usage than *Dichotomy,* have an unmistakable sound of Riegger. This is due in part to the fact that Riegger does not compose like an "intellectual," or think like a theoretician, but subordinates both theory and ingenuity to expressive ends. He has brought to twelve-tone composition certain elements that appear incongruous, and that do not occur in the works of other twelve-tone composers, but he has succeeded in evolving a homogeneous and clearly personal style.

The problem of form in atonal music can be solved in more than one way. Schoenberg himself derives motifs from a row, using these motifs as the important elements in composition rather than the row itself, which has another function as a reality for the composer

---

[9]The examples from *Dichotomy* are printed here by permission of New Music Edition, copyright owners.

rather than for the audience. Riegger uses such motifs consistently and practically in his musical construction, but often combines melodic elements so derived with rather arbitrary harmonic support. One of the pitfalls in atonal music is diffuseness, because of the abandonment of a conventional harmonic ground-plan; Riegger, however, has solved this difficulty by ingenious exploitation of a non-tonal harmonic drive, clearly foreshadowed in the *Study in Sonority,* lacking conventional resolutions, but obeying a logic that establishes itself, without too great difficulty, in the ear of the listener.

Any such harmonic logic clearly depends on rhythmic organization as well. Here, too, Riegger departs from dodecaphonic purity; there are elements in *Dichotomy* that certainly stem from the *Sacre.* Reconciliation of antagonisms so violently defended seems absurd, but in *Dichotomy* it is an effective fact. Riegger makes no virtue of consistency in appearance, but forges a consistency out of elements partly explored and partly his own. His deviations from the purest theory are usually aids to coherence. Characteristic is his emphatic construction of motifs from portions of a row, involving "forbidden" repetitions, even of groups of notes:[10]

---

[10] Ex. 6a, from the Duo for Flute and Clarinet, by permission of New Music Edition; Ex. 6b, from the First String Quartet. ℗ Copyright 1946 by Associated Music Publishers, Inc. Used by permission.

The last example shows Riegger's typical use of fragments of a row to establish a rhythmic pattern as thematic material. This may also be discerned in a fugue subject from the Third Symphony and a fugato subject from *Dichotomy*.[11]

Ex. 7a

It is obvious that the rhythmic inspiration comes from a source alien to Schoenberg. Very highly articulated and hammering rhythms, used in counterpoint, are fundamental in Riegger's style. Despite his use of repeated notes, his music is free of empty patches; the percussive rhythms are skilfully controlled. The music does not seem busy merely for the sake of exercise, or out of irritability, or from not knowing what else to do. Riegger's music is extremely compact; it has none of the tenuous quality, sparseness, or fragmentation often associated with the twelve-tone idiom, and although Riegger is evidently identified in important ways with twelve-tone music, his work is anti-systematic and independent. He makes clear, as all first-rate composers do, the difference between discipline and system, between adaptation and adherence. One's ideas of twelve-tone music are apt to be determined by the music of its founder and disciples. In this music of Central Europe one often senses an extreme involution, sometimes the expression of taut personality

---

[11]Ex. 7a, from the Third Symphony, by permission of Associated Music Publishers.

yearning for a commonness which it will not permit itself. Riegger's work displays in comparison to this type of "official" dodecaphony an almost rude vigor. He has removed his work from the atmosphere of tortured chromaticism, and given it an appearance of healthy extroversion.

Riegger is as fond of contrapuntal forms as any orthodox dodecaphonist; his work is full of canons, fugues, fugatos, passacaglias. None of these seem aimless, or undertaken in the spirit of exhibiting skill; their vivacity stems in part from a return to the kinetic origins of music: they reflect an infusion of dance forms and rhythms, and involve a drive that is as much physical as intellectual in appeal. Just so, in *Dichotomy*, attention is not drawn to the evolution of material, to its development in fugato, or to its transformation in the passacaglia with which the work concludes. *Dichotomy* compels the listener with its energy, its newness of sound, its directness, and its compact unity. It is a work with no false notes, either musical or psychological, and it goes straight to the point. One recognizes a contrapuntal formality, not as an end in itself, but as a natural method of expression always under the most sensitive control.

III

In 1933, Riegger was asked to write the music for a new work of Martha Graham, whose art he greatly admired. There began, as a result, a long period of collaboration with many of the figures prominent in the world of the modern dance. Riegger considered that composition for the dance was a challenge to ingenuity and inventiveness, although in a purely musical sense it also imposed limitations. He was more than successful in meeting its terms, if one can judge by the number of pieces he was asked to furnish. From his Opus 16, a work with the somewhat distressing title of *Frenetic Rhythms* (1933), through Opus 29 (1941) there is but one slight piece (Music for Voice and Flute, written to order for the *Boletin Latino-Americano de Música*) that was not composed for the dance stage.

The rhythmical impact of Riegger's music should, one supposes, make it highly satisfactory to dancers. Much of his dance music is, in any case, highly satisfactory to musicians, two of these scores at least, *New Dance* and *Evocation,* being worthy of some comment. The Finale of *New Dance* is perhaps Riegger's most widely known piece, and there is no reason, except its greater subtlety, why it should not be as popular as Ravel's *Bolero.* The composer arranged it, by request, for a variety of combinations. The piece has a great deal of bounce and humor, and a fresh and pungent sound; it is built over an ingenious *basso ostinato* which provides a powerful forward drive. This type of ground is a favorite with

Riegger, and is used effectively in his Passacaglia and Fugue for Band also.[12]

Evocation is held in high esteem by its composer as being unique among his works, a characterization with which one need not entirely agree. It is, not unlike other works, dissonantly atonal without using either the twelve-tone technique or a rigid dissonant counterpoint. It has a characteristic motival profile, again makes use of an invented "tonic" and "dominant," and extensively exploits what Riegger calls "cumulative sequence." This device, which is of course an old one, is used by Riegger consciously and often.[†]

Evocation uses perfect fourths rather more often than is usual for Riegger. It is a short piece, well enough knit to stand by itself in concert performance, and it indicates the quality of work Riegger gave to the dance, where more idly built productions might have served.

Riegger's addiction to composing for the dance ended abruptly in 1941; he has not written for it since. Towards the end of his "dance" period, he began to work on his First String Quartet, the composition that marks the beginning of the most productive period of his musical life. The years from 1939 through 1949 saw him produce not more than a half-

---

[12]Ex. 8a from New Dance. ©Copyright 1940, 1965 by Associated Music Publishers, Inc. Used by permission. Ex. 8b by permission of Merrymount (Mercury Music Corp.).
[†]Evocation. Copyright 1953 by Peer International Corporation. Used by permission.

dozen works of the scope ordinarily described as "major"; but the quality and decisiveness of these works is extraordinary. Prophecy, as George Eliot observed, may be of all mistakes the most gratuitous, but it is difficult not to believe that the Third Symphony, the two string quartets, and the Music for Brass Choir will, with *Dichotomy* and the *Study in Sonority,* join the small list of enduring American works. These late works are those of a master, still growing in independence of mind and command of musical resource.

The First Quartet employs a strict twelve-tone technique, and one of its great merits is that the technique never obtrudes. It is a work of exceptional finish, clarity, and expressiveness, combining style with humanity, logic with verve, and individuality with discipline. The Scherzo is brilliant, witty, exhilarating; in the Adagio, for the first time in his work, Riegger sounds the note of deep contemplation and serenity. The Quartet, like the *Study in Sonority* of twelve years earlier, shows another genuine self-discovery in Riegger; it marks the emergence of a fuller emotional range and intellectual power through the strictest trials and the severest self-examination. Nothing in the First Quartet can be condemned as the work of a man held in check or intent simply on objective perfection. Yet the outflowing feeling, which one senses to be the triumph of direct expression over technical hazards, does not result in any of the banalities of emotional over-writing or unrestrained enlargement. The composition, only sixteen minutes long, has consistency, sureness, proportion. The technical features of the Quartet (and of the other works of the last decade) are not greatly different from those of Riegger's earlier work. One notes still the fondness for alternating pure unaccompanied line and sheer mass, the ingenuity in variation and imitation, the telling use of repeated tones, the life-lit and perhaps dance-derived rhythmic variety, the frequency of fugato and stretto, the ability to invent fabulous sonorities. There is no abandonment of the elements of style already mastered and identifiable, but there is a greater richness in their application.

In no other large work of recent years has Riegger employed the twelve-tone technique as literally as he did in the First Quartet. The Sonatina for Violin and Piano (1947) has the appearance of inconsistency in that one of its two movements is clearly based on a tone series, while the other, just as clearly, is not. But one discovers this only with study, so homogeneous does the work as a whole sound in performance. The Second Quartet, completed ten years after the First, is a good example of the continuation of a technique that is not twelve-tonal at all, but freely atonal. It is one of Riegger's most immediately appealing works. It opens with a statement of the principal melodic subject in unison, goes on to a second subject derived intervallically from the first (Ex. 10).[13]

---

[13] Ex. 10 from Second Quartet. Ⓟ Copyright 1949 by Associated Music Publishers, Inc. Used by permission.

Ex. 10

The formal clarity of the work derives from much that is traditional, and from Riegger's quite unpretentious application of relatively simple devices. The opening subject reappears in the third movement, *fortissimo*, not only as the climax of the movement, but as the point to which the whole work builds; the lyrical subordinate subject of the first movement reappears in the finale as a counterpoint. Each movement, from the second on, begins either thematically or harmonically with the material concluding the previous movement.

There is a poise in the Second Quartet that is the mark of mature and almost retrospective work. The Quartet is wonderfully clear and varied for all its terseness; it has humor and liveliness, quiet and warmth, all wrought in superbly contrived string sound.

Riegger's calculation of sound, his daring in timbre, has resulted in one work that is completely without precedent. This is the Music for Brass Choir (1948-49), which brings to a peak Riegger's exploitation of a number of the elements characteristic of his style. Scored for the incredible combination of ten trumpets, four (or preferably eight) horns, ten trombones, two tubas, and timpani (all independent parts), this is no mere occasional piece written for a fortuitously available wealth of brass instruments, or a demonstration of how to write what it is now fashionable to call a "sound-piece," but a work that carries the structural technique of the tone-cluster to its highest point. It may be called the apotheosis of the minor second.

As in the *Study in Sonority,* Riegger begins with a simple unaccompanied melodic germ, which recurs throughout the piece. The motif is immediately answered by the harmonic suggestion that outlines what is to come:[14]

Ex. 11

---

[14]Ex. 14 by permission of Merrymount (Mercury Music Corp.).

This six-note cluster is the most extraordinary sound in the piece; similar clusters, of increasing length, appear, as Henry Cowell has pointed out,[15] to become more consonant as the work progresses, until the final and logical culmination in a twenty-six-note cluster seems, for all its fantastic strangeness of sonority, to be a consonance of indescribable richness.

To have conceived a work of this character for such a combination of instruments may well be considered a triumph of imagination. (It is also an interesting illumination of Riegger's characteristic unworldliness: for to have written without paid commission a major work that can, because of the instruments it requires, be performed but rarely, is an act of the greatest disinterestedness.) There are few composers who would attempt a similar venture or who, so doing, could succeed in producing a work that is, to quote Virgil Thomson,[16] "as impressive to the mind as it is invigorating to the ear."

This is a phrase that may be applied to much of Riegger's work, and certainly to the Third Symphony (1946-47), which is, in actuality, his First. His two earlier works of that name merit no consideration; they remain in the list of the composer's music only because, one supposes, no one wants to destroy completely such large bundles of manuscript paper. Riegger himself has no illusions about Symphonies One and Two; the First, undertaken at the age of fifty-nine, was to be considered, with typical modesty, a trial. It has never been performed, nor is it now offered for performance. The Second was written for high-school orchestras and entered in a competition held by a music publisher. As high-school *Gebrauchsmusik* it is possibly too good; the idiom is naive enough for a university. It is actually the sort of private joke of which Riegger is extremely fond.

The Third Symphony, however, is something else: it is a work of great power, and is in many ways a summation of Riegger's composition. It is the most imposing example of his creative adaptation of twelve-tone methods and the logical integration of all his previous explorations. It is by no means consistently twelve-tone; the first movement is based on a tone-series, although it departs from it in the middle section; the second movement uses a row intermittently; the third is fairly free, and the fourth returns to fairly strict tone-row construction. But the character of the symphony, as has been pointed out,[17] does not

---

[15] In *The Musical Quarterly*, XXXV (1949), 463.

[16] New York *Herald Tribune*, April 9, 1949.

[17] An analysis with examples, appeared in *The Musical Quarterly*, XXXIV (1948), 594 ff. The reader may also consult excellent discussions of the work by Henry Cowell (*Musical America*, Dec. 1948) and by Frederick Dorian (*Notes*, Vol. VI, No. 4, Sept. 1949).

depend on simple ingenuity in reconciling diverse technical methods; it derives, on the contrary, from the bold absorption and fusion of musical ideas by a strikingly original mind. Its clarity of intellectual expression makes it perhaps one of the most important scores of the last twenty years, yet for all of its intellectual appeal it is always musical and vivid, and admirably embodied in physical sound.

IV

The innocent prolixity that characterizes the work of so many composers is notably absent from Riegger's production. Composition, for Riegger, is hard work, to be undertaken responsibly and with constant discipline and self-criticism. He rewrites a great deal, edits meticulously, and attempts always to achieve the most succinct exposition of his ideas. He feels that the enlargement of the tonal vocabulary in the 20th century is not necessarily a license to greater freedom for the composer, but on the contrary imposes on him an ever greater need for control and clarity. In this sense his use of set forms acts as an integrating factor binding his work to a tradition from which, at first hearing, it may sometimes appear remote.

Riegger's music has been for over twenty years as "advanced" as any being written, and it remains consistently in this category at a time when many of his contemporaries and juniors have jelled in a mold or become more conservative with increase of years. It is unusual today to witness a career that starts in conservatism and becomes increasingly radical in development; the opposite seems the rule and Riegger is the exception. Everything about Riegger to the age of thirty-five has the stamp of traditional schooling. He still retains a mastery of what we can once again, with some aptness, call the *stile antico* (witness certain of his choral works and the Canon and Fugue for Strings, the latter a noble work that succeeds in evoking the atmosphere of the 17th century); and he retains a devotion to traditional forms. Yet his break, made in maturity, with all that no longer served his expressive ends was a thorough one, carried through in all its implications. It was self-generated and conscientious.

Riegger has consistently avoided the easy way of doing things; and if he has no purely musical regrets, it remains true that he has suffered in recognition and rewards. The prizes awarded his earliest works must have tempted him on, but he chose a path that plainly offered little hope of further awards. Few of his works were written for orchestra, the only medium that commands wide attention; and such attention, in fact, came to him only with his Third Symphony. (This work was, incidentally, the first major commission he ever received.)[18] He has had few associations that have been of help in furthering his career, and he has for most of his life given lessons and done editorial work in order to support himself and his family. Despite his association with the *New Music Quarterly* and the U.S. Section of the International Society for Contemporary Music (which, in a gesture of tribute, elected him President in 1948), he has been influenced by few musical personalities, and has himself had little influence on others. He stands somewhat apart from the minor currents and effects of a local scene, and represents in his music not only something independent but also something larger: his music is neither national nor local, neither provincial nor primitive.

It should become evident in time that Riegger's music is important, as the fully achieved body of work of an independent and skilful creator is always important. His scores reveal an originality that relates at the same time to the traditional and to the most important ideas of the 20th century. The synthesis is unique and instructive, instinctive enough to be free of artificiality, intelligent enough to carry authority. There is seldom anything *manqué* in the composition; the music almost always seems to have the rightness that is the mark of expert craftsmanship. The passion for perfection abides with Riegger, and the passage of years has seen him achieve in his work that degree of integration of which, in his early days, he sensed the need. Like every composer of high musical morality, he writes for himself, accepting the authority of conscience rather than that of audience, respecting tradition rather than serving it. He does not adopt the fashionable pose of the skilled craftsman, turning out music that is acceptable, agreeable, or "competent," designed to appeal either to the "culture"-ridden concertgoer or to the taste of a coterie. His recipe calls for neither marshmallow nor vinegar. Not valuing the common, the pretty, or the pretentious, he has acquired nothing of orchestration from Hollywood, nothing of gracefulness from the ballet, nothing of artlessness from imitation folk music. Personal integration of a high degree often produces an appearance of unworldliness, and Riegger, though doubtless aware of the importance of being important, declines to profit by this awareness. His integration is both musical and moral; his concentration is inward, his music refined by scruple: its goal is itself and not its effect. In his quiet and continuing search for completeness of expression, for artistic self-containment, Riegger has resisted classification and removed himself from large audiences with second-hand judgments. His music is unavailable on recordings and is seldom heard in broadcast or concert performance. Such instances of the distance between original minds and widespread appreciation are not unknown in our own or other times; one notes them with regret, but not without the hope that the distance may some day be lessened.

---

[18]The Symphony was commissioned by the Alice M. Ditson Fund in 1946.

The Music of Elliott Carter

The Musical Quarterly XLIII/2 (April 1957)

We have passed through one Age of Innocence in American music. The present period gives less cheer, but it is not impossible that the cheerfulness of the innocent age is yielding to a kind of gloomy knowledge that gives a truer account of what and where we are. The Age of Innocence was the age of Roy Harris, The League of Composers, the WPA, and of a hundred or so composers briefly hailed as Hopes or Geniuses, and now departed even from memory. In criticism, it was the age of Paul Rosenfeld and *Modern Music*. It seems, in retrospect, that almost everyone was happy, fighting for performances, raving against critics, forming organizations, and shouting, "Down with Wagner, Beethoven, Verdi!" and just about everybody between Bach and the year before last.

There was excitement, however, and some of the composers and many of the works remain with us. The honored Elders are established, and none of similar stature have emerged. In these late years, most American composers of the first or the second rank seem, in fact, to be standing fairly still. The 1950's have been uneventful. New works appear with regularity, but they say little new, and in some cases give evidence that the original vein is worked out. The younger composers for the most part are imitating their elders without much luck; the young Sessionses, Coplands, and Schumans are writing neutrally and eclectically; the middle-aged Weberns, Stravinskys, Bartóks, and Hindemiths for the most part are doing as well as they always do, which is not quite well enough. It is hard to think of any American composer under the age of thirty-five who seems absolutely first-class. There are plenty of minor talents, some with well-defined and interesting personalities, but, as is always the case, they compete for attention with the huge number of larger and noisier mediocrities. And, to be sure, there are the experimenters; but even these seem much less lively than the Cowells and Varèses of the Twenties.

The one composer of importance who has recently come to the fore is Elliott Carter, and his music represents what is perhaps the most significant American development of the last ten years. Carter is now forty-eight years of age, and has been writing music since 1933. Until 1946 he was another of the mass of more or less gifted composers, performed occasionally at concerts of The League of Composers, attracting mildly favorable attention, and representing well the Parisian-Stravinskian wing of American composition. He was admired, with considerable reservation, by most of his colleagues; the reservations were generally on the basis of something complicated and labored in his work. It is only now that we can see what this apparent complicatedness meant. This was nothing more or less than the foreshadowing of the successful solution of technical problems so ably presented in Carter's works beginning with the Piano Sonata of 1945-46.

Carter began serious work in music rather late, and acquired what may be called professional status as a composer considerably later. As the son of a well-to-do New York family, he was not faced with the economic necessity of choosing a career, and was able to pursue an education in the leisurely fashion no longer common. He is one of the few musicians, indeed one of the few persons of our time, who may still, in Jacques Barzun's sense of the phrase, be called an educated man. Carter's mind is neat, precise, and well-stocked; his interests cover a wide range, and his curiosity is restless. His formal education includes four years as an undergraduate and two years as a graduate at Harvard, where he majored originally in English. His interest in music developed during his high school days, and was encouraged by Charles Ives. But Carter never became a proficient pianist, or anything more than a gentlemanly dabbler until his last years at Harvard. He then took Walter Piston's courses and a composition course with Gustav Holst, who was for one year a visiting professor. Holst was slightly distressed by Carter's efforts, in both composition and piano playing, and considered that if the young man did not make so many mistakes while trying to play Beethoven he might perhaps not write so many of these mistakes into his own work. This comment has rather a familiar sound, and one can draw the familiar moral.

For three years after Harvard, from 1932 to 1935, Carter studied in Paris with Nadia Boulanger. During this time he acquired a sound technique, and composed the first work that remains acknowledged in his list of compositions. This was incidental music to Sophocles's *Philoctetes*, composed for a performance in 1933 by the Harvard Classical Club. Carter has returned often to classical subjects; he is able to deal with the classics in the original and has studied Greek meter and prosody as part of the formation of his musical language. In 1936 he did incidental music for another Harvard production, this time of Plautus's *Mostellaria*, and a *Tarantella* with text from Ovid. These early works are by and large diatonic, and incorporate fragments or stylistic paraphrases of extant Greek melodies. They have an interesting style of their own, not much like the Carter of the last ten years, but fresh and original despite the somewhat self-conscious classicism. Most important stylistically, the 1936 pieces show a humor that occasionally crops out in later works, especially in the delicious *Defense of Corinth*.

A number of works from the Thirties have been withdrawn, including a Flute Sonata and two String Quartets. The remaining works include the ballet *Pocahontas*, composed for the Ballet Caravan, of which Carter was for a time musical director, and some choral pieces.

Pocahontas is a large work in which, according to Abraham Skulsky, Carter "was concerned with finding his version of an American style."[1] But the main characteristics of the piece are Stravinskian. It is effective music, and shows sure professional competence. The first version of *Pocahontas* dates from 1936; the re-orchestrated Suite from the ballet, from 1939. It was apparently during these three years that Carter greatly developed his technique; after 1939, all of the music has a surer quality.

In the ACA *Bulletin* article devoted to Carter, Skulsky discusses sympathetically most of the early works, and devotes some attention to Carter's First Symphony, composed in 1942. This Symphony is generally simpler in idiom and less elaborate in orchestral dress than *Pocahontas.* It is the kind of work that prepares the composer for his next steps, and gets out of his system a number of obvious debts to other composers.

The first of Carter's pieces that ought surely to stand up as a repertory item is *The Defense of Corinth,* which is a real *tour de force.* This work, for narrator, men's chorus, and two pianos, based on an English translation of a passage from Rabelais, was composed in 1941, while Carter was teaching at St. John's College in Annapolis, Maryland. (It is interesting to note that at St. John's, in addition to heading the Music Department, Carter also taught Greek, mathematics, physics, and philosophy, and conducted the Glee Club.) *The Defense of Corinth* is exuberant, original, and delightful, and a perfect setting of the text. It is full of rhythmic invention and lively sounds. Using solo and choral declamation, recitative, part-song, and fugal techniques, with the pianos providing energetic support, the piece is so highly imaginative and full of life and humor that it cannot fail to enchant an audience, provided that it is well performed (see Ex. 1).[2]

The best of Carter's work for the next few years is found in other choral pieces, notably *The Harmony of Morning* (1944) and *Musicians Wrestle Everywhere* (1945). *The Harmony of Morning,* to a text of Mark van Doren, for women's voices and chamber orchestra, sums up Carter's achievement at this period of his development. It is considerably more elaborate contrapuntally and harmonically than most of Carter's earlier works, and while echoes

---

[1] Abraham Skulsky, *Elliott Carter,* in the ACA *Bulletin,* Summer 1953.

[2] The examples are copyrighted as follows: Ex. 1 © 1950 by Merrymount Music Press; Exx. 2 and 3 © 1948 by Music Press Inc.; Exx. 4 and 5 © 1949 by Music Press Inc.; Exx. 7 and 8 © 1956 by Associated Music Publishers, Inc., New York; Exx. 9 and 10 © 1957 by Associated Music Publishers, Inc., New York. Ex. 1 is printed by permission of Merrymount Music, Inc.; Exx. 2-5 by permission of Mercury Music Corporation; and Exx. 6-10 by permission of Associated Music Publishers, Inc., New York.

Ex. 1 (Allegro)

of Copland are still heard, it represents the largest step yet taken towards a recognizably personal idiom. The technique is one of *cantus firmus* variation, and there is a good deal of very effective canonic writing. The mood of van Doren's eloquent poem is admirably captured, and as usual the prosody and line are fine and sensitive. There is still a certain coolness about the work in terms of expression, but it is not inappropriate and it is evidently controlled rather than inhibited.

Musicians Wrestle Everywhere, to a poem by Emily Dickinson, is set for five-part chorus *a cappella* or with strings. It is freer in polyphony than *The Harmony of Morning* and represents a new high point of achievement in the combination of rhythmic displacements. The line is varied, pliable, irregular, with shifted accents that combine to make a highly successful cross-accented counterpoint. It is in this work that Carter, on a small scale, first seems to solve some of the problems that have preoccupied him. The relation with the Piano Sonata is clear (see Ex. 2).

Ex. 2

In 1943, while serving with the Office of War Information, Carter composed some charming songs to poems by Robert Frost, which may well be recommended to singers seeking unhackneyed American works for recital programs. They present no special difficulties, and have an elegance usually lacking in American compositions of this genre. Two larger pieces for solo voice, to texts of Whitman and Hart Crane, are more elaborate and taxing, and perhaps not quite as viable. But all of these works exhibit a great sensitivity to text, a refined prosody, and a musical imagination constantly growing richer and more sure of itself.

The *Holiday Overture* of 1944 I have discussed briefly in the Current Chronicle.[3] The ingenuity in rhythmic design is very evident in this brilliant piece, and the orchestral writing is considerably more assured than in the First Symphony. The Overture is an exuberant piece, in which the complexities are made to appear casual. From the standpoint of technique, the work is extremely impressive; aside from *The Defense of Corinth,* it is also Carter's gayest work.

All of the compositions that have been mentioned above may be regarded as representing Carter's "first period." In a sense this is unfair, but it is hard to escape the feeling that with the Piano Sonata of 1945-46 Carter emerges as a more important and interesting composer, one who has completed his *Lehrjahre,* and one who takes a place not occupied before. Carter himself sees a line of continuous development, and indeed such a line must necessarily exist. But none of the works before the Piano Sonata unite *all* of the qualities

---

[3] *The Musical Quarterly,* July 1950. This article appears in this volume on pp. 66-69.

that make the later Carter style. There are masterful exhibitions of certain traits of style and technique in all of the earlier pieces, and many of the shorter ones hold together in a compelling fashion; but the longer ones almost all fail of complete and convincing success. With the Piano Sonata, there is a new force and coherence, a completed mastering of technical problems and a consequently higher power of clarity and expressiveness.

I have discussed Carter's Piano and 'Cello Sonatas at some length in the pages of *The Musical Quarterly* (for January 1951),[†] and must of necessity refer the reader to this earlier article. My impressions of these pieces remain unchanged, and I cannot find better ways of describing the novel techniques involved. Since the appearance of my article, others have written about the two Sonatas, and on the basis of turnabout being fair play, I take the liberty of quoting. In the Fall 1956 issue of *The Juilliard Review,* Joseph Bloch, in the course of discussing American piano sonatas, wrote:

> First and foremost is the Sonata (1945-46) of Elliott Carter. That this is a master work is no news. Nearly every pianist and every composer and every critic admires it . . . The complexities are still there, but they no longer seem so terrifying and unprecedented as they did ten years ago, and even in the blackest moments it is all laid out gratefully for the piano.

Skulsky, in the article mentioned above, writes:

> The *Piano Sonata,* composed in 1945-46 . . . marks still another turning point in Carter's musical thinking . . . It presents the composer coming to grips with the problem of writing for the modern piano. For it, he invented a purely pianistic style that gives full rein to the virtuoso aspect of the instrument, employing its entire range of sonorous possibilities. . .

> This *Piano Sonata* carries the principle of irregular scansion, of cross-accented counterpoint, of shifted accents to the furthest limit that Carter has gone using an unchanging unit as a basis. In its first movement, this unit is a fast sixteenth of about MM. 528, while in most previous examples of the kind found not only in his own music but in that of other contemporaries who go in for this device, the unit is usually no faster than MM. 400. This means that in the sonata the irregularities are not perceived and are not meant to be perceived as shifting accents but as a kind of rubato of phrases although the unit is to be played at an unchanging speed. Previous to this Carter had been interested in molding rhyth-

[†]This article appears in this volume on pp. 69-74.

mic groupings into very irregular lengths and in the cross-accented counterpoint which resulted. Both were derived from the English madrigal school where such devices abound.

William Glock, in *A Note on Elliott Carter*, writes:

> In his earlier works, Carter already shows himself, in Lou Harrison's phrase, 'sensitive to the force and weight of well-disposed and varied rhythmic material'; but I am not aware that he uses any techniques that could not be attributed to the examples of Copland or of the English madrigalists. With the *Piano Sonata* of 1945-6, however, he takes a great stride forward, almost as though he had passed through a sudden dramatic change of musical consciousness. The first movement runs mainly at one tempo, ♩=66; but within this tempo Carter writes two kinds of music, one *Maestoso*, the other *Legato scorrevole*; and in the second kind he is evidently hearing a very rapid semiquaver (♪ =528) as his metrical unit. There are no time-signatures, and the bars vary both in length and in the grouping of the semiquavers within them. Thus the music of these quick sections has an inimitable quality, like a toccata that sways and bends and seems to consist of a perpetual subtle *rubato* because of the irregular groupings—mostly from three to eight semiquavers together, but with a preponderance of five and seven.[4]

For an example of the *scorrevole,* the following may be cited:

Ex. 3

Tempo I, *scorrevole*

---

[4]*The Score and I.M.A. Magazine*, No. 12, June 1955.

Glock surmises that "it may have been the size and brilliance of his undertaking in this Sonata that stimulated Carter to such an extent that unaccountable things happened." But this is putting things in reverse order; the preparation represented by earlier pieces (particularly such works as *Musicians Wrestle Everywhere*) might indeed, with a composer less capable of logic, less consistent and energetic intellectually, or less aware of the nature and uses of technique, have led to nothing more than an increase in fussiness and an expenditure of ideas in a series of musical vacuums. But the value of Carter's achievement is precisely that at this point, roughly the years 1945-46, the larger design became possible through a summing up of the work that had gone before. And what characterizes the Piano Sonata, the 'Cello Sonata, and the String Quartet is not alone the novelty of the metrical methods, but the scope and wholeness of the architecture. These are all works on a grand scale, very personal in style, and esthetically notable for the subordination of immense ingenuity to intense expressiveness. Glock puts this very well:

> The true criterion is whether the music says something worth saying. In Carter's case there seems no doubt on this point, for one can hardly help being impressed by the intensity of expression and by the imaginative power of the music, in terms both of sheer sound and of grandeur and subtlety of organization.

Between the Piano Sonata and the 'Cello Sonata, Carter composed two large works of somewhat unequal interest. The first, a ballet on the subject of *The Minotaur,* was written for the Ballet Society in 1947; a suite from the ballet was later extracted, and since it has been recorded commercially, is now perhaps the best-known of Carter's works. *The Minotaur* is a good score, of which almost any American composer might be proud, but it is not altogether representative of the essential Carter style. It might have been written by someone else of the general neo-Classic persuasion. It is not Apollo, but Stravinsky, who is the Leader of the Muses in our day, and who seems to have determined for the time being the musical style for classical subjects. *The Minotaur* comes complete with the noble sounds of the Master, and the expected devices of *ostinato,* chorale, and ground bass. But everything is well handled, the effects are sure, and the writing shows great confidence. It should be noted that *The Minotaur* was completed six months before Stravinsky's *Orpheus,* the work it most resembles.

Emblems, composed in the same year (1947), is a different story. It belongs with the Piano Sonata as an original, striking, and unsurpassed piece in its medium, and carries the fine and powerful things in the earlier choral pieces to a new dimension. *Emblems* is a setting of three poems by Allen Tate, for men's voices and piano. The opening movement is *a cappella,* of great breadth, and extremely difficult:

Ex. 4 Largo *sostenuto*

The second movement opens with a solo passage for the piano, which continues to have an important role for the remainder of the piece. The problem of writing for chorus with piano is here solved with remarkable success. There is a vigorous strength in the entire piece that recalls the very best of Ives, but it is much less tentative than Ives usually is, more consistently wrought, and more finely shaded. The textures may be illustrated by Example 5.

For the final movement, Carter develops highly syncopated rhythms in what may accurately be described as an authentic "American" style, no less "American" for the fact that both Honegger and Walton have also used it with success. *Emblems,* in every way, is recognizably the work of an American, and represents Carter's most obvious success in achieving this kind of national expression, which has always seemed important to him. The piece is dramatic and stirring, and is a complete answer to those who have at times in the past had an impression of Carter as a composer full of skill and ingenuity, but lacking in passion and freedom.

Aside from the 'Cello Sonata, the year 1948 saw Carter produce an exhilarating and deftly written Woodwind Quintet in two movements. The work ranks with the best written for this difficult instrumental combination, not only in the expert handling of the sonorities, but in the solid substance of the ideas. Here again the interest is in cross-accented, highly dissonant counterpoint, to which the medium may be made to lend itself.

The 'Cello Sonata has been described more often than it has been played, since there are as yet few 'cellists and pianists willing or able to give it the concentrated study and preparation needed for public performance. (There is, however, an excellent recording by its original performers, Bernard Greenhouse and Anthony Makas.) This sonata may well be

Ex. 5 a)

b)

one of the influential works of the century, for in it Carter used for the first time a principle that he had been developing for some time. This principle has been described as "metrical modulation," and for a thorough discussion, I must refer the reader to my already-mentioned 1951 article in *The Musical Quarterly*, and again to William Glock. Both of these articles are illustrated with enlightening examples.

The idea of "metrical modulation" may be described concisely as a means of going smoothly, but with complete accuracy, from one absolute metronomic speed to another, by lengthening or shortening the value of the basic note unit. A simple example from the Eight Etudes and a Fantasy for Woodwind Quartet (1950) may serve to make the principle clear:

Ex. 6

The principle is applied on a large scale in the 'Cello Sonata, where large sections are constructed on the basis of change, not of tempo, but of relative note-lengths in proportions not easily exploited in conventional notation.

All of this would be mere ingenuity in arithmetic were it not that the 'Cello Sonata is also a moving piece, and it is this that should be emphasized here. The Sonata is big, dark, and musically of the most sustained and compelling quality. The technique gives it a subtlety of motion that is extraordinary and fascinating.

The 1951 String Quartet carries all of Carter's technical preoccupations to a logical culmination. This work is almost without doubt the most important and imposing accomplishment of American music in the last decade; it has aroused the keenest interest and discussion in both Europe and the United States. George Rochberg's review of the recording of the Quartet (*The Musical Quarterly* for January 1957) may be cited, as may the above-mentioned article by William Glock.

The quartet goes very much further than the 'Cello Sonata, and in the most completely logical way. It involves a texture in which non-simultaneous changes of speed ("metrical modulations") in the four instruments become the essence of the contrapuntal texture. This factor of absolute speed (which of course becomes also *relative* speed in the ensemble) is superimposed on the usual devices of polyrhythm and cross-accent. Needless to say, the apprehension or absorption of this idiom requires effort of both players and listeners; but most of those who have made a serious try have found the effort rewarding. The work is very long, between forty-five and fifty minutes, and is conceived as continuous, although there are clearly defined movements. The designated pauses, however, come in the middle of movements, and one assumes that these are designated mainly to give players and hearers some respite from intense concentration. Organically the work is dense and unified. The fantastic independence of the four parts is balanced by their interchanges of material. The technique here is a kind of super-invertible counterpoint, to which the new element of absolute and independent speeds has been added.

The Quartet has a dark intensity and power. The result, as communicative music, appears to justify the vast expenditure of ingenuity. This, in sum, is the measure of Carter's success. Examples from so complex and sustained a work are not easy to choose. Perhaps, however, the two here given may help to give some idea of characteristic textures.

Ex. 7

II

Ex. 8 (♩ = 120)

Coming between the String Quartet and the magnificent Variations for Orchestra (1955-56), the Sonata for Flute, Oboe, 'Cello, and Harpsichord (1952) appears to be in the nature of an occasional piece, although it is by no means without its own interest. Carter has never been one to shirk a difficult problem, and here the question of sonority and balance is obviously a poser. The Sonata won the Walter W. Naumburg Musical Foundation Award for 1956, and will soon be available on a recording.

Carter's most recently completed and performed work is his Variations for Orchestra, commissioned and recorded by the Louisville Orchestra. This is an overwhelming piece. I should have no hesitation in ranking it with the most remarkable works composed by any American musician, and as a piece of the first rank in any time and place. Rochberg's words about the Quartet certainly also apply here: "One recognizes it as a marker, a milestone . . ." In the Variations Carter has stunningly summed up all of his experience and produced an orchestral masterpiece that is constantly stimulating, marvelously sonorous, and kindling to the imagination. It is bound to the masters of the present and the recent past, but it also points to the future; here is one of those works of genuine assimilation and synthesis that so many musicians have been seeking. It is not imitation; again to quote Rochberg: "Surely the best guarantee of carrying on a genuine tradition is to accept its influence and use that influence as a springboard for a step towards a new milestone." This is what we feel has happened in the Variations, where the shadows of Berg, Bartók, Schoenberg are dissolved in the background, and indistinguishable; they are now the point of departure for a new, dominant, strong, and sure personality.

The work consists of an Introduction, Theme, nine Variations, and a Finale, and runs approximately twenty-three minutes. The style is basically dissonant, chromatic, and shows considerable influence (though not literal following) of twelve-tone techniques. One of its strengths is precisely that the influence appears to be so comfortable, so well-assimilated, without self-consciousness or theoretical roadblocks. The Variations are certainly the work of an assured composer, and may well represent the commencement of a "third period" in Carter's growth. In any case, the Variations show control of a certain prolixity noticeable even in so strongly built a work as the String Quartet.

The atmosphere of the Variations is dark and dramatic, with effective changes of pace and color. The theme itself is lengthy and complex, and cannot conveniently be reduced for illustration. The Variations use about every known contrapuntal, structural, and metrical device, and a few new ones. There are a few "metrical modulations," not too many, since they are difficult to negotiate orchestrally. But the fourth and sixth variations use a novel technique of retarding and acceleration:

Ex. 9

In Variation Six this is reversed:

Ex. 10

It is always unfair to pick out one or two small examples from a work of this scope. The entire piece is constructed with great mastery, and every bit of it is assured and powerful. It represents another enormous step forward for the composer, and this in itself is great good news for American music in general. Carter may certainly be hailed as the most original and daring musical mind at work in the United States today, and he has unquestionably produced more important works in the past ten years than any other American composer. The list of these works is not long, but each is unique, and more impressive than the one preceding. At least four of them—the Piano Sonata, the 'Cello Sonata, the String Quartet, and the Variations for Orchestra—are, in such limits as we can use the term, masterpieces; if we quarrel with this characterization, there can however be no question that each stands among the most important and dominating American works of its kind.

Current Chronicle: New York
[Review of Wallingford Riegger's Third Symphony]
Musical Quarterly XXXIV/4 (October 1948)

The New York Music Critics Circle gave its annual orchestral award this year to Wallingford Riegger's Third Symphony, commissioned by the Alice M. Ditson Fund of Columbia University and presented for the first time at the university's Festival of Contemporary American Music in May. For this happy conjunction let due praise be offered, and let us note the almost unique occasion of a commission, a festival, and an award uniting upon a work of the greatest excellence by a composer whose adequate recognition has long been merited. Riegger's Third surely must stand among the half-dozen most impressive symphonies of recent years. It is forceful, original, serious, terse, moving, and skilful. It will, of course, find no easy road to popularity, for while skill impresses and originality sometimes amuses, passion frightens and independence offends many frequenters of concert halls. In unpopular virtues, Riegger's work abounds.

Riegger exemplifies the independent composer whose attention is focused inward, on work rather than on its effect, and on music rather than on allegiances. He is not of those who can be easily and conveniently classified; nor is his list of works sufficiently long to impose by quantity. He is thus less known, by name or performance, than many highly touted or more conforming contemporaries whom he surpasses in thought and craftsmanship. He is too sincere a musician to coin musical small change for the machines of mass distribution. Among a large number of musicians, this sincerity is acknowledged and respected; but it is well known that sincerity is not a way to wide recognition unless the artist be sincerely commonplace, which Riegger is not. Recognition has been sporadic, and of a somewhat special flavor; Riegger's music for the dance has had a certain admiration and influence; *Dichotomy,* written in 1932, aroused some enthusiasm at Yaddo in 1947. Riegger has gone his way almost as one indifferent, in a musical sense, to fashion; his Trio in B minor (Society for the Publication of American Music publication award, 1931) shocks one with its straight traditionalism, as does *Dichotomy* with its abundance of new sounds and energies. Yet this contrast does not point to inconsistency, or to the bewilderment of a composer before a choice of styles or poses. Riegger's music always sounds like no one's but his own; he has never been tutored by style or mastered by technique.

This is particularly true of the music Riegger has written in recent years, using the twelve-tone technique which has so often made the composer its servant. Many of the accusations made against the twelve-tone technique and its practitioners—that it is mechanical, that it conveniently false-fronts for inadequacies of mind, of ear, and of heart—appear true in the light of inferior work, but appear particularly ill-founded when viewed against a work like Riegger's symphony. Granted that the pursuit of a theory or the practice of a technique may be, as ends in themselves or as disguises, both empty and self-defeating, why should the moral be pointed only for atonalists? Was this not just as true of classical theory and practice? The first consideration in music is obviously not method, but music itself. Whatever music is, it begins with the creative individual who is not afraid of being himself, and who has mastered whatever technique is necessary for the realization of his own artistic, intellectual, or spiritual ends. It is the impact of the individual on techniques that occasionally produces art.

Riegger's employment of twelve-tone techniques in his symphony is neither dull nor mechanical; it is an individual piece, not a school piece. The strength of the score is not in its ingenuity but in its vitality; it has an abundance of memorable musical ideas that do not flounder, but proceed, and proceed with force as well as with logic. It is true that ingenuity or the exercise of intellectual subtlety in the manipulation of material is a primary element of great music, but such exercise on dull premises produces only tedium. Technique and cleverness in themselves cannot be expected to convey pleasure to any but those who practise a craft, and they may then of course produce only envy. At the worst, the cultivation of these ends becomes the ingrown pastime of devotees with a special jargon; and it is a picture of this sort that excited twelve-tone apologists and detractors equally often evoke. But why must any practice always be at its worst, except for purposes of reverse propaganda? Riegger's symphony has ingenuity and craft enough to please the most fastidious fancier of musical puzzles, but one of its merits lies in its concealment of artifice, which is given life and made apparent as music. One questions whether the logical connection of these chords[1]

Ex. 1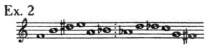

with the tone-series will be apparent to many ears, but the relevance of the connection to listening satisfaction may be doubted. The tone-series on which the first movement is based is

Ex. 2

[1]The excerpts from Riegger's Third Symphony are printed here by courtesy of Associated Music Publishers, Inc., copyright owner 1948.

and the connection becomes quite evident to the eye. But is this discovery not something extra, a pleasure for the student examining the score, rather than a self-revealing attraction for the listener?

Santayana most persuasively called attention to the limitations of musical sensibility, and the dangers of intellectual over-elaboration exceeding the synthetic powers of apprehension. This is a trap into which many composers have fallen in an enthusiasm for the exploration of possibilities, but it is one that Riegger avoids. His structure is essentially simple, his melodic outlines clear. The opening movement begins with a direct statement which the ear retains:

Ex. 3

The three opening bars announce a "motto" to which frequent melodic and rhythmic reference is made; the entire passage quoted serves as an introduction of the utmost thematic clarity. Following it, the violins introduce the main tempo in a figure of sixteenth notes, suggesting how faithfully the row will be followed in further development:

Ex. 4

The structure of the first movement is a large but simple *ABA*; sonata form, if it takes one's fancy to call it so, easy to grasp and completely satisfying in conveying a sense of fulfillment. The middle section builds up on lines of crossing and ascending major seconds to a tense climax that is brilliantly released in a return to the opening bars. From material in the middle section:

Ex. 5

comes the elegant and expressive opening of the second movement:

Ex. 6

Vigorous fugato passages on a new twelve-tone row contrast with the predominant lyricism of this movement, which ends, with a quiet beauty, on a simple repetition, more sonorous instrumentally, of the opening sixteen bars.

What gives this symphony its special character is its extraordinary rhythmic organization, its fusion of the spirit of the dance with the fugal techniques of the twelve-tone system. It is always sharp and clear in beat and pulse, kinetically driving. There is a total absence of the arhythmic browsing chromaticism or contrapuntal meandering that in some twelve-tone works loses the listener in a labyrinth made more difficult by artificial fog. Echoes of a generalized *New Dance* are discernible in each movement, still something quite personally Riegger's. It is an abstracted drive: *the* dance rather than *a* dance, remote from choreography. The third movement has humor as well; real humor, neither wisecracks nor facile sarcasm; even better, not self-burlesque. It is the good humor of a composer completely sure of his technique, knowing that he can afford to have a bit of fun with it. Few things in music meet more rarely with success.

The contrapuntal and rhythmic characteristics of the first three movements are summed up in the fourth, a passacaglia and fugue of fresh inventiveness, modest in dimension, and requiring no guidebook. The end[2] may be a bit noisy and abrupt, but one leaves the entire work with the feeling that one will return to it, and return often. Rehearings are urgently needed; there is much to be discovered, much to be savored, in this twenty-five minute score. It is by no means a work that should remain "difficult" or "harsh" for a moderately intelligent audience, for it has buoyancy, motion, and life, physical appeal to the senses as well as interest to the mind. If there are no plushy sounds to sing the hearer into daydreams, or artillery to pound him into insensibility, there is also no stale or sterile padding to make him restless. As a matter of course, Riegger uses the complete bag of tricks of the atonal contrapuntist, but the effect of his symphony cannot possibly depend on the listener's ability to diagnose them as they pass. The unity and individuality of the style are striking both before and beyond analysis.

If the symphony has shortcomings (and no doubt many criticisms have been and will be made), its orchestral nature is certainly not among them. It is not "orchestrated" music, but music written with great expertness for orchestra. The sounds are wonderful: clean, exciting, and imaginative. How pleasant it is to find a score that does not abound in orchestral "effects" as a substitute for ideas, that manages to stagger along with mere pairs of woodwinds, conventional brasses, no harp, no piano, no built-in nightingales. One wishes perhaps that Riegger had dispensed also with the whole percussion section, which, given the nature of the music, appears almost redundant.

Riegger, at sixty-three, is now working on his Fourth Symphony, which will be awaited with considerable interest. His Third, meanwhile, should wear well. The test of wear is one that all our recent symphonies need, and few receive. Let us hope that to this test Riegger's Third will soon and often be subjected.

---

[2] This has since been revised.

Current Chronicle: New York

[Review of Peter Mennin's Third Symphony]
Musical Quarterly XXXV/1 (January 1949)

With his Third Symphony, completed in his twenty-third year (1946), Peter Mennin may be said to have established himself as a genuine musical personality. The Symphony has had an unusually large number of performances, in New York and elsewhere, and now the printed score has arrived. It must be said that this work looks as well as it sounds. Mennin obviously has extraordinary gifts and immense facility. As long as this technical command and fluency remain at the service of his taste and talent, we may expect great things. The Third Symphony impresses by its evidence of real melodic inventiveness and by its management of long lines in a contrapuntal texture that is both learned and complex without seeming labored or contrived. It is surprisingly free of the naivetés and obvious derivativeness one expects to find in the work of young symphonists. The Symphony indicates the composer's maturity by avoiding studied efforts to be "original" at all costs, and on the other hand, by not being merely stylish, Mennin has already indicated that he is developing an idiom of his own.

To say that Mennin's work lacks obvious derivativeness is not to imply that it lacks ancestry. The work of any composer reflects what he likes in all the music he has heard. This must be transformed, synthesized, or developed in a new creative process. Mennin, like many another contemporary, admits his indebtedness to Renaissance and Baroque music; he also expresses a great admiration for the work of Vaughan Williams. This is rather refreshing in the United States, where Vaughan Williams is rather undervalued, but where Hindemith, Schoenberg, and Stravinsky are repeated or diluted in daily compositional rituals, and where their reactions to earlier music are often accepted as bases for imitation. It is obvious that Mennin's acquaintance with Renaissance and Baroque music is not limited to a few records from the *Anthologie Sonore,* or to the paraphrases and creative adaptations of contemporaries. He has in some way found time to acquire a scholar's knowledge of principles and a craftsman's mastery of techniques that are wholly remarkable; he can talk intelligently and enthusiastically about "old" music and yet write music of his own that is neither academic nor self-consciously mannered.

It has been correctly observed that the sonata form of the 18th and 19th centuries depends more on harmony than on melody (so that the extraction of purely melodic "themes" is more or less meaningless) and Mennin, knowing this, wisely avoids trying to force his musical ideas into a semblance of sonata form. Each of the three movements of his symphony has a melodic and contrapuntal architecture that owes much more to the canzona or the fantasia than to the sonata. The work remains thematically clear because the subjects are beautifully profiled and stated in clear non-chordal relief. There is a unity of style here that is based on a modal concept of pitch center rather than on one of tonality, and on melodic variation and transformation rather than on directed harmonic drive. The real polyphonic character of the work, deriving from pre-fugal procedures, is clarified by Mennin's understanding that the bar-line is harmonic. Although his time signature in each movement remains constant, his melodies themselves are a negation of bar-line feeling.

The first movement opens with a subject stated in unison (strings, bassoons, with rhythmic accents in horns, tuba, and timpani):[1]

Horns and woodwinds follow immediately with a closely related subject, stated over an evenly striding bass in the low strings:

This very direct and closely knit presentation leads without elaboration or commentary to the statement of a third subject in m. 29. The new subject is a long melodic line (20 measures) played by the violins over a canonic *ostinato* (derived from the first subject) in violas and 'cellos, and a repeated figure in the basses:

---

[1] The excerpts from Peter Mennin's Third Symphony are copyright, 1948, by Hargail Music Press and are used here by permission.

Ex. 3

This long subject is taken up canonically by the low strings, and the subsequent development throughout the movement is one of contrapuntal intensification. The examples quoted may be taken as representative of the writing throughout the symphony. The second movement, like the first, opens with a contrapuntal subject stated without harmonic background or linear elaboration, and continues with statements of two further subjects of considerable length. The similarity of subjects in all three movements indicates clearly Mennin's awareness of the principles of melodic unity in pre-classical music. He has made his choice between construction in long and relatively non-climactic polyphonic lines, and the later principle of melodic and harmonic contrast that is implicit in sonata form. By sacrificing drama, he gains continuity; the consistency of treatment here is unusual and admirable.

The variation or transformation technique appears again in the third movement, which presents two long subjects clearly related to melodic elements of the preceding movements. The first is stated over another canonic *ostinato*, with a large augmentation of a subsidiary idea in the bass:

Ex. 4

All of this seems almost too ingenious when analyzed, yet the symphony has not the slightest sound of paper-music. This is a tribute to Mennin's command of his idiom and his understanding of musical realities behind dexterities of technique. One feels spontaneity and life in the music rather than cleverness; although the cleverness is formidable, it never makes one feel that it is displayed as an end in itself. The work is primarily that of a melodist who knows how to construct skilfully with his melodic material. The contours of Mennin's melodies are interesting; they are modal without sounding archaic, and occasionally they become somewhat operatic. They bring to mind a host of associations without suggesting any specific derivation. He uses an assortment of flat seconds, raised fourths, alternate major and minor thirds—all melodically and without harmonic reinforcement, avoiding chromaticism and quite clearly without any kinship with the atonalists. Using many augmented and diminished melodic intervals, he avoids sounding like Ernest Bloch and despite the superficial similarity of modal feeling also does not sound like Roy Harris. One has the impression nevertheless that both of these composers should be proud to claim some influence.

Mennin's Fourth Symphony has already been completed, but not yet, at this writing, performed. A fine Fantasia for Strings, having much in common with the Third Symphony, was written on commission from The League of Composers, and performed last winter. With compositions of this quality already written at the age of twenty-five, Mennin should have quieted any suspicion that he is a young talent not quite ready for large works. Perhaps with four symphonies written he will feel sufficiently secure and have sufficient leisure to try sonatas and quartets. It will be interesting to see what he does in these fields; there is ample justification for expecting more first-rate music.

Current Chronicle: New York
[Review of Igor Stravinsky's *Mass*]
Musical Quarterly XXXV/3 (July 1949)

The new Mass (1948) by Igor Stravinsky was performed in February for the first time in New York[1] and met with what may fairly be described as a reception lacking in enthusi-

---

[1] Since performed on the radio (April) and at the Columbia University Festival (May). None of these performances, unfortunately, did full justice to the work.

asm. The nature of the comment in the press I found illuminating as a reflection of many problems in the criticism of contemporary music as well as of many difficulties faced by the composer in his secondary relations with the public. Neither the apologists nor the detractors seem to have contributed much to this occasion but column-yards of irrelevancies for which not they, but the traditions of their occupation, must be blamed. In general, one observed a determination to use terms either totally lacking in meaning or applicability, or of so specialized a nature as to constitute a discouraging mumbo-jumbo to the reader unfamiliar with pseudo-musicological jargon.

Since the Mass appears to me to be both beautiful and original, it seems to me worthwhile to consider some of the problems of vocabulary and point of view that any really new work is bound to encounter after its early hearings. Not only standards of the past, but histories of the past, enter into discussions and judgments; adjectival confusion flourishes, and words that are at best applicable only to extrinsic elements of the music are used as evaluations of a final sort. In the case of a Mass these tendencies will naturally overwhelm criticism and embitter conversation, since both religion and music are basic things which are disguised by their histories, entwined in their relations, and personal in their manifestations and vocabularies. Although the symphony and the sonata belong to anyone who claims them, the Mass traditionally belongs to an idea of God and a way of worship. There is an immediate and justified question as to whether or not a Mass, being an act of liturgy, must be written only for performance in and by a church. Is there such a thing conceivable as a Concert Mass; and if there is, what are its emotional, social, or esthetic terms? Since churches for several centuries have more or less consistently recognized only "approved" styles and regarded new music with hostility, does not the composer who writes a personal Mass challenge both religion and lay audience in a way best calculated to displease both?

I hope it is evident that I am leading up to the question of why so many people found Stravinsky's Mass lacking in "spirituality" or wanting in grandeur, and why anyone should assume it just to use such terms as criticism. Certainly the matter of "religious" music and its "spiritual" values is one of association and language, and not one of either religion or music. It is clearly affected by the acceptance of certain arbitrary, though traditional, criteria. But if the Pope Marcellus Mass is taken as the measure of "spirituality," and the B minor Mass as the measure of grandeur, what becomes of the Masses of Machaut, or Dufay, or Josquin? The minimum reasonable demand for "religious" music, given the changing world of creation, if not of criticism, would seem to be a discernible elevation of tone and seriousness of intention. These qualities are found in more than one style of liturgical or ecclesiastical music, and since Stravinsky's Mass possesses them, it suggests as much religion as music ever can. It is, after all, the words and not the music that are always specifically religious; the music represents an attitude towards them in much the same way as the sculpture of Chartres or that of Bernini makes visible an attitude towards saints and towards architecture. Stravinsky's attitude is made clear in the austere beauty of his created sound, lacking in lusciousness and devoid of drama; but who shall say that this is inappropriate to religion? Perhaps the objection to this kind of religion is only, in reality, that it is neither analgesic nor consoling.

One is tempted to digress here, because the hearing of a new Mass involves questions of tradition, of association, and of unthinking acceptance that affect all arts very deeply. One has but to think of the ideas of church architecture, once flexible, syncretistic like religion itself, as they are reduced today to the feeble imitation of earlier models. A steeply gabled roof gives an interior supposed to lead thought upward; a wall is removed and replaced with stained glass which is intended to lead outward to the infinite (for glass is a communication with exterior light). But would it necessarily be less "religious" to build a church directed down, not up, over an abyss, to provide a place of danger and darkness in which to worship, with the reminders of mortality and of ignorance? Perhaps religion should be, if a safeguard to the community, a perilous experience to the individual; perhaps it should isolate him even within the shelter of the spiritual community, so that he achieves his own peace and safety; perhaps the artist, too, even the composer, should have his dark night of the soul.

In this sense perhaps a contemporary Mass should be deeply disquieting in its musical setting, and go beyond mere imitative acceptance of a blunted vocabulary. For surely language has changed, not its purpose. And we can come by this step to Stravinsky's language, about which much has already been written, and much confusion spread. The Mass has been discussed in terms of its conscious (or self-conscious?) archaism; it has been represented as the work of a composer lately devoted to the work of 14th-century masters, a kind of *Ars Novissima.* I cannot depose as to the extent of Stravinsky's study of Machaut, or, for that matter, of Perotinus, but I am not, on the other hand, convinced that this is a matter of great importance. I am aware, in the Mass, of melodic elements, contrapuntal relations, mannerisms of rhythm, cadences, and open sounds that suggest at times what medieval music is supposed to have been; but I am far more aware of music that only Stravinsky could have written, and of elements that have for many years been apparent in his style. Since the title of *Mass* will itself plausibly suggest the history of this early major form of Western music, it is not surprising, in a musicology-conscious culture, that there may arise a fashionable wish to re-create a period of history which, because it is essentially unknowable, appears the more fascinating. One cannot, I suppose, deny the attractiveness for modern musicians of music until recently so neglected; but one may ask whether it is attractive because of its similarities to contemporary style, because of its differences, or because, like all of the really new music of the 20th century, it represents an escape from the burden of a "classical-romantic" tradition to which, for many years, nothing new has been added.

Let us look at the matter in another light: a composer can lend a helping hand in the praiseworthy work of restoring past beauties which we have allowed to become obscure. The musicologist can take this renovating process only so far, removing centuries of dust to reveal the original glow. But his is only a suggestion that has to be realized by the performing artist or artists. The gulf separating the present-day listener from a piece of Gothic music, even when well performed, may remain considerable. But the composer who can acquire by pure instinct a feeling for styles long extinct can give us not fact but illusion—perhaps even a convincing illusion of Gothic music. This, however, is art and not antiquarianism, though it may serve both ends. With Stravinsky there is no pointless (or, to use the word of accusation: "sterile") imitation; if there is mannerism, it is mannerism of a sort that has become integrated into a completely personal expression. There is much less inconsistency of "style" in Stravinsky than in many composers who repeat themselves more obviously. It is always well to remember that the most esteemed painters of the early Renaissance in Italy pleased themselves with the thought that they were the inheritors and exponents of classical principles; but the differences between Quattrocento and Hellenic art, and the self-contained quality of each, would hardly seem to require demonstration.

It appears to me, in any case, that there is little paraphrase, commentary, or re-issue of anything in Stravinsky's newest work. Stravinsky has never needed the excuse of some predecessor's work for his own boldnesses, and I conceive as a strong possibility his invention, without the authority of another century, of the following cadences:

Ex. 1a

Ex 1b

and the following polyphonic lines:

Ex. 2

which to me are fine, sensitive, and moving, without reference to the settings of these same words by composers from there to here. There is also, in this Mass, much chanting; but the rhythmic chant that Stravinsky employs here is not the exclusive property of the Catholic tradition; if there is a familiar sound to it, it is that of most ritualistic intonation. Stravinsky himself gave a version of the type, in another context, in *Les Noces* a good many years ago. From the Mass, we may take this example:[2]

---

[2]The examples from Stravinsky's Mass are printed here by permission of the copyright owners, Boosey & Hawkes.

Ex. 3

Something remains to be said about the beauty of texture and freshness of color in this extraordinary work. The chorus (in four parts throughout, with occasional solo passages, and with children's voices called for in treble and alto parts) is supported by an ensemble of five double reeds and five brasses: two oboes, English horn, two bassoons, two trumpets, three trombones. No one in our day has so productive an imagination in respect of timbre as Stravinsky. The use of these instruments is a stroke of genius; the successive sounds, with or without the voices, the combinations, alterations, and permutations are breath-taking, and of a nature that even a musician fairly versed in orchestration does not anticipate. I do not think that Stravinsky got these sounds anywhere but in his inner ear; I doubt that they were heard, even accidentally, anywhere else before. Here again we have evidence of the direction appropriate for new music; we have had it before, of course, in works of Bartók, Berg, Varèse, and Webern as well as Stravinsky: it is away from the bloated conventional symphony orchestra, which has the vulgarity and noisiness of all mass media, and in which there is nothing new, but merely globs of heavy sound highly conventionalized since Strauss. Symphonic orchestration now tends to become a technique to conceal lack of musical talent. It is interesting to note how often the most original and vital composers write for small, new, odd combinations in which line and timbre are exposed rather than smothered. *L'Histoire du Soldat,* the *Octuor,* and the new Mass are brilliant examples. In the Mass we have combinations such as these, with variety in spacing and effect well worth noting:

The Mass is full of such things, which are not new in Stravinsky's style, but which are here unified with perhaps greater economy and tenseness than ever before. This consistent individuality, this intense certainty of direction and effect, one finds in the work of few contemporary composers—the handful who, like Stravinsky, may with all justice be termed masters.

Current Chronicle: New York

[Review of Leon Kirchner's Duo for Violin and Piano (1947) and Piano Sonata (1948)]
Musical Quarterly XXXV/4 (October 1949)

At a guess, I should say that each year in the United States a hundred or more hopeful
young composers, recently graduated or still studying with one or more masters, begin
submitting works (and large ones, more often than not) to publishers and to organizations,
like The League of Composers. The number of these young and often intellectually dis-
placed persons who set out to create symphonies (or novels or murals or theories of history)
is in effect a reflection of unrest, or of dissatisfaction with the prospect of following the
two key professions of our time, atomic science and advertising. What is most interesting
about the production of the hundreds of young composers is that a good deal of it finally
gets heard. It is heard, of course, as a result of the ceaseless agitation and propaganda for
contemporary music which are (despite, or perhaps because of, the performances) more
than ever necessary.

The level of work by younger composers is doubtless no more depressing today than it
ever was; in the United States, however, the situation of having a very large number of
such composers is a new one, and there are no comparable generations against which to
measure the current crop. The impression may occasionally arise that one deals not with
composers, but with crowds of composers. The fear of being an individual (or is it, fatally,
an inability to be one?) prevents all but a few from ever reaching maturity; we live in an
age of committees, of forum groups, of congresses, laboratories, clinics, and explanatory
notes. The atmosphere of the school persists, often that of the school of minnows. Mr.
Burkat, in *The Musical Quarterly* some months back, correctly noted the allegiance of
much young American music to Rochester and *Appalachian Spring*; he might, I feel, have
added the third force: Central Europe via Southern California. The pursuers of trends
have always existed, and have always forgathered after their fashion, which is internally
inimical but united in crying down other trends and unauthorized impingements on posted
property. But despite the sniping, which is usually very highbrow, these committees,
groups, adherents, addicts, evangelists, societies, or what you will, formally or informally
organized, have a useful function: they provide, collectively, a sort of central underbrush
or second growth, in which the rare accident of a tall tree may easily be seen.

Such a comparatively dominating height appears in the person and works of a newcomer
to the New York scene, a Guggenheim Fellow from California named Leon Kirchner. It
is not necessary to urge remembrance of the name; it will be heard often enough to im-

press itself. It is a joy not to have to write that Kirchner is talented or promising; one can write that of at least several dozen others. Kirchner is already the real thing; he is a composer whose works can stand being heard on programs with the music of anyone writing today. The compositions heard in New York, a Duo for Violin and Piano (1947 and a Piano Sonata (1948), remain in the memory as towering over the music of any new or young composer heard during the past year. The works need no special protection, although we are indebted to The League of Composers and to the Composers' Forum respectively for the presentations in New York. These concerts gave us additionally the opportunity of making the acquaintance of the composer as a brilliant pianist.

Kirchner arrived in New York from California, but he was born, exactly thirty years ago, in Brooklyn. Having gone west, he studied first with Bloch, then with Schoenberg and Sessions. Some strength of purpose, and confidence in that strength, is indicated by the fact that he worked in the mornings with Bloch after coming off the night shift in a war plant. Induction into the army interrupted these studies, resumed, following his discharge, with Schoenberg and Sessions under somewhat less difficult conditions. One respects Kirchner repudiating all of his work before the Violin and Piano Duo of 1947; among the juvenilia are a piano concerto and other works of the type that one needs courage not to preserve and rewrite. Kirchner's total of acknowledged works is therefore impressive only by quality; aside from the Duo and the Sonata, he now presents only a string quartet, completed this year, and a set of small piano pieces.

What strikes one about the Duo is its intensity, its daring, and its containment. Few composers can proportion music of rhapsodic glow so that it does not weary by excess of tone or of length. It is his sense of proportion, perhaps more than any of his other gifts, that stamps Kirchner as a composer who commands himself and his medium absolutely. This control is apparent in the absence of padding, of vulgarisms, of passages that sound labored, of noise designed to be shocking or merely to be soothing. The Duo is all meat. Refreshingly, it cannot be classified; one could not name Kirchner's teachers by hearing his work, and that is the mark of the discovered individual and of the artist. The quality of sound recalls Bartók, the most elusive of 20th-century composers, who cannot be imitated, and who can only rarely be evoked. Kirchner's music has something of the same darkness, the same poetry, the same disquieting hiddenness, but with Kirchner, as with Bartók, this is a product of temperament and not simply of mannerism.

The idiom is chromatic, violently dissonant, drivingly rhythmic; the design is clean, the elements succinct. There is every mark of high style, and no evidence of writing to a theory. The writing for both piano and violin is masterfully competent, although the demands on the performers are considerable. The sound is often thick, sometimes clusterish in effect through the use of seconds, but the massiveness is relieved by the most sensitive filigree and ornamentation. The extraction of excerpts presents a difficult problem of choice, and is possibly of no great point, but the following may convey useful suggestions:[1]

Of the Piano Sonata, one can say that it is an even stronger work than the Duo. It is one of the half-dozen piano sonatas written in this country that one expects to be hearing some years from now. Here again, despite the opening with a tone-row (which, incidentally, seems to disappear immediately), one cannot find a school to which the work seems indubitably to belong. Kirchner profited by his studies with Schoenberg not to become doctrinaire, but to think and work like a composer. In the Piano Sonata there are signs of a more developed Kirchner style: a peculiar placing of trills, an odd and effective use of *style brisé* and unconventional ornamentation, a further exploitation of the repeated note and the chord built on major or minor seconds. The Sonata is the work of a man of forceful, definite, and yet sensitively constituted personality; the music requires thoughtful assimilation by anyone who essays to play it, but it repays the thought and rewards study.

---

[1] The excerpts from Kirchner's Duo are printed here by permission of the copyright owner, Merrymount Music Press.

Current Chronicle: New York

[Festival of Contemporary American Music]
Musical Quarterly XXXVI/3 (July 1950)

The annual Festival of Contemporary American Music, sponsored by the Alice M. Ditson Fund of Columbia University, always attracts a good deal of attention and serves as a wind-up of the winter season of "serious" music in New York. It is invariably well attended by composers and other professionals who come to exchange greetings and au revoirs, and also to hear the works presented. But one can hardly escape the conclusion that the meeting is more sociable than musical in significance, and that the perfunctory exchange of congratulations is the important business of the assembly. The atmosphere is somewhat that of the gathering of a very large family, not all the members of which are on quite cordial speaking terms. It is also rather "official" and increasingly academic, the more so since the awards of the National Institute of Arts and Letters, the Ditson Fund, the Pulitzer Prize, and others are either directly or somewhat vaguely involved in the proceedings. One is staggered both by the amount of patronage that is thus put on view, and by the implication that it represents a family fortune in which all the well-behaved relations may eventually share.

Now that the Institute concert has been incorporated into the Festival, the character of the latter has become even more neutral than heretofore, and one may describe the 1950 programs as mixed without being representative and curious without being novel. Most of the music seemed either mildly good or mildly dull; little was deeply exciting or interestingly irritating. It is difficult to know what musical position, if any, is represented by the Institute; its awards seem to be more or less the equivalent of the Army's Good Conduct Medal. As to the Festival, one feels that it has the aspect of rather restrained patriotic festivity. The coincidence of the Festival with "I Am An American" Day (May 21), could only lead one to recall the comment made by someone a few years back: that it sounded like "I-Am-An-American-Who-Studied-With-Hindemith" Day. (To which a more malicious person added: "But perhaps not quite enough.")

No one, however, could say that Hindemith was present in spirit at this year's concerts. The foreigners who could be made out in the background appeared more to resemble Debussy, Strauss, Fauré, Holst, d'Indy, and Stravinsky. Could they have been consulted, it is possible that they would have had interesting contributions to make to the absorbing discussion of what is American music, a question that can probably be resolved only by a Congressional committee with full access to everything, and complete authority to separate the alien corn from the domestic.

The chamber music concert, sponsored jointly by the Academy, the Institute, and the University, presented what was, in principle, an agreeable juxtaposition of generations. Arthur Shepherd's *Triptych for Soprano and String Quartet,* on poems by Tagore, came off as the most successful piece from the standpoint of consistent taste and stylistic achievement; it is well made, sensitive, and pleasantly vocal, and worth hearing because it is representative of the best music of an older generation of American composers. Edward Burlingame Hill's Sextet for Winds and Piano, although jolly in its opening movement, lags as it continues; it also had the rather great disadvantage of being performed at a constant *mezzo-piano.* Andrew Imbrie's Divertimento is not, one hopes, a representative piece, either of American music or of Imbrie. Ben Weber's[1] romantic *Concert Aria after Solomon,* Op. 29, is not a quite characteristic piece for a composer who is usually associated with the younger 12-tone group. In any case, the *Concert Aria* is a satisfying work, uninhibited and sensuous, with echoes of *Salome.* The aria is sectional, clearly defined by skilfully used instrumental motifs, and well built to its climaxes. The instrumental texture is rich, varied, and interesting throughout, with the voice line (elegantly and intelligently sung by Bethany Beardslee) exhibiting the desirable combination of simultaneous integration and independence. The opening bars of Weber's work indicate the type of harmony and motif profile used in general throughout:[†]

The orchestral program included Elliott Carter's *Holiday Overture* and symphonies by William Bergsma and Henry Cowell, all admirably performed under Izler Solomon, despite the trying conditions imposed by broadcasting hurry, which necessitated cuts in Cowell's work and stepped-up tempos in Bergsma's. Cowell's Fifth Symphony provided a very striking contrast to anything and everything else on the Festival programs. As a consequence of its standing uncompromisingly on the composer's highly individual esthetic position,

---

[1]Weber, Imbrie, and Elliott Carter were the 1950 recipients of "Arts and Letters" grants in music from the Institute.

it appeared to shock many listeners perfectly used to the conventional derivations of what is accepted as "modern" music.

Cowell is an Irish minstrel and an international folklorist, with a prodigious recollection, both racial and personal, and an intellectual energy that enables him to take a quite serious interest in the most diverse manifestations of the art and practice of music. The application of a theoretical mind to the utilization of folk-inspired material is as a rule apt to produce the unhappiest of results, but Cowell has more than occasionally (perhaps because his theorizing is entirely without pseudo-philosophical cant) demonstrated his ability to produce convincingly natural music. The Fifth Symphony is one of his most successful essays in the reconciliation of historical and regional (including Oriental) styles. The melodies, usually modal and harmonized traditionally (with an occasional spicing of sonorous clusters), are fresh and unforced; the rhythms, including a sprightly opening section in 11/8, are clean and contrasted, and the transitions are smooth. It takes great sureness to bring off this sort of musical populism, which, with Cowell, is neither conscious primitivism nor technical ingenuousness. Whether Cowell's most successful efforts in this style will fall squarely between two audiences—the innocent and the sophisticated—is an interesting problem in musical sociology. Cowell has written, in his Celtic folk vein, some genuine masterpieces for band, which although moderately successful are still really over the heads of band audiences. It is of course a truism that popular culture and intellectual populism actually never meet; it is perhaps sadder that in practice the "intelligentsia" seldom know which is which.

Elliott Carter's *Holiday Overture* illustrates another aspect of this problem in his effort to appeal to a large audience within the limits of a highly self-conscious and conventionally modern (contrapuntal, dissonant, and much orchestrated) style. The overture is full of razzle-dazzle and noise, quite brilliant and good fun of a serious sort. In general spirit it recalls Chabrier, with passing compliments to Copland. The contrapuntal complexities are handled with an appearance of casual expertness; the orchestral writing is extremely brilliant. But the piece needs, for a smashing success in our concert halls, an admixture of witlessness and vulgarity which its composer will never, even with the best intentions, acquire.

William Bergsma is another composer of whom the same may be said. His First Symphony disappoints in that there is so much in it that can be called beautiful, skilful, and complete; but there are awkward spots and indications of a too self-conscious striving and elaboration. These are failings that are not infrequent in the works of earnest composers, young or old, but one does not often find them in the work of a composer with so genuine a lyrical gift as Bergsma's. In the case of such a composer, one has a confident feeling that the artifice will soon disappear (or at least be more knowingly concealed) and that the borrowings, of which there are not a few in this work, will be more gently domesticated. Bergsma is so clearly a musician of the first quality that one waits impatiently for the works he must now be writing.

Current Chronicle: New York
[Review of Elliott Carter's Sonata for Violoncello and Piano]
Musical Quarterly XXXVII/1 (January 1951)

Elliott Carter's Sonata for Violoncello and Piano, composed in 1948 and heard several times in New York during the past year,[1] is one of those rare works that tempt one to extremes of praise. It is a mature and distinctive work of an original, responsible, serious, and adult composer whose gifts have not been fully understood or widely appreciated. One senses on first hearing that the 'Cello Sonata is far above the common run of contemporary premières; it is a happy confirmation of the quality of all of Carter's recent work and a happier augury for the future, for it seems to mark the full emergence of a deeply conscious personal style and the final subordination of great ingenuity to equally great expressiveness. Carter has for many years enjoyed a large measure of respect among musicians, but performances of his works have never been numerous. (New York is still awaiting, at this writing, its first hearing of the brilliant *Defense of Corinth,* composed in 1941.) He has had the reputation of being an intellectual composer with a gift for calculated complexity applied to a background of Boulanger and Piston, a composer of music never lacking in skill but sometimes ingeniously uninteresting. Such a reputation may, however, often be unjustly earned, and its origin, in an age like ours, is always suspect as being the poverty and sloth that will prefer dogmatic simple-mindedness on all counts. A work like the 'Cello Sonata does not, in any case, appear suddenly, without anticipation of its characteristics in earlier works; and many of these, especially the Piano Sonata (1945-6), show that the horrible charge of "intellectualism" is not particularly damning in Carter's case. Works such as the two sonatas and the woodwind quintet show richness as well as exactitude of mind, imagination as well as taste, gravity as well as wit; they are of a quality

---

[1] First performed in recital by Bernard Greenhouse, for whom it was written; and later, by the same artist, at a concert of The League of Composers and elsewhere.

equalled by few of his compatriots, and each is close to being the best in its own medium that we have had from American composers.

It is true that Carter is an intellectual in the sense that he regards each new work as being in some respects a problem peculiar to itself, and considers that intellect is often useful in arriving at solutions. But he is certainly not an intellectual with a formula or a doctrine. It is clear that he regards these with as little enthusiasm as he does any other variety of spiritual petrifaction. Each problem, in Carter's work, must find its own musical solution; consistency of method is not a goal, nor is method itself. Most important, one does not feel that the solution is at any time held to be the aim and end of the composition. Lack of consistency in method, lack of formula in aim, need not indicate a creativity that is either nervous or nerveless; they may equally well be the result of a great refinement of the inquiring spirit.

Among artists, aware of the smothering nature of today's mass audience, the temptation unquestionably exists, as strongly as ever before in history, to exploit cleverness as a defense or refuge, by emphasizing the separation of creativeness from mass-mindedness. The composer of so-called intellectual tendencies is perhaps more apt even than other artists to succumb to this temptation, but it is, of course, possible to resist. The solution of puzzles is seldom more than a personal satisfaction, without communicable value. It is a retreat that is a typical manifestation of the artist's spiritual isolation. One may be sure that any composer whose music shows thought has at times explored the abstractions of disembodied sound, in the remotest detachment from expressiveness or even from considerations of utility. But he comes back, if he is a composer, to apply whatever gains he has made in this flight, to the more prosaic, but also more human, problem of performable music sufficiently within a tradition to be understood.

There is every evidence in Carter's music of something like this process as an underlying artistic and intellectual practice. There is a niceness of detail and a care for proportion, both serving a total plan always held in view, that bespeak thought more than intuition. But why do we so often deprecate thought or overpraise the intuitive? Is it because popularized psychological jargons help produce popularized art? What we object to, of course, is the exhibition of the process of thinking rather than its concealment in an artistic result. It is possibly true that in an occasional earlier work, Carter showed less mastery of this type of concealment than he has since displayed. Certainly one finds in his more recent works a largeness of design, admirably coherent, and one does not find one's attention wandering from effect to device. The structure and unity may be philosophically conceived, but the musical achievement resides in the translation into notes that are their own justification.

It is in these terms that Carter has so notably grown. The Piano Sonata is a decisive work; it has sweep and scale; there is nothing small or fussy about it to detract from its effect. It is dramatic and intense, broad and vigorous. There are many sounds that, as isolated sounds, recall Stravinsky or Copland, but they are integrated in a fashion both personal and striking. This is achieved without sacrifice of lucidity; the reverse is obviously true: it is precisely the lucidity of the composer that enables him to attain a moving and original expressiveness tending away from the esthetic of neo-Classicism. The 'Cello Sonata has many of the same qualities; it is thoroughly big, rather dark, extremely bold. It makes, moreover, several interesting structural departures, which need to be dealt with more fully.

Carter gives much attention to problems of balance, sonority, and idiom for each instrumental combination that he uses. The 'Cello Sonata is much concerned with balances of sonority and timbre between the 'cello and the piano; the newer *Eight Etudes and a Fantasy* for woodwind quartet (1950) is even more extraordinary as an achievement in this respect, though it has its anticipation in the Woodwind Quintet (1948). But the principal idea that has engaged Carter from 1945 to the present has been that of using meter—ideas of absolute and relative time—as the groundwork of form. The Piano Sonata uses tempo sections in an unusual way to construct a large two-movement form; it has been described as a sonata consisting of a fantasia followed by a fantasia, but this is merely a way of suggesting that it is too unorthodox for conventional analysis, or type-casting. The first movement presents other difficulties, both for the performer and the anatomist. It has no time signature, but gives a metronomic unit for the half or quarter note: bar lines are used, but are placed without regularity. The following example[2] is taken somewhat at random:

Ex.1 Piano Sonata
Tempo I, scorrevole

legato
pp
poco a poco cresc.

[2]Reprinted by permission of the Mercury Music Corporation, owners of copyright.

Here we have a bar with sixteen 16th notes (apparently equal to 4/4), divided into patterns of seven, four, and five; and a bar of twelve 16ths (apparently equal to 3/4) divided seven and five. The divisions in the following bars are indicated with equal definiteness. Clearly the effect desired by Carter—emphasis on duration of note rather than pulse—is not new except in terms of 18th- and 19th-century thinking, but his realization of it is more rational than those one usually finds. The bars are *not* 4/4 or 3/4, and cannot be played as such without total distortion. The barring and grouping of the 16ths in the rapid-running sections of the movement (marked *legato scorrevole*) show the attention to detail that is characteristic of Carter; each fragment of phrase seems carefully thought out, but continuity is thereby achieved rather than impeded, and the visual presentation is the most helpful possible to the player. Yet it takes a flexible-minded performer to acquire the necessary style of playing. Carter is aware that the style or technique of this work is possible only in music for a single player. It is too difficult of execution to be reasonably expected in ensemble performance with conventionally trained players.

Hence a new technique, or a new solution of the original problem, is evolved by the composer for works involving two or more players. Part of the problem is that of using conventional notation for non-conventional ideas of metric alteration, and for dividing note-values in the proportions of five and seven as well as the customary two, three, and four. Carter has developed, in his most recent works, the idea of "metrical modulation." This concept is based on the use of absolute or metronomic time in readily legible and easily playable divisions marked off by conventional bar lines; through its application the length of the basic note unit may be shortened or increased by almost any fraction. An example from the *Eight Etudes and a Fantasy* for woodwind quartet may make the principle clear through a simple application:[†]

This principle is applied on a large scale throughout the four movements of the 'Cello Sonata, and becomes a formal element in the composition. Large sections are constructed on the basis of change, not of *tempo,* but of relative note-length in proportions not easily exploited in conventional notation. The metrical inter-relation of the movements themselves is also made explicit. An example from the slow movement may be used to show the technique of lengthening the eighth note in the proportion of 7:6:

[†] Exx. 2 and 3 reprinted by permission of Associated Music Publishers, Inc., owners of copyright.

This is one of the more devious "modulations" used in the piece; in performance, however, it moves with perfect smoothness and arouses no sense of strain or pointless artifice. It would appear quite clearly that the use of this type of "modulation" could become a simple game; it is to Carter's credit that he has not let it become one in his music. He has found it a useful adjunct to the achievement of expressive aims and has succeeded in making it function unobtrusively as a technique. It is praise of the sonata to point out that its excellence has been widely perceived without reference to its technical novelties; its coherence of form is felt with the same immediacy as its intensity and eloquence.

A discreet use of "cyclical" devices is found in both sonatas. In the Piano Sonata, the slow sections of the first and second movements are clearly related; they may, in fact, be said to be made of the same material, differently colored. There is skilful variation of sonority throughout the piece, and extremely effective employment of the overtones produced by silently depressed keys. The first subject of the 'Cello Sonata reappears on the closing page with the roles of the instruments reversed; many motifs in the work appear in varied shapes in two or more movements. These are all, to be sure, intellectual devices, yet many of them may be (as they are here) excellent musical ones as well.

Carter has just completed a string quartet, not yet performed, in which the idea of "metrical modulation" is further developed. As a by-product of his preoccupation with the idea he has also written a set of six pieces for kettle-drums. It should be interesting to discover in the quartet whether the musical vocabulary and esthetic perspective of the two sonatas still holds the composer's interest, or whether there are further surprises in store.

Current Chronicle: New York
[Musical scene in New York and review of William Schuman's *Judith*]
Musical Quarterly XXXVII/2 (April 1951)

The concert presented in New York by the Louisville Orchestra, being a "commercial" venture, was interesting in that as well as in other respects. What this orchestra has done deserves wide notice and celebration. Rather than cease operations, the orchestra has been reduced to fifty players, so that willy-nilly it represents a sane musical and economic balance for a community of moderate size, and challenges the untruth that an orchestra must be constituted as if it had to play the *Sacre* at each concert. We know that most of the standard repertory can be played by a group of fifty, and that huge works are in any case best left to the few large and highly polished orchestras that can deal with them (and whose performances can be disseminated through broadcasts or recordings). But the Louisville Orchestra improves even on the idea of using a suitable ready-made repertory: far from sacrificing a choice of contemporary repertory, it commissions its own. At the rate of six each year, it has already reached the impressive total of eighteen new works.

A selection of these works was presented to New York at the end of December: six scores of which only one had previously been heard here. In view of the inevitable gamble involved in commissioning new works, the Louisville Orchestra came out well. Thomson's distinguished *Wheat Field at Noon* was the one familiar work listed; this has already achieved a number of performances, and it is to be hoped that others of the Louisville commissions will enjoy equal success. Exception must be made for Diamond's *Timon of Athens—A Symphonic Portrait After Shakespeare,* suitably described by the composer as a "psych-orchestral" study. Comment on this description appears unnecessary. The juvenile pomposity of the author's program note, explaining Shakespeare to the unlettered, is matched by the music, the progress of which from cliché to cliché (misunderstanding and noble tears) is interrupted only by pointless bursts of activity in the percussion section. One gets weary of composers who, when they can think of nothing else, call out the drums and cymbals. Claude Almond's *John Gilbert: A Steamboat Overture* is less interesting, since it is less preposterous; it is a typical piece of the "native American" school, completely academic, a work that any of forty or fifty composers might have written.´ These scores represent the minus side of the Louisville Orchestra's efforts. The works by Martinu and Persichetti were characteristically skilful, but were overshadowed by the scale of William Schuman's *Judith,* commissioned jointly of Schuman and Martha Graham as a "choreographic poem" for presentation by Miss Graham as soloist with the orchestra.

The novelty of this conception is, in my view, quite irrelevant; the score is a fine and strong one and can get along handsomely with or without gestures. I suppose that in a certain sense a collaborative effort must be considered for what it appears to be or in terms of what it seeks to achieve, but I cannot avoid the conviction that the collaboration is an unequal one and that Schuman's music will easily outlive the circumstances that called it forth. *Judith* has the virtues of Schuman at his best. The obvious fact about Schuman is that he is a big composer, vehement, self-confident, and emphatically positive. He is, in a sense, a musical Walt Whitman; he has the same athleticism, the same exuberance, the same love of sound, and also the same capacity for the elegiac and the poignant. Schuman, like Whitman, is sometimes too much himself, in the sense that he will use a machine-gun to kill a mosquito and be happy about it because the gun makes such a nice loud rat-tat-tat. Enthusiasm is occasionally substituted for suitability. But the score of *Judith* is well-knit and well-proportioned´in every respect. It is forceful, dramatic, imaginative, and brilliantly written for orchestra, not merely "orchestrated." Its economy of material makes

A Passage from William Schuman's *Judith* (see p. 78)

for coherence throughout the multi-sectional structure, and since the music was composed before the "scenario," it is clear that the latter could have had no effect on the musical form, except in the most general way. The most important musical fact is that the score may be abstracted from the dance without loss of clarity. Viewed musically, it remains extremely vivid, coherent, and disciplined.

The underlying harmonic scheme in Schuman's work is often quite simple, consisting of common triads with single dissonant notes at the interval of a semitone from any member of the chord. For example:[1]

Schuman likes to space the dissonance widely, often keeping the dissonating notes in the outer voices, especially in slow or lyrical passages; he tends to close the position where greater weight or agitation is sought. This is not, however, an invariable practice. In general, Schuman greatly prefers spacing in major sevenths and minor ninths to the closer position of the minor second. As examples, one may cite the tranquil opening of the score (Ex. 2a) and a chord succession taken from a passage of obvious dramatic stress (Ex. 2b):

The melodic possibilities of such chord combinations are fully explored; the melodies may be said to be generated out of the necessity of supplying tones dissonant to the triads. Figures such as:

are common. In the passage illustrated on pp. 76-77 the relation of melody to triad is made very clear. The arbitrary connections between the triadic harmonies, and the more or less constant tension produced by the melodic dissonances, work together to preserve

---

[1]The examples from *Judith* are copyright 1950 by G. Schirmer, Inc. Used by permission.

the consistent forward motion that characterizes Schuman's music; they often enable him to lengthen his line beyond what is the expected point of relaxation or resolution. This technique is exploited to considerable advantage in many of Schuman's scores.

Thematically, *Judith* is based on a series of ideas presented in rapid succession after a brief introduction in which they are foreshadowed. It is possible to say that the entire composition is based on the ideas stated in the passage illustrated.

This material passes through many transformations, rhythmically and intervallically; there is much freedom of octave transposition, and little literal repetition except in the concluding section of the score. But the transformations remain recognizably related to the germinal ideas. Throughout the score appear Schuman's characteristic sudden and violent contrasts in dynamics: *pp* to *fff* in an alternation that is so rapid and frequent as to become a mannerism. The shifts of orchestral timbre are handled in much the same way, though always with extreme skill, and often with telling effect. Schuman's orchestral imagination is certainly superior to that of any other American composer. The display of virtuosity is sometimes such that it dazzles, or even distracts, rather than beguiles the listener. Schuman demands great effort of conductors and orchestral players, as in such a passage:

Ex. 4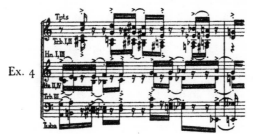

but the excitement of such an exchange of timbre, subtle even at a high pitch, is clearly well worth the effort. The score of *Judith,* like all of Schuman's orchestral scores, abounds in similarly striking passages.

A good deal has already been written about the restless, nervous, emphatic quality of rhythmic activity in Schuman's music. The score of *Judith* is characteristic in this respect, but there is a satisfactory balance of quieter elements, giving not only relief in the simplest terms of lessening of tension, but making much more effective, through well-conceived proportioning, the excitement produced by the complex counterpoint of rhythm and timbre. It is in this way, among others, that *Judith* seems one of the most wholly satisfactory of Schuman's scores. It should be heard again, and (with all respect to the Louisville Orchestra) with a few more strings; as concert music it will stand with the best American scores of the past many years.

Current Chronicle: New York
[Review of Luigi Dallapiccola's *Canti di Prigionia* and *Il Prigioniero*]
Musical Quarterly XXXVII/3 (July 1951)

The most memorable first American performances heard by this chronicler during the past season were those of two large works by Luigi Dallapiccola, a composer hitherto almost unrepresented on our programs, although his work has been discussed, and his European reputation known, for some years. In January the *Canti di Prigionia,* for mixed chorus, two pianos, two harps, and percussion, were presented by the U. S. Section of the International Society for Contemporary Music at the invitation of the Juilliard School of Music (and with Juilliard performers), and in March the Juilliard Opera Theatre gave four performances in English of *Il Prigioniero,* a one-act opera with prologue first staged at the Florentine May Festival of 1950. It seems not inappropriate to record an indebtedness to Juilliard and to the initiative of Frederic Cohen and Frederic Waldman for performing these remarkable works, which surely indicate that Dallapiccola is one of the vital composers of our time. Both the *Canti* and the opera reveal Dallapiccola as a prodigious musical personality, a man of high intellect and imagination, formidable technique, and broadly cultivated humanity. His is a genuinely new and important voice in contemporary music.

The juxtaposition of *The Prisoner* (composed in 1946-47) and the earlier *Canti* (1939-41) affords an interesting view of Dallapiccola's style and its evolution. Such tags as "leading exponent of the twelve-tone system in Italy" (which have become attached to him, and which may well be true) give a misleading notion of his music, which, like all great art, is personal and yet within a tradition. It is much less important that he has used one technique or another than that his music is impressively his own. The slogan-description, in Dallapiccola's case, seems to have aroused some curiosity about the possible Italianization of the twelve-tone technique in his work. *The Prisoner* is dodecaphonic, clearly so; whether it is noticeably Italianate or Italianized seems much less clear. It is worth remembering that Dallapiccola was born (in 1904) in Pisino d'Istria, lived in Graz as a young man, and undertook his first musical studies in Trieste. A good deal of Austrian commerce flows from Vienna through Trieste, no matter what flag flies over the port. There is of course no reason why a composer born in Calabria or Andalusia should not compose successfully in the twelve-tone style; we are interested if he does so only because of the discontinuity with local traditions that is implied. Central European tradition and its continuity may lead naturally and easily to Schoenberg and Webern and Dallapiccola. In that simple idea of tradition lies the advantage of every European composer not totally alienated from his ancestry and his culture. It is very difficult simply to *adopt* another heritage. One feels more strongly each day, with the disintegration of our external standards and values, that tradition and the memory of cultural stability form a necessary basis for evolving a personal style that is intelligible. That is perhaps one of the explanations of Dallapiccola's strength, as it is of Stravinsky's, Bartók's, or Berg's.

The *Songs of Captivity* are unhesitating and overwhelming expressions of traditional faith. They are not songs of documentary captivity; they contain no allusions to circumstance. The Latin texts of the songs are the Prayer of Mary Stuart, the Invocation of Boethius, and the Leave-Taking of Savonarola. The *prigionia* with which they deal is an everlasting one, and its expression is in the central ethical tradition of European civilization. Dallapiccola's music suggests that same vast and still meaningful background; it has the quality of the universal in that, despite its extraordinary sounds, one does not immediately classify it as contemporary or "modern" music. It is new, and yet it is a synthesis; it is aware of the whole 20th century, not merely of Stravinsky or of Schoenberg, but of every other original thought, and of the past as well. Adherents of any school or doctrine may easily find suggestions of what they most admire, but such simple terms of admiration as these exclude all that is truly important in the absorption of the suggestions by a major personality. The note of high tragedy, which has almost disappeared from our art, is in these songs recaptured and reaffirmed with nobility and daring. We are accustomed to skill, such as we find here, but we rarely have grandeur, or imagination of such evocative power. Nothing stale, nothing cold, nothing specious or cleverly invented diminishes the force of this grave and exalting music. If this is Italian music, we have had little of its sort since Monteverdi.

Perhaps it is not far-fetched to suggest that Dallapiccola is in fact, both technically and spiritually, in Monteverdi's direct line. Monteverdi's preoccupation with vocal line, his amazing sense of timbre, his daring in the treatment of affective harmony, are all found in Dallapiccola. The *Songs of Captivity* are extraordinary in all these respects: the vocal lines, combining in a virtuoso counterpoint, are of the utmost refinement in contour and expressiveness; the harmonic idiom is alternately taut and relaxed; its balance between tonality and atonality is in some ways an echo of Monteverdi's tense position between the tonal and the pre-tonal. It is the timbre of Dallapiccola's *Canti* that makes them unique; this is the product of an imagination in sound that has had few equals. The songs use an "orchestra" of two pianos, two harps, xylophone, vibraphone, six timpani, ten large chimes, three tam-tams (large, medium, and small), cymbals (free and suspended), triangle, and various drums. It is useless to attempt a description of the sounds that Dallapiccola makes these instruments produce. In a sense they are evidence, in a different context, of the genius of Varèse, who may first have suggested them. The indebtedness of Dallapiccola, if indebtedness there is, should surely be credited to *Ionisation* rather than to *Les Noces.* But whatever stylistic influence we may try to discern or to deny, the impressive fact remains that from the standpoint of sonority, among others, we have here music that is new and moving and beautiful.

The Prisoner will probably cause controversy wherever it is heard, but it will almost surely be respected. It is perhaps less perfect than the *Canti,* but its imperfections may stem from the imperfect and complex nature of opera itself. Certainly *The Prisoner* is a good illustration of the enormous difficulties and hazards that any composer of opera must knowingly accept; he puts himself at the mercy of singer-actors, stage directors, costumers, and especially of librettists and translators, in addition to the usual conductors and instrumental performers. The Juilliard Opera Theatre's production of the Dallapiccola opera was under the musical direction of a gifted and devoted conductor, Frederic Waldman, but despite his remarkable achievement in presenting the work with student performers, it must be admitted that the opera was poorly acted and in some roles not well sung. The English translation was a liability at all times, the over-all stage management was ineffective (although the set by Frederick Kiesler was brilliant), and the choral singing was indecisive. These are not unusual disadvantages for composers of opera to face; they are of his own courting, but they are of course not of his making.

The disadvantage of the composer's own making is usually the libretto, whether he chooses this ready-made, supervises the work of a collaborator, or writes it himself. Where the dramatic and musical pretense is innocent, the conditions governing (and governed by) the libretto are simpler; but Dallapiccola's aspirations, like those of most modern opera composers, are intensely serious as to drama and symbolism. His libretto, written by himself after a story of Villiers de l'Isle-Adam (*La Torture par l'Espérance*) and an episode from Charles de Coster's *Ulenspiegel,* must therefore be judged on a serious basis. Any libretto will be intensified beyond what it is worth, or it will be reduced to insignificance, if it does not match the dramatic power of the composer's music. Dallapiccola's "plot," at first glance, seems important and able to stand musical intensification. It deals with a prisoner of Phillip II, in the subterranean vaults of the *Official* in Saragossa; the prisoner is called

"Brother" by a guard, begins to hope for freedom, escapes from his cell with apparent connivance, but upon reaching the outside of the prison falls into the waiting arms of the Grand Inquisitor, who is none other than the guard who first gave him hope. This is bitter enough and has special meaning enough for the 20th century; but it is not as strong as it seems. Dallapiccola the librettist makes a fatal mistake, not of dramatic construction, but of morality, in seeming to present this fable to indicate that hope itself is the final torture.[1] The material of the fable is too real and too terrible to permit such a questionable moral thesis, and it is this that undermines the truthfulness, the ultimate convincingness, of the work of art as opera.

The music of *The Prisoner* is magnificent. Its technique is primarily dodecaphonic, but it is effective in much the same ways as the non-twelve-tone *Canti*. The opera calls for three principals, large chorus and chamber chorus, and an orchestra of the usual proportions, to which are added saxophones, on-stage organ and brass, and the same extensive apparatus of percussion that was used in the earlier work. This prodigality is justified by the fantastic and intoxicating sounds that this master of timbre and sonority produces. Even in the reduced orchestral version commissioned by the Juilliard in view of its limited pit and stage facilities, much of this incandescence remained. The original is, however, clearly to be preferred, and it is to be hoped that American audiences will soon have an opportunity to hear it. Nothing in Dallapiccola's use of his resources sounds unnatural, contrived, noisy, or merely luscious; it is "orchestration" only in the sense of using vocal and instrumental combinations, and in this case with genius.

Dallapiccola's twelve-tone technique is strict and easy to follow in terms of conventional analysis. To the ear it seems flowing and natural, although the vocal lines are not always easy to sing and are occasionally lacking in dramatic force. The rhythms are on the whole strongly marked; and there are occasional reiterations of dissonant chord combinations (derived from tone-rows) that produce an effect of a simpler harmonic style. The opera as a whole is very tightly constructed, with motifs recurring in simple form and in complex contrapuntal alterations. The usual inversions, retrogressions, and other devices essential in row transformation are of course abundant. Formal types used include ricercari, a ballata, and a strophic aria. Some of the principal motifs may be illustrated:[2]

---

[1] It is still possible that Dallapiccola did not intend this sense to emerge. Nevertheless, the crucial lines of the libretto (in the original) are: (1) *Vivere devi, per poter sperare;* and at the last (2) *S'è fatta luce! Vedo! La speranza, l'ultima tortura / Di quante mai sofferte, la più atroce . . .*

[2] The examples are printed by permission of Boosey and Hawkes, Inc.

These three motifs are used in the three ricercari in the third scene, and have recognizable symbolic as well as musical significance throughout the opera. One of the stunning things in *The Prisoner* is Dallapiccola's introduction of two choral interludes that are almost completely consonant and triadic. The impact of these is, in the context, even more astonishing and dramatic than one would, theoretically, suppose it to be. They are timed, moreover, with a real sense of theater. Dallapiccola wants the audience to be literally overwhelmed, and inserts a note in the score: "The sonority of the second Choral Intermezzo should be formidable; each listener should feel literally run through and submerged by the immensity of the sound. To effect this, one should not hesitate to use mechanical aids, such as loudspeakers, etc." The vastly magnified entrance of the chorus on a C-major triad (Juilliard did, in fact, use amplifiers) is a theatrical effect that is really blood-chilling.

The function of the chorus is the antique one of commentary, the comment in this case being derived from Psalm texts, sung in Latin. The first is placed after the Prologue: *Fiat misericordia tua, Domine, super nos . . .* The second, as the Prisoner bursts from his cell: *Domine, labia mea aperies, et os meum annuntiabit laudem tuam.* Precisely at the point where the Grand Inquisitor takes the Prisoner's hand to lead him to the stake, the chamber chorus enters with a quotation from the Prayer of Mary Stuart from the *Songs of Captivity.* As this progresses, the large chorus once more takes up the text and music of the second Intermezzo, *pianississimo.*

Whatever shortcomings *The Prisoner* may have, it is probably safe to say that not since *Wozzeck* has anything so remarkable been written for the musical stage. We must hope for more; and we must await rehearing of *The Prisoner* in its original language and orchestral completeness.

Current Chronicle: New York
[Review of two New Music Society concerts]
Musical Quarterly XXXVII/4 (October 1951)

The two concerts presented (on May 8 and 10) by the New Music Society afforded comparatively large audiences a chance to hear some oddments of the past and future of "modern music," interspersed among pieces less determinedly original, and perhaps more seriously musical. A peculiar hodgepodge, but refreshing in its way, and full of material for profound reflection on the part of anyone who likes his music with a dash of sociology, or vice versa. Modernism for its own sake being, as we know, so much a matter of intent, dead-pan humor or dead-end earnestness, comedy or hatred, clarification or destructiveness, dedication or artistic amorality, what matters in concerts like these is that the audience is given no clue; and this was a wise, if perhaps accidental, disposition on the part of Frank Wigglesworth and his associates of the Society. Audiences are, in a vital respect, at least as fair game for the critic as what they listen to; the beginnings of an illuminating cultural history may well lie in the camouflaged tape-recorder planted squarely in the middle of the parterre. At some concerts (and those of the New Music Society lead the list) one would, in addition to the conversation for its own sake, have recorded a counterpoint to the stage performance which one could then present to John Cage, who would almost surely find a use for it. But this is a project that I humbly propose for another critic, another year.

There was much pleasure in hearing again at these concerts such pieces as Ruggles's *Lilacs,* Cowell's Sinfonietta of the early 1920s, and Thomson's *Capital Capitals.* These works have, in various ways, survived being "modern," and cannot now be described as quaint, which is, one feels, a circumstance rather disappointing to many people. One missed hearing representative pieces of Varèse, and perhaps of Charles Seeger and Rudhyar, to round out the picture; Varèse's *Offrandes* was originally scheduled, but unfortunately withdrawn. Ruggles's gift has always seemed to me a small, though distinctive, one; *Lilacs* sounds very much like *Angels* or another of his compositions, but there is a recognizable and personal feeling in all of these. At the risk of bringing down wrath from all quarters, I should say that the sound is in the end rather more pretty than rugged or impressive. The consistent dissonance in Ruggles's pieces is, after thirty years, the mildest kind of auditory excitement. If one misses the more violent excitement that these works caused in the '20s, one can now perhaps at least hear them better for the lack of it.

Cowell's Sinfonietta is to my mind one of his most interesting and satisfying scores; it stands up more than remarkably well after an absence of twenty-five years. To 1951's younger musicians it explains, better than Cowell's recent works, the composer's reputation and position as an experimenter, innovator, and ornament of the *avant-garde*. Webern thought highly enough of the Sinfonietta to perform it in Vienna in 1926, as representative of new American music; the score was published in 1931 by Adler, in Berlin. Its neglect in America is hard to explain; it is not a period piece, or in any sense a curiosity, except in one respect: it contains an interpolated third movement in which a cantilena for solo 'cello is accompanied by the whirling of thundersticks. (This movement does not appear in the printed score.) The thundersticks, I suspect, represent an experiment, not in sound, and not even in mystification, but simply in seeing how far the audience will let itself be distracted; this, I am sure, is just the sort of comedy that might appeal to Cowell as a wry commentary on certain aspects of fashion and modernism. It is perhaps ironic that the comedy succeeds too well, and that the solid musical substance of the three conventional movements is apt to suffer a lessening of attention. The Sinfonietta has resource and invention, in addition to thundersticks; it is skilfully contrapuntal and almost constantly at a maximum dissonance. In many ways it is unique. Nowhere has Cowell, or anyone else, given more bite and brilliance to the tone-cluster; and I think that nowhere else in his work is there so much freedom and elegance in the interweaving of rhythmically interesting contrapuntal lines.

If Cowell uses thundersticks, his disciple Lou Harrison advances technologically through the ages to the employment of brake-drums, iron pipes, packing-boxes, bells, wood-blocks, assorted drums, along with a guitar and an ocarina. Using these not as an interpolation in a larger piece, or as added "effects," but as the entire orchestra of his *Canticle No. 3*, Harrison miraculously succeeds in producing a succession of charming and obviously well organized sounds. One does not at once think of the word "sensitive" as a likely one in connection with so much old metal, but that is precisely the word to describe Harrison's calculation of his effects. The ocarina, floating melodic fragments over the rather muffled percussive sounds, becomes, moreover, not a comic substitute for a flute or a recorder, but the beautifully right instrument for the occasion. This music of Harrison's may perhaps be described without disparagement as a gentle variety of Varèse, with Oriental overtones. It is extremely subtle, refined, and full of grace and imagination.

A good deal of the more conventional music heard at the New Music concerts had notably fewer enduring qualities than Harrison's. But Ellis Kohs's Chamber Concerto for Solo Viola and String Nonet is made of good stuff, and is convincing enough evidence that Kohs (born 1916) is one of the younger American composers who is arriving at maturity and is worth hearing. This Concerto is a work of considerable distinction, warm, full of virtuosity, well-designed. Its style is a personal composite, free from marks of any one school, synthetic like that of Kirchner and others of the rising generation, an individual reshaping of the variety of main forces that 20th-century music has produced.

The second of the New Music concerts (at which the Kohs and Harrison works were heard) went on far into the night. Some of the more interesting exhibits, coming at the end, were regrettably telescoped. Toch's *Fuge aus der Geographie* and McLaren's experiments in writing sound directly on film were inadequately presented, but both deserve extended comment on another occasion. Neither represents pointless experiment, and McLaren's is distinctly ominous. The climax of the evening was John Cage's composition for 12 radios, 24 players. Suffice it to say that this work seems to me highly symptomatic, and I am sure that its presentation constitutes one of the most pointedly desperate comments ever made on the narrowing world in which the intellect is still permitted freely to live. Cage's opus, itself a consequence, should bear interesting fruit. Who can tell where this will end? In what progressive nursery school will two radios (four hands) first be used to teach counterpoint?

Current Chronicle: New York
[Review of Leon Kirchner's Sinfonia]
Musical Quarterly XXXVIII/2 (April 1952)

Considerable anticipation attended the performance by the New York Philharmonic, under Mitropoulos, of Leon Kirchner's first orchestral work, a Sinfonia in Two Parts, written on commission from Rodgers and Hammerstein, awarded through The League of Composers. A number of questions and reservations, after hearing and studying the score, prompted me to a re-reading of Kirchner's Piano Sonata and his Duo for Violin and Piano, about which I had occasion to write in enthusiastic terms a few years ago.[1] Review of these works has in no way lessened my esteem for them. On the contrary, it seems to me that they represent a musical gift of the highest order. Works of such quality cannot be written by accident, and they must represent at least one permanent aspect of the composer's musical language. In the light of them the Sinfonia appears to be in many ways a regression.

With Kirchner's earlier works, one could say confidently: "Here is a composer"; on the evidence of the Sinfonia alone, one would say, still admiringly, "Here is an impressive talent." The Sinfonia, viewed as development, is disappointing, but it is still full of indications that Kirchner, of all recently arrived American composers, is the one most worth watching.

It is possible that the pressure attendant upon the production of a first orchestral work, with the added responsibility of a commission, and the certainty of a performance that will attract much attention, is somewhat insalubrious. There is in the Sinfonia a slight air of desperation, as if the composer felt the necessity of cramming everything into one piece; and an air of tentativeness in the sense that at one time or another almost everything is tried. In writing of the earlier and smaller works, I mentioned Kirchner's fine sense of "containment," especially as applied to the difficult problem of handling material that is by nature almost rhapsodic. It is precisely this sort of containment and control that the Sinfonia lacks. It sprawls and ambles; it is often forceful, always wayward; one leaves it with the feeling that it is less a Sinfonia than a music for the theater, or even for the films. One assumes that programmatic ideas did not influence the composition (unless they existed subconsciously), but it is difficult otherwise to account for the occasional banalities, abruptnesses, or picturesque clichés that are all too evident. The ending, re-minding one of nothing so much as *Tod und Verklärung,* is as tepid as a movie finale, and unfortunately succeeds in bringing to recall the weakest aspects of the music that has led to it. This is the more regrettable in that there is so much in the score that might better be remembered.

Disunity and disparity of elements are the most disturbing aspects of the score. It is true that the eye discerns a continuity of constructive ideas (motifs, harmonic complexes), but the ear does not. One hears successive treatments of material that recall not only technical

---

[1] *The Musical Quarterly,* XXXV (1949), 617ff. [See pp. 63-65 in this volume.]

procedures, but also specific pages, of Wagner, Stravinsky, Ravel, Bartók (of *The Miraculous Mandarin*), and especially Richard Strauss. The Sinfonia seems to come from *Tristan* by way of *The Rite of Spring,* or perhaps, if one can suggest it without the imputation of facetiousness, from *The Rite of Spring* by way of *Tristan.* There is certainly something in the score that goes backwards, or unsteadily. The matter of "influences" is not particularly important. The effort of this generation in music is perhaps ultimately directed towards a synthesis of all of its shaping influences. This will be achieved, and it is by no means impossible that Kirchner may lead the way, without incongruities, in a fusion that will be the highest expression of the completely personal. But in the Sinfonia styles are merely forced to live together; they are not fused, and some of the juxtapositions are alarming. In writing of the earlier pieces, I observed that one could not identify Kirchner's teachers through his music; that is still true of the Sinfonia, but for a different reason: here one senses a student still undecided among an almost impossible multiplicity of masters, not yet absorbed and dominated by a new personality.

Tonality has apparently become a preoccupation of Kirchner in the period between the String Quartet (1949) and the Sinfonia. The Sinfonia seems to represent an extended concept of D major-minor. The note D is emphasized as a center of gravity at the beginning, and the final pages sustain (too long perhaps) a D-major triad to which a C♯ is added. An unresolved relation of C♯, and often G♯, to the fundamental D triad seems to be one of the bases on which the harmonic explorations develop. The opening gives one a motif that recurs frequently:[2]

Ex. 1

A second major idea is foreshadowed in the sixth measure, and is fully stated in measures 11-15:

Ex. 2

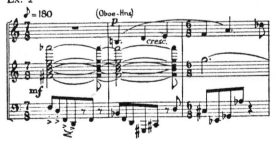

---

[2] The examples from Kirchner's Sinfonia are used by permission of Mercury Music Corporation.

There is a development of these ideas, but no restatement in clear terms. The material becomes somewhat dissipated in what appears to be an indecision about the function of rhythm in tonality, and a disquieting conflict between diatonic and chromatic thinking. The only passages in the work that are strongly pulsed are those produced by the use of nearly conventional tonal progressions; a rhythmic languor characterizes the more chromatic passages throughout.

The second movement, linked to the first by a sustained B, is related to the first in materials, but the relation is by no means made clear. Much of the development is ingenious and beautiful, but expected high points do not arrive. One feels that the work has been full of promises almost wilfully unfulfilled.

Kirchner's preoccupation with rhythmic and metric problems was evident in his earlier pieces, and in them he achieved notably successful and exciting results through a combination of vigor and subtlety in manipulating odd and regular patterns. The preoccupation is still marked in the score of the Sinfonia, but the results are only occasionally effective. It is only fair to note that the most successful passages are really brilliant. The score is fearsomely complicated in appearance, not only as to changes of time-signature, but in the almost constant counter-play of subdivisions within the bar: individual voices against other voices, choir against choir. It is here that the calculation goes astray, for the voices tend to cancel one another out; in the end they produce, for all their individual vigor, a neutral and almost anti-rhythmic effect. One misses a pulse, and one is also reminded that a rhythmic pattern, before it can effectively be shifted, must first be established. It is possible that Kirchner was seeking a special kind of rhythmic blankness, though his technique then seems like a long way round to such a goal. It seems more reasonable to assume that the constitution of the orchestra, with its numerous voices, proved to be too much of a temptation towards experiment with simultaneous complexities.

This would appear to be true also of the manipulation of timbre in the Sinfonia. A continuous effort to find novel and interesting combinations defeats its own end. There are sections of the Sinfonia that are wonderfully imaginative and very beautiful in orchestral sound. But they appear in surprising places, not as culminations, but almost as happy accidents. There are other spots in the score that simply do not come off, though one senses the intention, if only through the eye. (I have felt for a long time, and have suggested in these pages, that "orchestration," as such, is a major blight on American musical thinking. It arises perhaps from our commercial emphasis on "arranging," which filters through with only slightly diminished intensity to the thinking of serious and even introspective composers. I do not, certainly, argue for the neglect of orchestral resources; I feel only that the temptation of the cheap effect should be resisted, even if this means withholding delight from a public corrupted, up to the concert-hall level, by radio and movies. Among other things, snare-drum rolls are a poor substitute for musical transitions.) Kirchner does know instruments; his writing for them is, in technical terms, daring and skilful. But there is perhaps too much effort to be fancy, and occasionally, with drums and chimes, there is a flashiness that one feels to be really misconceived and not at all in character.

For the Sinfonia is, despite its theatricality, a sober work. One does not doubt the intensity of its mood or the thoughtfulness of its design. Kirchner thinks musically and abstractly, and feels honestly and deeply. If the Sinfonia fails, it is perhaps because of certain pressures in our musical society reacting in a disturbing way upon a greatly gifted composer.

Current Chronicle: New York
[Review of music by Samuel Barber and Wallingford Riegger]
Musical Quarterly XXXVIII/3 (July 1952)

American and English composers have occasionally ventured to set French verses, but this risky undertaking has seldom had as successful an outcome as Samuel Barber's *Mélodies passagères*, a cycle of five songs on poems (in French) of Rilke. This cycle, completed in 1951 and published as Barber's Opus 27, received its first complete performance at the New York recital of Pierre Bernac and Francis Poulenc. It is high praise to write that Barber's songs seemed perfectly at home, or completely naturalized, and that on a program with songs of French composers, including Poulenc himself, they remained distinguished. Barber's French songs seem to me to have a kinship with the best of Sauguet's; with for example, *Les Pénitents en Maillot Rose.* Passages such as Ex. 1, from the first in Barber's set, may point up the comparison, which is not at all to Barber's disadvantage.[1]

---

[1] The examples from *Mélodies passagères* are copyright 1952 by G. Schirmer, Inc. Used by permission.

The distinction of Barber's songs lies above all in a consistent delicacy and lack of pretentious mannerism. The music seems natural and simple, though it is neither. It is the work
of an experienced, assured, and subtle craftsman whose taste is equal to his technique, and
whose sensibilities are in balance with his ingenuity. There is nothing new in the elements
with which Barber works, either for Barber or for other composers; there is a fine quality
of line, intelligent prosody, a harmonic consistency that preserves freshness within the
limits of conventional tonality. But it is rare to find these elements in so fine a balance
that one is not tempted to hear them or think of them as elements at all. Each song is that
kind of whole which is more than the sum of its parts; each "frames itself," and achieves
a musical communication that requires no translation or analysis, but merely attention.

Barber is able to resist the temptation to become conventionally "expressive." The under-
emphasis of these songs is one of the qualities in them that gives most delight. They rather
pointedly avoid declamation and rhetoric, quietly escape sentimentalizing, and, except for

the fourth song (which will doubtless prove to be the most frequently heard in Town Hall), employ no obvious "pictorialization." The positive qualities of expressiveness may be illustrated by the artful monotony of such a vocal line as:

or the tensely controlled and haunting opening of the last song:

Barber's music remains, in these songs, neither startling nor novel. But its qualities remain far beyond competence, or what is now praised as "craftsmanship." Barber's music has always had a feeling of rightness about it, of achieving an intention completely, of curiously combining directness and sophistication. It is perhaps possible to sense, especially in the last of these songs, still further refinements to come.

Occasionally a Current Chronicle may be of service by calling attention to performances of considerable interest by virtue of their not having taken place. New York, in this sense, has distinguished itself by not having heard a single work completed by Wallingford Riegger in the past three years.[2] Riegger's Third Symphony, scheduled by the Philharmonic, also quietly disappeared from the programs. The continuing indifference to the music of this solitary and original composer, viewed against the continuing flood of mediocrity presented by dedicated organizations and nicely endowed festivals, constitutes one of the least gratifying aspects of the New York scene.

The indifference to Riegger's music, past and present, continues despite a great increase of critical recognition and a small number of prizes and awards. But there are hopeful signs. The Third Symphony, as a consequence of a Naumburg award, has finally been recorded, in an excellent performance by Howard Hanson and the Rochester Philharmonic. Hanson's willingness to undertake this recording should remain forever to his credit. It is rumored that *Dichotomy* and the Study in Sonority will be recorded in Europe by Walter Hendl. Looking at the releases of recording companies, small and large, with their now extensive listings of contemporary music, good, bad, and indifferent, we note that these (if they are pressed) will be the first commercial recordings of any music of Riegger, who is now in his sixty-eighth year. Perhaps we may yet look forward to recordings of the Quartets.

Since the beginning of 1949, Riegger has composed four works. During the past academic year, Riegger has been visiting professor of composition at Northwestern University in Evanston, Illinois, where all of the new works have been performed.

The Cantata Opus 46, *In Certainty of Song* is a handsome and effective work, standing midway in style between Riegger's conventionally tonal music and his radically dissonant idiom. Its five short movements are well rounded and show a sure hand; the affirmative character of the text is given fittingly positive and forceful setting. A vigorous passacaglia and fugue forms the central portion of the cantata. The "adagio" of the work is a gentle and touching lullaby in unadulterated F minor. The harmonic decrescendo and accelerando by which Riegger reaches and leaves this simple tonal interlude is very skilful. Portions of the work may be rather difficult to sing, particularly passages of tone-clusters such as:[3]

---

[2] Since this article went to press, a performance of the Cantata *In Certainty of Song* was given at Town Hall by the Inter-Racial Chorus under Harold Aks.

[3] In Certainty of Song, Cantata. Copyright 1951 by Peer International Corporation. Used by permission.

Ex. 4

The small choral work, *Non Vincit Malitia,* is generally triadic and more or less in the key of C. By contrast, the Nonet for Brass employs twelve-tone technique in fairly strict application. (Can it be that Riegger's "undependability" about developing a single style makes people nervous about his music?) Riegger has already shown what he can do with an outsize group of brasses; curiously enough that work, the extraordinary Music for Brass Choir, Opus 45, has received more performances in the United States than almost any of Riegger's conventionally scored pieces. Perhaps it is this that encouraged Riegger to write a work for a more generally available small ensemble of brasses. The Nonet calls for 3 trumpets, 2 horns, 3 trombones, and tuba. It is not unreminiscent in spots of the Music for Brass Choir, and is equally brilliant, if not as overpowering. It uses a tone-row full of semitones, which make inevitable a consistent recurrence of tone-clusters.[4]

Ex. 5

The motivic material is developed with great logic and drive in a simple form. The central fugato has a nervously jagged subject rather reminiscent of *Dichotomy,* and very characteristic of Riegger:

Ex. 7

---

[4]Examples from the Nonet copyright by Associated Music Publishers, Inc., New York.

For a performance of the Nonet at Northwestern University, the composer wrote a brief program-note that may be of interest:

> What intrigues the composer about twelve-tone techniques is [their] severe restrictions. To keep within them is a challenge, as it is to a poet to stick to the rhyming scheme, once decided upon, of a sonnet. Can it be done without sacrificing plausibility, "spontaneity" or expressive content? To avoid clichés, yet to cover up traces of effort, is the goal of every artist, regardless of medium or technique. Has he succeeded? Only a second or third generation can decide. Formally, there is nothing unusual about the Nonet. A slow introduction, an allegro with a fugato section, the close recalling the opening, followed by an animated "come-on-boys-all-together"—this is the scheme.

Current Chronicle: New York
[Review of Jacques de Menasce's Sonata for Viola and Piano]
Musical Quarterly XLI/3 (July 1955)

Jacques de Menasce's new Sonata for Viola and Piano is a distinguished and beautiful work. Completed in March 1955, and performed for the first time, by the composer and Lillian Fuchs, at a concert of The Musicians Guild in April, the Sonata makes the impression of a completely realized, completely successful essay in this difficult medium. One feels that it may well prove to be an enduring work, not merely because it is a successful viola sonata, but because it is first-rate chamber music from beginning to end, so wholly satisfying as music that one forgets that it is also a *tour de force*.

It is several years since de Menasce has produced a work of this size or scope. Because of ill health the composer has confined himself recently to songs—some very extraordinary ones—and small piano pieces. It is at least ten years (if my memory serves) since the Violin Sonata, and considerably longer since the Second Piano Concerto. It is therefore interesting to note the crystallization, clarification, and intensification of style that is evident in this latest work. The Viola Sonata is de Menasce's most moving and most eloquent expression; it has greater depth and passion, consistently and persuasively, in addition to all of the polish, the refinement, the sensitive calculation that one admires in earlier compositions.

The Viola Sonata is the work of a man who is both musical and human, who adds to a great technical skill a deep wisdom and an unconstrained warmth. De Menasce's craftsmanship, his *expertise* in writing, the coherence of his musical thought, the consistency and clarity of his language, have always been impressive. He is one of the not many composers, for all that his output has been comparatively small, who are really original and who have a completely personal style. Like all such styles, de Menasce's is difficult to describe; one is not tempted to refer the reader to other composers for comparisons, since de Menasce's music does not sound like Berg's (with whom he studied) nor like Stravinsky's or Bartók's or Hindemith's. The Viola Sonata is the music of a definite and recognizable personality.

The texture of the Sonata is extremely rich. The harmonic idiom derives basically from the superposition of perfect and augmented fourths; chords so constructed are handled with remarkable subtlety and variety, so that they sound at times acrid and biting and at other times gentle and veiled. A counterpoint of considerable complexity forms, and is formed by, this consistently dissonant fabric. There is no triad or simple seventh chord in the work, yet there is also no great effect of dissonance for its own (or for experiment's) sake. There are also no tricks, no bizarre sonorities, no tortured lines, no instrumental "effects." The clue to the work's distinction is perhaps its control, which one senses to be absolute. The freedom of the 20th century with respect to every aspect of the technique of composition has imposed the need for this sort of control on every composer. Perhaps what we mean when we speak of a composer's attaining maturity is precisely his achievement of a sense of what noise or novelties to eliminate. We have no ready-made musical syntax, although it is suggested that we are evolving one; this seems to me to be still a rather distant (and not necessarily desirable) prospect. A much more real phenomenon, which needs no justification outside itself, is the evolution of a consistent and controlled style through invention and selection. Since the 20th century has invented much, perhaps it is selection and control that we should now recognize as mastery of medium.

Clarity of form, as against complexity of form, is an aspect of this mastery. It is fairly easy to be complex, difficult to be clear; "devices" are numerous and come to hand easily, but it requires instinct or intelligence to achieve lucidity. De Menasce's Viola Sonata is strikingly clear, sure, and satisfying in its organization. It is a one-movement work, of about nine minutes; this is a rather dangerous outline for any but the surest and most highly skilled craftsman. De Menasce presents his most important structural material in the opening seven measures (see Ex. 1).[†]

The *adagio* quickens gradually to *allegro molto* and subordinate material is introduced. The middle section, *allegro moderato* (see Ex. 2), is a lengthy contrapuntal development of a subject derived from the viola line in measure 7 (see Ex. 1):

[†]Exx. 1 and 2 copyright Durand et Cie. Used by permission of the publisher. Theodore Presser Company, sole agent, USA.

Ex. 1

Ex. 2

The composer calls this section *fugato,* though it is perhaps more ample than this term indicates. A second *allegro* restates the first one, though not literally, and one tone higher, and the Sonata concludes with an *adagio* that is a truncated evocation of the opening. The form is thus basically simple and regular: A-B-C-B-A; an arch, if one will. These "analytical" descriptions do not help one greatly; inferior works also fall into patterns. It is the relevance of "form" to "content" for which only music speaks, and here it speaks persuasively. It is not a derogation to say that in this respect this music is not difficult.

The work should go into the repertory and it should be recorded. One may hope that a recording will be made by Miss Fuchs and the composer. One may hope too that this Sonata will be the first in a new succession of larger works by de Menasce, whose contribution to the music of our time is already larger than is generally perceived.

Current Chronicle: New York
[Review of Igor Stravinsky's *In Memoriam Dylan Thomas*]
Musical Quarterly XLII/2 (April 1956)

Much that is visible in music becomes audible only after a considerable lapse of time, if at all. Illustrations may be found in profusion from the Gothic period to our own day. Some of these examples eventually impose themselves as works of art, when the ear catches up with the eye; others remain forever paper music. A classic example of music for the eye has been given us by our most Gothic composer, Igor Stravinsky, in his recent piece entitled *In Memoriam Dylan Thomas*. This short work, written in 1954 and heard for the first time in New York on November 30, 1955, has already been the subject of much discussion and analysis in various periodicals, and the manner of its construction has aroused much interest. Stravinsky's use of what has generally been described as "serial technique" undoubtedly marks a new direction in his evolution, though not as new as has been supposed. With Stravinsky this technique becomes at once so personal and so simple as to remind us again that he is the greatest master and creator of style that the 20th century has produced. It is ridiculous to discover, as some of the analysts have done, an influence of Schoenberg or Webern here. Stravinsky's latest phase is as un-Viennese as any of his earlier ones; it is a state of mind as well as a manifestation of technique, and the state of mind is evidently medieval.

The principle of the six-minute *In Memoriam* is a simple one, and it is put into practice with such strictness that one completes a study of the score with the feeling that the work is an exercise. The "subject" is a cell of five notes: E, E♭, C, C♯, D. These notes are first stated within the smallest compass, from C to E, and what this "row" therefore amounts to is a rearrangement of the intervals in the span of a major third. It will occur to the reader that two overlapping transpositions (on C, E, and G♯.), dividing the octave into major thirds, will produce all twelve tones. This is a neat, plausible, and simple scheme, and makes the basis for a splendid exercise in symmetry. It is almost the sort of thing that a very imaginative teacher might propose to a highly gifted student. Take the cell, use it in its original form, its inversion, its retrograde, and its retrograde inversion, simultaneously and with transpositions, and one has canons; *Dirge-Canons* if they are slow and sad. And the eye, moreover, can recognize them even if the ear can not.

At any rate, it is with *Dirge-Canons* that the work begins and ends. These are scored for four trombones and a string quartet, which perform antiphonally. The trombones are allowed note repetitions; the strings are not. An element of number mysticism, quite Gothic in character, is evidently involved in the relation of the five-note cell and the time signatures of 5/4 and 3/2 plus 2/2. The opening of the piece illustrates the calculations presented:[1]

The complete "answer" by the strings is contained in three measures:

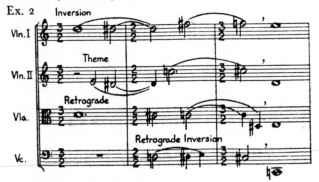

To call these statements "canons" is, by any standards, stretching a point. Perhaps they can be described as "isomelic" but it may be doubted that this will be of great help to any-

---

[1]Examples copyright 1954 by Boosey & Hawkes, Inc. Used by permission.

one merely trying to listen to them. The ear takes the impression of rhythmic imitation rather more easily than that of pitch imitation, and here the pitch relations are by no means easy to perceive, even with the aid of "analysis."

The aural difficulty persists through the *Song,* a setting of Thomas's poem "Do not go gentle into that good night . . ." for tenor voice with the string quartet, which is heard between the opening and closing *Dirge-Canons.* Again, all the material comes from the five-note cell, which is often used in a curiously overlapping manner, as for example here at the entrance of the voice, where the Inversion and Retrograde combine to make a phrase:

I must confess that my enthusiasm for playing the game of "Find the Subject" waned after a page or so, but I have been assured by more patient colleagues that every note is properly accounted for; that is, except one. I am unable to draw any conclusion from this except that it must represent whimsy rather than carelessness, for Stravinsky is not a careless composer. On the other hand, neither is this a whimsical piece. It appears to be engineered with rather grim determination, in order to prove or to demonstrate a theorem, a method, or a hypothesis. It is consistent, ingenious, and made to order for the kind of "analysis" that is a fashionable substitute for listening and hearing. The current preoccupation with musical machinery is interesting and symptomatic; at times one feels that the major obligation of the composer is to provide stimulating opportunities for the analyst; certainly a whole school of critics and propagandists reserves its greatest admiration for those works that provide the neatest possibilities of demonstration. It is, one may suppose, no accident that the Age of Anxiety and the Age of Analysis are one and the same.

It is worth noting that Stravinsky himself challenges the reader to accept his work on "constructivist" grounds by providing the necessary "clues" in the score. On the lowest level, it is offered as a puzzle, with the key provided. Yet it is obvious, as it always has been, that preoccupation with techniques, style, devices, need not preclude expressiveness or even passion. There is this problem, and there is reconciliation, in Josquin, in Lassus, and in Bach. The problem exists, in fact, in all "severe" styles employing highly developed contrapuntal techniques. It does not appear to have a successful solution in Stravinsky's latest work; the *In Memoriam,* alas, not only looks like an exercise, but sounds like one: a neutral, complicated, morally indifferent, and laborious exhibition. Perhaps it is merely preparation for the next manifestation; one cannot believe that Stravinsky will rest with what this work represents.

The concert at which the *In Memoriam* was heard—presented by a new group called Camera Concerts, with the talented young Jacques Monod as conductor—included *Pierrot Lunaire* and the local première of Varèse's *Deserts*. It was one of those occasions on which one is tempted to conclude that all is wrong with the *avant-garde*. *Pierrot* and the Stravinsky offered a contrast that was at once enlightening and depressing: hysterical "expressionism" on the one hand, and frigid "unexpressionism" on the other. The two combined to produce an impression of real sickness. *Pierrot,* in addition, is painfully dated, and although doubtless a masterpiece of a sort, is a fearfully boring one. It is a pity that Schoenberg's literary tastes were so atrocious at times—consider also *Erwartung*—for it asks much of anyone to accept as a whole work of art a combination of words and music that depends so much on a miscalculation of tone and appropriateness. (The English translation of *Pierrot* included in the program read like something whipped up by S. J. Perelman.) Art has an obligation to be serious, and its humor must be intentional. To be earnest is not quite the same thing as being serious, any more than being nervous is quite the same as being sensitive. There is a terrible quality of earnestness (and nervousness) in both *Pierrot* and the *In Memoriam;* and perhaps all they prove in the long run is that all of the lovely and impressive technique that they demonstrate can be misdirected. They offer an uninviting choice: either Schoenberg becoming hysterical over bats and pallid washer-wenches, or Stravinsky, imperturbable, poker-faced, and perhaps after all not really interested, while death strikes and hell gapes. Neither is a brave, noble, or even adult posture. But Stravinsky's is perhaps more *chic*.

Current Chronicle: New York

[Discussion of the Juilliard School's Festival of American Music and review of William Bergsma's opera *The Wife of Martin Guerre*]
Musical Quarterly XLII/3 (July 1956)

Juilliard School's Festival of American Music presented a large number of new works (almost all commissioned for the occasion) including a piano concerto by Roger Sessions, a 'cello concerto by Peter Mennin, Walter Piston's Fifth Symphony, and William Schuman's revised Violin Concerto. There were also assorted orchestral and chamber music works, as well as songs, by a score of other composers. The new pieces ranged from very good to very bad, and in this respect were perfectly representative of American music today, as they also were in their range from the gentle and pretty to the ugly and brutal. While a few "big" American composers were not represented (most, however, had been asked), all the major lines of effort were present, and the over-all impression was what might have been predicted of any mass production by American or Russian or Ugro-Finnic or any other breed of composers.

One knows by now pretty much what to expect from Sessions or Piston or Schuman, or even from some of the younger men like Mennin. In respect to these composers, the Festival provided no news. Mennin's 'cello concerto has drive and polish, plenty of virtuoso activity for the soloist, and some distinguished ideas solidly exploited. It tells us nothing new about the composer. Neither does Sessions's piano concerto, which runs along rather predictable lines. What was unpredictable, and perhaps worthy of note, is that most of the composers gave of their best for these commissions, and that the new works were for the most part excellently representative.

The musical discovery of the Festival was without a doubt William Bergsma's three-act opera *The Wife of Martin Guerre,* on which the composer had worked since 1951, and which was not commissioned for the occasion. Bergsma has enjoyed a reputation as an interesting and talented "young composer," but his opera should establish him as something a good deal more than that. He has now emerged as an original and distinctive figure, with a fresh and personal idiom and an ability to work on a large scale. *The Wife of Martin Guerre* should establish him as a major personality in American music.

Bergsma possesses what is possibly the rarest thing in American music: a genuine lyrical gift of the utmost refinement. The sensitiveness of his line is extraordinary, as is the delicacy and clarity of his contrapuntal texture. He uses, in his opera, a small orchestra, skilfully manipulated to preserve a perfect clarity of line and color; yet the opera itself is not on a small scale. Bergsma ranges from unaffected gentleness to intense passion without descending to the commonplace or straining for "big" effects. There is a remarkable intensity, conviction, and individuality in the opera, with no false notes and with no miscalculations of tone or style. Bergsma's taste is supremely fine and his idiom is thoroughly consistent. The music is for the most part linear and highly dissonant, but the spacing of voices and harmonies is unusually subtle, so that the tensions are widely varied. The angularity of line that was apparent in some of Bergsma's earlier pieces has been refined in this work, but the texture remains as clear and the colors as bright as in his best previous work. Perhaps here too, *The Wife of Martin Guerre* represents an advance in control and invention, just as it brings to a new focus all those elements of skill, subtlety, warmth, and freshness that made Bergsma's earlier works interesting.

The Wife of Martin Guerre is remarkable for its avoidance of cliché, and more remarkable in that this avoidance does not seem to have cost Bergsma a great deal of effort. (In many composers, one senses the furious effort to pretend, by distortion, that the cliché isn't really there.) Bergsma has style, intelligence, and imagination, and, in the way that only very good composers can, exploits his own strengths, which a cultivated and sophisticated critical mind has evidently enabled him to perceive. It is this that makes *The Wife of Martin Guerre* a strong and individual work, unaffected by *Wozzeck, I Pagliacci,* the dear old folks at home, or Gilbert and Sullivan cum Tchaikovsky. To be sure, there is abnegation here too; but a delicacy and fineness of mind make this appear as willing control rather than inhibition. On the most obvious level, one can mention that Bergsma uses only one percussion player in his opera orchestra. Surely, for an American composer this must represent the absolute top in renunciation. But it serves to underline the fact that Bergsma's bigness is real and not factitious.

The vocal writing in the opera is sensitive, expressive, singable (though not always easy), and dramatically appropriate. The quintet in the third act is as good as anything of the kind yet done by an American composer; indeed, as effective operatic ensemble writing it can hold its own with most models in the repertory. There is a great luminosity in the writing of all the parts, and the flow of music is neither broken nor forced beyond a natural inclination.

All in all, *The Wife of Martin Guerre* is by a wide margin the best opera by an American that I have heard. A good share of the credit must be given to the librettist, Janet Lewis, who should receive an award of some sort for producing what is probably the most distinguished libretto in the annals of American opera. The story itself is dramatic and moving; but beyond that, the language has style. Miss Lewis has written no libretto-ese, no doggerel, no inflated trivialities; she has given us simple, well-rhythmed language, free of artiness and of vulgarities of expression. Miss Lewis gives this synopsis of the story:

> The external events of the story treated in the opera are historically true. In 1548, Martin Guerre, a young peasant of the village of Artigues in southern France, left his wife and infant son in order to evade the anger of his father over a minor theft. He planned to be gone only a week. Eight years, however, elapsed before his family had any news of him. Then, as far as his family could judge, he returned, improved by the years, and took control of his farm, his father having

died during his absence. It was not until she was pregnant by him that his wife, in bewilderment and torment, came to the conviction that it was not her husband who had returned, but another man. To her guilt and horror at this conviction was added the realization that she loved him more than she had loved her husband, and the belief in her own household that she had gone mad. One day, a wandering blackguard, rebuffed by her husband, called him an impostor. Distraught, she brought against him her strange and tragic accusation.

Two trials followed. The first, at Rieux, condemned the man to death; the second, which decided for the prisoner, was interrupted by her true husband's return. The wife knelt at her true husband's feet, exhausted by the suffering she had endured to restore his honor, and met with his cold statement: "The error into which you plunged could only have been wilful blindness. You and you alone, Madame, are responsible for the dishonor which has befallen me."

A few critics objected to the pace of the opera, and found dramatic deficiencies in the unfolding of the plot. I cannot imagine what they were thinking of, unless the corruptions of television, *verismo,* and detective stories have made anything but the crudest melodrama too subtle to follow. What do they think of *Pelléas*? Miss Lewis, it is true, avoids bludgeoning the audience with the obvious, and has centered the interest on the emotional and psychological problem of the wife, rather than on the surface of events. The last act is chillingly dramatic, but it depends for its effectiveness on the skill with which its tensions have been built. Good last acts do not arrive from nowhere, either musically or dramatically.

Certainly in comparison to *Tosca* or *Wozzeck* or *Il Trovatore, The Wife of Martin Guerre* is theatrically understated. But such comparisons are as absurd as they are profitless. The musical theater has room for *The Marriage of Figaro* as well as *Elektra,* and no one seriously complains about the dramatic effectiveness of *La Bohème* or *Götterdämmerung,* both of which reek of bathos, pomposity, dramatic irrelevancies, and horrors of linguistic inflation. What Bergsma's opera so happily avoids is precisely the fault of inflation, which is the curse not only of most Romantic and contemporary operas, but of American music in general. *The Wife of Martin Guerre* is theatrically credible, out of the ordinary, elevated in tone and style, effective, and memorable.

An abridged version of the opera has been recorded by Composers' Recordings for release in late summer or early fall. It is to be hoped that the complete libretto will be made available to purchasers of the recording, so that the continuity may be made explicit. The recording should be an important one in American music.

[Review of Hugo Weisgall's opera *Six Characters in Search of an Author*]
Musical Quarterly XLV/3 (July 1959)

Considering the number of words written annually about opera in general, and about American opera in particular, it is not surprising that Hugo Weisgall's *Six Characters in Search of an Author,* an extraordinary work given its world première on April 26 by the New York City Opera Company, aroused some of the most peculiar comments heard in many seasons. So great is the earnestness and the confusion about our American "musical theater" that when a real masterpiece of music and theater comes along it is almost certain to be unrecognized. This is about what happened with *Six Characters,* although most of the musicians who heard it admired the work greatly, and it should be stated that the press, with a few exceptions, did not give the opera an openly hostile reception. By far the greater number found it interesting, daring, and technically of immense competence; the reservations were, I think it fair to say, based on confusion about the nature of the "musical theater" with which everyone was absorbed during the City Center's decidedly illuminating season of American works.

Weisgall's opera is a work of great originality and superb craftsmanship, and certainly, if there is any musical justice, it will be kept in the repertory until it is recognized for what it is. One cannot expect a piece of extreme sophistication and relative complexity to "succeed" as rapidly or as simply as many more innocently composed works are able to do. Weisgall's opera was by far the most difficult attempted by the City Opera, and the very greatest credit is due Mr. Rudel and his associates not only for undertaking it, but also for managing what was on the whole a brilliantly executed presentation.

Before attempting to praise Weisgall's work, it is perhaps necessary to consider the prejudices and contradictions of prevalent thinking about opera. We have not moved since Wagner's day, or for that matter since Monteverdi's. "Opera as drama" is still pitted against "opera as opera"; the serious and the frivolous are in their usual camps, the one abandoning Donizetti and the other Alban Berg, with Verdi looking down from heaven and presenting to the first camp the music, and to the second the libretto, of *La Forza del Destino.* Weisgall's opera received the benefit of the delightful simplifications of both sides. It is worth noting that there were some who felt the piece to be too much drama, and too little opera, for this is patently the end of a line of reasoning much in vogue. When is an opera not an opera? One must at least admit that this is difficult to determine, provided one accepts the idea that opera should be drama. Can the libretto be too good, or too interesting?

And if one wants light musical entertainment, with agreeable tunes to whistle, then why bring in irrelevancies?

The apparent contradictions can, it seems to me, be resolved by the application of a little common sense. Everything about an opera should be interesting: plot, language, music, mise-en-scène, acting, singing. What is, however, true is that most operas are interesting only as music, yet they survive despite this. For this reason it is absurd to demand that they be given here, for example, in English, since if the words are not worth listening to (and they seldom are, or if they are, they lose their worth in translation) there is no gain in understanding them. Verbal trash is no easier to take than musical trash, and it is often a blessing when the words can *not* be understood. This is also true of operatic action in many cases, as it is true of operatic acting. But has anyone ever abandoned a love for opera because of silly plots, fourth-rate verses, or a complete lack of dramatic illusion on stage? I am not thinking of those sober souls for whom there are only six or eight operas worth talking about; on a less rarefied level there would appear to be a good many more aspects of opera to take into account.

Weisgall's opera is interesting on every count, and in terms of tone, atmosphere, and intent it is not like any opera that comes to mind. This is, of course, what makes it "difficult." The Pirandello play is presumably well known, and it is not difficult to imagine the change of focus from theater stage and speaking characters to opera stage and singers. Denis Johnston's adaptation of the play is brilliantly successful: a tight, witty, literate libretto, in good idiomatic English, with no false notes or translations into librettoese. He has managed to strengthen and sharpen the play, taking as his license some ideas written by Pirandello himself in his foreword. Johnston has played down the pseudo-philosophizing about illusion and reality, greatly toned up the wit and satire, and left the melodrama alone. Even so, the mixture is rather wild, but theatrically exciting, and a tremendous challenge to the composer. For the composer is in a sense forced to deal with ideas, and this, by and large, is not operatic territory. We admit that drama can deal with ideas; must we say that opera as drama can be only a certain kind of drama, or that an opera based on *Hamlet* can turn out to be only Ambroise Thomas'? True, Richard Strauss tried "opera as idea" in *Capriccio*, where the matter was also, as in *Six Characters*, ideas about theater, opera, words, and music; but Strauss left out the melodrama and the satire. (*I Pagliacci* is also about something; but it seems to leave out a good deal.) The Weisgall-Johnston-Pirandello mixture is astonishing and improbable, and is marvelous theater. It is very much more effective, exciting, and moving than the play; and this, quite simply, is its test and its achievement as an opera, the measure of its *musical* success.

In the end, it is always the music itself that does the acting, and that is, in the most real sense, the plot. This is why, again, so much of the current rage for operatic *acting* is beside the point, confusing, and contradictory. It is also why Weisgall's work gave rise to so many misunderstandings; because it hit so exactly the mark no one really expects an opera to hit, and that, perhaps, no one really wants it to hit. The City Center troupe, being excellent actors, in a sense contributed all too effectively to making the opera a "drama." For what is wanted in opera is not actors, but singers; and it is here, unfortunately, that the cast was not quite strong enough. Weisgall's work demands big voices first and foremost, voices that can project resonantly; it can almost dispense with clever acting and skilful gesture. (Of course one would be happy to have all of these things; but how often in history does this happen?) Action and gesture are there, in the score; it is the musical venture, the operatic achievement, to *sing* them into being on the stage.

What is most remarkable about *Six Characters* is its completeness and force as a stage work; and what needs to be emphasized is that it is the music that provides the force. Weisgall's comprehension of the intricacies of his libretto is evident in every note, and the dissonant, often bi-tonal idiom he uses is ideal and full of invention. There is the greatest skill shown in the balancing of voices and orchestra, in the variety of orchestral sound itself, in the choral writing (which was universally admired), and in the differentiation of characters. In this last, there is much subtlety; so much so that one cannot expect everything to be apparent on a single hearing. Basically, Weisgall has written all of the "real" music for the six "characters"; while the "real" people have a kind of imitation music, full of mockery, witticism, and musical allusion. The characters themselves are persuasively drawn; the protagonists live musically and assume their reality through their music, which is exactly what opera asks them to do.

Pirandello, I think, would have been delighted by the way in which Weisgall, through his music, underlines the ironies and ambiguities of the play, as well as its melodrama. The commentary of the music is extraordinarily acute and invariably apt, and it is no mean achievement for music to add an intellectual or perhaps a quasi-philosophical reinforcement to an already challenging play. But this is its "creation of atmosphere," and far-fetched as it may seem, it succeeds here precisely as Debussy miraculously succeeded with *Pelléas.* And one might well ask here: is *Pelléas* an opera? I am under the impression that it is admitted to the canon despite the fact that it is a total setting of a play entirely lacking the characteristics, either in construction or language, of a conventional opera libretto. The moral, I think, is that we must be narrow-minded about only one thing at a time, and that we should perhaps admit that music can do many things, communicate in various manners, and that opera is potentially a larger field than its simpler definitions would suggest.

Pirandello's "characters" are, in his own words, "born alive, and seeking to live," but they must live in the pre-ordained way in which the author conceived and left them. Hence they seek a dramatic company (or here an opera company) for a working out of their destinies. The juxtaposition of the "characters," obsessed with reality, and the members of the opera company, professionally occupied with illusion and convention, calls for a musical imagination of considerable richness and sophistication. Weisgall rises to this challenge as only a composer of superior gifts and broad culture could do. It would be easy, all too easy, to convert *Six Characters* into a kind of *Pagliacci,* and one has the feeling that this is what many people wished that Weisgall had done.

It is not every day that we hear an opera with so much in it, and we are not used to it. This, too, is perhaps what caused so many odd reactions to Weisgall's work. The pace of the score is tremendously swift, and many seemed to regret that the action did not slow up for lush set pieces. But there are set pieces, and eloquent ones, in *Six Characters*: they are brief, but they are forceful, and they are "in character." (The Father, after all, can not do the Prologue to *Pagliacci.*) They are not "romantic" or heroic pieces, but *Six Characters,* like *Wozzeck,* is not a romantic or heroic opera any more than it is a folksy one; and this, perhaps, constitutes an additional difficulty for some. But in this difficulty it has the best of company, and it is worthy of nothing less than that company. Time will, I think, establish it as a major achievement of the contemporary musical theater.

Current Chronicle: New York
[Review of works performed at the New School: Roger Sessions's Quintet, Leon Kirchner's Second String Quartet, Ernst Krenek's Sixth String Quartet, and Milton Babbitt's Composition for Four Instruments]
Musical Quarterly XLVI/1 (January 1960)

The New School, with the generous aid of the Fromm Music Foundation, recently gave New York an opportunity of hearing for the first time Roger Sessions's Quintet, Leon Kirchner's Second String Quartet (both completed in 1958), and Ernst Krenek's Sixth String Quartet, completed in 1936. The fourth work of the evening, Milton Babbitt's Composition for Four Instruments, written in 1948, was the only one previously performed in this city.

The evening was one of the most rewarding in many seasons. It is not often that one hears first performances of two important and attractive new works in a single evening, surrounded by one other work of considerable interest and another of striking craftsmanship and origi-nality. The performances, too, by the young Lenox String Quartet (making its New York début), with excellent assisting artists, were remarkably good.

Sessions's Quintet is one of his most immediately appealing, accessible, and delightful works. The adjective "delightful," I know, has not often been applied to the music of this serious, dedicated, and uncompromising composer. But it is time that the musical public, certainly that portion of the "public" able to listen to serious music at all, cast aside its pre-concep-tions about Mr. Sessions, and return to listen to that portion of his music which best dis-plays his remarkable gifts. For the best of Sessions (and I should list the Quintet in this category) is not only serious, uncompromising, built with logic and strength; it also has motion, warmth, and expressiveness of many kinds. Further, works like the Quintet are so clearly in the Classical tradition of chamber music that even the semi-educated listener should be able to find his bearings.

The accessibility of the Quintet does not make it less severe, serious, or important, or de-tract in any way from its originality or power. I feel very strongly, on the other hand, that this clarity of writing is a merit of the most significant nature. There is a misguided senti-ment prevalent among an insecure minority of the avant-garde which amounts to a decla-ration that that which can be understood is not worth understanding. The stature of Mr. Sessions is fortunately such that he can even afford to be understood without any loss of prestige. And while inwardness and self-sufficiency are none the less surely marks of the greatest artists, there remains always the problem of communication and meaning, not only for posterity, but even for a handful more than the "happy few" among contemporaries.

If I have suggested that the Quintet is an easy work, I shall have done Mr. Sessions an in-justice. The Quintet is not music for the millions, and it will probably not be a staple in Town Hall for quite a number of years to come. But the materials have grace, and the con-struction transparency and economy. The work has warmth, animation, and nobility. It shows at all times the hand of a master, one who is not only not afraid to be complicated, but who is also not afraid to be direct.

Technically, the Quintet is dodecaphonic, and there appears to be a serial connection among all three movements. There is plenty of evidence in the score of rigorous procedural logic. But if the composer must be interested in procedures and techniques, the listener should be interested in results. The most recondite construction must sound like a happy inevitability, or at least like an uninhibited and lifelike invention. Sessions has succeeded marvelously in the Quintet in drawing the listener's attention away from device and towards effect, an achievement not as common as one might wish in the more serious manifestations of present-day music. The secret is partly in finely profiled, distinguished melodic lines, in rhythmic vigor and clarity, and in a relatively Classic procedure as to form. The three movements are, in effect, a sonata-allegro, an aria, and a rondo; not quite in the style of Haydn to be sure, but recognizable enough as deriving from traditional principles. In this respect, one notes an important move away from the idea of continuous development and variation. This move is not necessarily "reactionary," and it will be more than interesting to follow its progress in the work of Sessions and the many composers on whom he exercises a beneficent influence.

The thematic character of the Quintet may be suggested by the quotation of its opening page (see Ex. 1).[1]

Ex. 1

---

[1]Copyright Edward B. Marks Music Corporation. Used by permission.

Leon Kirchner's Second String Quartet is in a quite different way an equally excellent and satisfying work. Admirers of some of Kirchner's earlier pieces, including his First String Quartet, may find it something of a surprise. It is infinitely more relaxed and lyrical, and uses no serial techniques at all. Kirchner has never been a "systematic" composer, but he has been influenced by various branches of dodecaphony, and has been spiritually kin to its best practitioners. Kirchner was in fact a student of both Sessions and Schoenberg. He has, however, always shown great individuality and independence, and the new quartet is further evidence of these qualities.

The quartet is light and transparent in texture, brief, delicately calculated in sound, and, like the Sessions Quintet, relatively traditional in structure and accessible to the moderately educated ear. The two works (Sessions's and Kirchner's) have in fact curious sub-surface similarities despite their almost diametrically opposed technique and rationale. The approaches of the composers (if one may pretend to imagine their methods of work, as might a musicologist of the future) seem to represent opposite poles of musical thought. If Sessions seems to approach composition from the standpoint of logic generating sound, Kirchner, in his new quartet, seems to assume that sound generates logic. By this I mean that while the procedures and construction in Sessions's Quintet are entirely susceptible to conventional analysis in terms of a row and its development, Kirchner appears to use no method but that dictated by his ear. Yet Sessions's logic produces beautiful sounds, and Kirchner's sounds unfold with convincing logic. If one feels that either composer would have sacrificed one part of his effect for another, one can be happy that in these two works no such compromise proved necessary. That is of course why both works seem so whole and so satisfactory.

Kirchner appears to be seeking something quite new in this quartet. He achieves delicate and beautiful sounds, created by rather subtle melodic lines in a carefully balanced polyphony. The harmonic calculation is curious and original, and is unsystematic enough to include even major triads. It rather pleases me that I cannot say with security that the work is tonal, non-tonal, polytonal, or pan-tonal, for I feel that it is time that we ceased worrying about these things, and especially that we desist from the attempt to classify each new work according to a doctrine. In a time in which all harmonic license is allowed there are many problems: of control, of intelligibility, and of motion. But what seems to preoccupy Kirchner here is the *quality* rather than the function of the sound masses. Kirchner is of course not alone in this concern, but his new quartet seems to illustrate it in a most direct way, and also to provide a most successful coming to terms with the problem. It is, I think, a major achievement to appear to be able to dispense with formulas, either of acceptance or avoidance, and to write a fresh kind of sound dictated by instinct alone. In any case, it shows complete independence and maturity on the part of the composer.

If Kirchner's harmony is not traditional, even by recent tradition, the structure of his quartet, like that of the Sessions Quintet, makes use of traditional recapitulations or at least of references to subjects in unaltered or almost unaltered forms. This is, for Kirchner, a fairly new procedure. All in all, the quartet seems full of confidence: the confidence of a composer assured enough to employ repetitions and major triads in a context from which they are usually excluded. If this is true, it is a happy development for American music, although the doctrinaire will disapprove and the musical anatomists be perplexed.

The Quartet is in three movements, played without a pause. The conclusion of the first movement (Ex. 2) may serve to illustrate the texture and style of the work.†

The second movement is a poetic and flowing adagio, with many *accelerandi* and *ritardandi*, and with many of the rhapsodic and almost improvisatory or exclamatory rapid-note figures in groups of five, six, seven, and eleven that have been characteristic of Kirchner's other works. These constitute a rather risky device, but Kirchner has always been able to use it effectively and expressively, without losing pace or continuity. Examples of the usage also occur in the final movement. This movement, which has a perfectly clear recapitulation and coda, also quotes briefly from the preceding adagio. We have thus an apparent return to a Romantically oriented sonata form, and one could with some truth say that the quartet as a whole reflects this orientation.

Milton Babbitt's Composition for Four Instruments is certainly more "advanced" than either the Sessions Quintet or the Kirchner Quartet. It is of course completely serial and post-Webern in technique. On paper it seems forbidding, and one would expect that the extreme delicacy of the composer's calculations would make it almost impossible to perform. Today's performers, however, manage complications that would have been insurmountable even twenty years ago, and although the performance was not literally perfect

---

†Example reprinted by permission of Associated Music Publishers, Inc.

Ex. 2

in terms of dynamics or rhythm, it is the measure of Babbitt's success that the piece sounds coherent and interesting, even fascinating. One would need a careful study to pretend to understand more than the general principles involved in its construction, but what is important is the conviction that such study would be worthwhile, and that increased familiarity with the composition would be rewarding.

The Sixth Quartet of Ernst Krenek is full of skill, and opens with arresting ideas. One admires the sure professionalism of the composer, the easy handling of the quartet medium, the ingenuity in all technical matters. But the quartet seems diffuse and over-long, and the last movement, a *fuga a quattro soggetti,* seems academic and gratuitous. It should be said that the work came at the end of a long and extremely stimulating evening, and the attention of even the most willing listener is bound to flag after a certain period of intense listening. But let us *not* suggest, given the kind of fare we normally experience, that we can have too much of good things!

Current Chronicle: New York

[Review of Igor Stravinsky's *Movements for Piano and Orchestra* and *Double Canon*]
Musical Quarterly XLVI/2 (April 1960)

In 1913 we had the Rites of Spring; in the last weeks of 1959 and the first of 1960 we had the Rites of Winter. The three Sunday afternoon events presented by Columbia Records seemed to be not concerts in honor of Igor Stravinsky but religious ceremonies presided over by Robert Craft. Little was needed but incense and candles to complete the illusion of attendance at a series of solemn public acts and rituals. Events move faster in the 20th century than they did in the 4th, but one was reminded of the Age of Constantine and of the proclamation and official public adoption of a new religion, complete with its saints and martyrs, interpreted for all the devout by those most recently, but most ardently, converted.

The apparent center of interest of the three ceremonies was the first performance of the new (1958-59) *Movements for Piano and Orchestra,* with the première of the *Double Canon* in memory of Raoul Dufy, and the first New York performance of the *Epitaphium* for good measure. There is no question but that the *Movements* are of very great interest, but the circumstances of the presentation, the company in which they appeared, the atmosphere of the unveiling, all provide perhaps even more food for thought.

Aside from the three new works of Stravinsky, plus performances of *Les Noces* and *Le Sacre,* the programs gave us Mr. Craft, venerating Schoenberg, Berg, and Webern, and honoring their forerunners, Monteverdi, Gesualdo, Schütz, and J. S. Bach. There is no doubt now, for the highest authority has spoken, about the canon of taste for the faithful. We should, according to the program notes, add Baude Cordier, who is cited by Stravinsky as a musical precedent, along with the Cyprus Codex. There is an enormous void where formerly Haydn, Mozart, and Beethoven were thought to occupy places, and one wonders that Bach remains among the elect. For the choices are symptomatic: we are interested in the processes of change and displacement with respect to harmony, with the growth (and perhaps with the decay) of the central achievements of our musical culture, and if all this is mingled with some regret, we must do our best to conceal our emotion under a brilliant display of luminous objectivity, expressed, if not in the passion and perfection of performance, then at least in the ardor of the program notes. And in effect these were much more interesting than the performances.

It is a temptation to dwell on the symptomatic, symbolic, and possibly historic significance of these concerts, not only because of the significance of Stravinsky himself who, at the age of 77, has once more attempted to put himself in absolute command of the musical scene, but also because of the quality of the commentary on this same scene that is implicit in the Master's latest avatar. From *The Firebird* to the *Movements* is a long journey indeed, both musically and psychologically; it constitutes a history of taste in our time, or perhaps a history of music itself conceived as a commentary on style. Stravinsky's interests, and his commentaries, need no recounting. But the most recent manifestation is actually something different, and is not exactly a commentary, since the historical precedent and example are closer to us in time, and there is the question of immediate example and direct influence in addition to the old manner of reinterpretation and reintegration of apparently disparate sources as a basis for the adoption of a stylistic attitude. It is precisely attitude itself that is in question here, for the latest Stravinsky seems less the adoption of an attitude than the expression of an intent, and this intent has the remarkable effect of beaming an equivocal light on everything that Stravinsky has done before. It becomes necessary to say that both *Les Noces* and *Le Sacre* sounded somewhat aged when heard in juxtaposition with the *Movements.*

Stravinsky has had the good fortune to outlive the already sainted trio of Schoenberg, Berg, and Webern, and it is he, apparently, who is appointed to carry on their teachings. There seems to be no mistaking the intent; and if, in the process, the younger disciples of Webern are swept away, or learn their lesson, it will be interesting to see what follows. Stravinsky has genius enough to carry this off; his own disciples will of course follow, and many have already done so. As for the already confirmed serialists, there appears to be both satisfaction and alarm. The *Movements* is a clear portent: we must hope that Stravinsky will be spared sufficient years for his inevitable further steps, past serialism, into electronic music, the direction of which he must undoubtedly attempt to influence both by his genius and by his authority.

The musical questions raised by Stravinsky's recent works are many. One must concede the inevitability, in our anxious and history-conscious age, of the artistic ransacking of the past in search of a companionship (or perhaps a togetherness) that Mozart and Beethoven no longer provide. They are not only too big for us, on a different scale, but represent a different relation to civilization. This is why we cuddle up to Baude Cordier and the Cyprus Codex; we require rather Gothic shapes and symbols of authority, and our submission must be absolute. But we must not question that Baude Cordier and the 14th century lead nowhere musically; the acceptance of the static condition is a fundamental premise. Serialism is equally a condition of security, and Webern equally a symbol of order finally imposed. It is probably natural that the varied stylistic adventures of Stravinsky should end here, that the need for Order which he has so often proclaimed should bring him at last to a Gothic mysticism and its contemporary equivalent.

One must also concede the possibility that all this is as it should be, and that a new Order is now historically as well as psychologically necessary. It is futile to try to guess the next generation's judgments ahead of time. It is possible that the ear is once again greatly behind the times, as has happened often enough before, and that serial music of all sorts, including the Webern *Trio-Satz* and the *Movements for Piano and Orchestra,* will some day be aurally clear without previous and intense visual analysis. Or again, this may be neither desirable nor necessary. The aural *demonstration* or unfolding of something intellectually apprehended beforehand may, indeed, be a new dimension of musical experience, which we will enjoy on a scale only dimly suggested until now. It seems to me that although this is possible, it is also unlikely, because we now move too quickly from adventure to adventure in art (always in search of the ultimate and elusive authority) just as we do in technology, which also in our times moves too rapidly for either understanding or control, and which in turn casts its doubts as well as its methods on our entire culture. We cannot rest long enough where we are, because we are not particularly comfortable, and we cannot adopt what is necessary to the understanding of either art or science, an attitude of receptivity, because the first requirement, a set of terms at least partly defined, keeps getting lost behind us.

The *Double Canon* for string quartet represents, in its simple way, the search for method and security, and at the same time the lack of finality or conclusiveness in Stravinsky's present technique. It sets forth an ordinary twelve-note row with a duration of fifteen quarter notes. This is taken up in canon a major second below and at a time interval of four beats. The double canon is produced by the entries of the other instruments using the row in exact retrograde both as to pitch and as to rhythm. It is all a perfectly mechanical manipulation of twelve notes and fifteen beats. But what is inconclusive about the exercise is that it *sounds* just as well if different intervals of imitation are used, so that one is left wondering why all the calculation was necessary in the first place, since not even a point about method seems to be proved. In any case, both the *Double Canon* and the *Epitaphium* are inconsequential demonstrations that seem more appropriate as entries in a composer's sketch-book.

The *Movements for Piano and Orchestra,* a full-scale work of about twelve minutes, like all bold applications of serial principles, attempts to deal with musical time in a new way, and thus raises fundamental questions about our perceptions. Music, up to now, like the physical time in which it exists, has been considered irreversible. Our understanding of harmony is of course based on this irreversibility. But with the popularization and distortion of notions of relativity, coupled with half-digested concepts of modern mathematics, it is perhaps now the conceit to make music reversible as well as discontinuous. (The *Double Canon,* incidentally, is every bit as interesting, euphonious, and logical backwards as forwards.) This supposition explains the denial of harmony as an element of construction, which is basic in the post-Webern world. It is worth observing that Mr. Craft, in his fascinating program notes, praises Webern as "the most purely contrapuntal composer of his time . . ." One supposes that this is praise, or at least an expression of values sought, and yet it seems curiously aimless. Who is our most syntactical poet? Or our least objective painter? Our most serial composer?

It is certainly possible that harmony is dead, that the composers of the 18th and 19th centuries have explored all the possibilities of what we have come to call traditional harmony, and that the composer today can add nothing to what they have left us. But Stravinsky's career as a composer has, until lately, been nothing less than a demonstration that this is not true at all, since all of his work has been based on a conception of harmony and rhythm generally within the framework of conventional tonality. His change of heart, at a comparatively late stage in his career, is thus the more striking, apparently even to himself, for he notes about the *Movements:* "Perhaps the most significant aspect of my new work is its 'anti-tonality.' I am amazed at this myself, in view of the fact that in *Threni,* triadic references occur in every bar."

The *Movements* are "anti-tonal" and also anti-harmonic, and represent direct and obvious continuation of Webern's techniques and esthetics. There are no triads here, and in fact there is very little impression of any kind of vertical sound, despite Stravinsky's statement that "unlike several younger colleagues, I compose my polyrhythmic combinations to be heard vertically." Granting the intention, one can only say that the vertical result is elusive. Perhaps it is all elusive, because it appears so very self-conscious. It is difficult for anyone to say what this music communicates or intends to communicate, because we are faced with that peculiar phenomenon in contemporary art, the desire to transfer the artist's proper concern with technique to the listener, reader, or viewer, whose proper concern it is not. The artist becomes both creator and commentator, and the unfortunate listener to music is no longer commanded to listen, but to understand. His relation with the composer is thus compromised and his function in the world of art is made unclear: he is subject and object at once, the insider and the outsider, with little prospect of a place from which to achieve a perspective. It is clear that he is to be content with "analysis," a rather small crumb, and, alas, usually a stale one.

Here again, Mr. Craft gives us our invaluable clue. Of Webern, he writes, "Perhaps, too, one might say that Webern has so analyzed music that only style remains. Is the *Trio-Satz* a-thematic? Obviously the answer would require an Information Theory definition of 'thematic.' Certainly a new analysis of the musical elements is attempted in this short movement, however, and this analysis is of the greatest importance for contemporary music."

I fear that he is right, and that enough like-minded activists on the peripheries of art will succeed in analyzing music out of existence, or at least in restoring it to that healthy state represented by the musical achievements of the age of Baude Cordier.

Current Chronicle: New York
[Review of Elliott Carter's Second String Quartet]
Musical Quarterly XLVI/3 (July 1960)

Elliott Carter's Second String Quartet, completed in 1959 and heard for the first time in March of this year, is even finer and more impressive than his First Quartet. The brilliance and importance of the new quartet can come as no surprise to those who have followed Carter's work since the Piano Sonata of 1945-46, for each successive composition has shown development and growth. Carter's work of the past fifteen years places him as the most original and significant American composer of his generation. The Second Quartet, climaxing these years of maturity, is the work of an assured master who has created an idiom completely his own, in which passion, intelligence, and taste unite to form an expression of power, intensity, and lucidity. The reception accorded the Second Quartet would now seem to make Carter's position of eminence apparent to all.

There is particular cause for rejoicing in the fact that Carter has gone his own way for so long a period, and has emerged with so definite a profile. His recent music is obviously the fruit of much assimilation, of many varied techniques and esthetics of our time, but the synthesis is entirely new, and is based on none of the fashionable systems or attitudes current among us. To review Carter's musical development is perhaps at this point superfluous; but the reader may wish to refer to my full-length study of Carter and his music in the April 1957 issue of *The Musical Quarterly,* or to an earlier Current Chronicle (January 1951).[†] During his years of growth and experiment, Carter was in-

---

[†] [In this volume pp. 33-47 and pp. 69-74]

fluenced strongly by middle-period Stravinsky; he has certainly experienced the attraction of Schoenberg and his school; he is aware of Bartók and Hindemith and of the advanced forms of serialism as well; he has even at times expressed concern about achieving the authentic American style. Surely this is a wide range to order or to assimilate, and it perhaps explains two striking things about the composer: first, his comparatively late emergence as a musical personality of the first rank; and second, the apparent security and permanence of that emergence. Carter's use of the 20th century's varieties of musical experience is a remarkable achievement made possible only by the combination of a penetrating intelligence and a broad culture with unusual musicianship. It is as much the quality of Carter's mind as his command of musical techniques that gives one such confidence in the permanence of his musical achievement to date and in the promise of his continuing development and productivity.

The Second Quartet is certainly not a simple piece, although it is considerably more accessible than the First. It is, in the first place, much shorter and more compact, running about twenty minutes to the First Quartet's forty. Although its technique is perhaps even more complex, it gives the impression of less denseness. There is certainly no levity, but there is more air and light. The Quartet carries the notion of extreme independence of parts, and the technique of simultaneous planes of meter and speed, to a point of extreme subtlety far beyond the relatively simple applications of the already complex idea of metrical modulation. Carter's prefatory note in the score gives a clue to what occurs in the music:

> So that contrasts of tempi and polyrhythmic textures will stand out clearly, all indications of tempi and relationships of note values must be observed quite strictly. However, in the cello part as well as in the Coda of the fourth movement, various kinds of *rubati* are indicated; these are to be observed only at the points so notated and not otherwise. Within this fairly strict observance of tempi, each instrument must maintain a slightly different character of playing from the others, for the most part. This is indicated to a certain extent in the parts. To bring these differences clearly to the listener's attention the performers may be more widely spaced than usual on the stage so that each is definitely separated from the others in space as well as in character, although this is not necessary.

As the note clearly states, the instruments are separated by "character" or style of playing; each is also assigned characteristic intervals and rhythmic figures. Thus, the first violin (which has the most varied character) plays sometimes "with insistent rigidity . . . but more often in a bravura style"; its characteristic intervals are minor thirds, perfect fifths, and major ninths; it often alternates long and short notes, but never in relations of double or half values. The second violin is written mostly in regular rhythms, stresses major thirds, minor sixths, and major sevenths, and performs four types of pizzicato in alternation with bowed notes. The viola's part is "predominantly expressive" with many *glissandi* and *portamenti*; its principal intervals are the augmented fourth and the minor seventh. The 'cello uses perfect fourths and major sixths as its characteristic intervals; in this part the rhythmic character is determined by various *gruppetti* of accelerating and retarding notes which are indicated as follows:[†]

Ex. 1

Again to quote Carter:

> Here the dotted arrow line starts over the first note value, a quarter tied to an eighth, which is to be played its full length, then goes to the final note of the group (a sixteenth) which is also to be played its full metronomic length. The intervening notes are to be played as a continuous *accelerando* (in other places, where the notation indicates it, as a *ritardando*); the notation indicating approximately whether the *accelerando* is regular, or more active at the beginning or end of the passage. The first note value, over which the arrow starts, and the last, to which it goes, are to be played in the metrical scheme where they occur. When no arrow is written, the 'cello should play in strict time. In the above example, the first note starts on the second beat and is held for its full duration; then follow the next five each faster, leading smoothly to the first beat of the next measure, at which time 16th note speed has been reached. Exactly the same type of notation (in reverse) is used for retardation.

It will seem clear to readers that this is a formidable scheme and perhaps a forbidding one. From a description, one can sense nothing about the music except that it is "constructed"; that is, that there is a plan and a technique in which ratiocination has perhaps a more important role than "inspiration." The result could be interesting musically, or it could not. Collapse could occur for several reasons, the most obvious being the possibility that the imagination in sound might not match the boldness of the design. But it is equally possible that the design itself may not reach completion because of its complexity. Only a musical gift of the highest quality could meet the challenge posed by the hypotheses of the work. Carter has this gift, and the Quartet not only is logical and intelligible, but moving and eloquent as well. The parts remain as independent as the author designed them, and yet combine to make a convincing whole. The work is as rewarding to the ear as it is fascinating to the eye.

[†]Exx. 1-3 reprinted by permission of Associated Music Publishers, Inc.

Another formal feature of the Quartet is its division into four set movements, separated by cadenzas for viola, 'cello, and violin in that order, with an Introduction and Conclusion, all to be played without pause. Carter indicates that the principal division of the work is approximately at the halfway point, making two main movements. Each of the subsidiary movements is "dominated" by one of the instruments of the Quartet: the first, *Allegro fantastico,* by the first violin; the second, *Presto scherzando,* by the second violin; the third and fourth by viola and 'cello respectively. The Quartet is conceived as a "series of events"; other than the unifying element of the instrumental "characters" there is no recapitulation, no traditional device of fugue or sonata. Carter has evolved an organic form which is completely original in terms of his completely original material. That this is an extraordinary accomplishment surely does not need emphasis.

The material of the work is derived in essential features from the following schema, which illustrates the genesis of changing speeds in the Quartet:

It will be noted that this excerpt includes all of the simple intervals, from minor second to major seventh. A second schema gives a source of additional material:

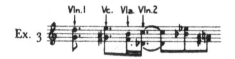

Cells such as these have no special meaning for the listener, but are fascinating for the serious student. Only many hearings of the Quartet will reveal to the ear all of the ramifications of the central ideas; meanwhile study of the score will be of the greatest interest to all who follow contemporary music with hope.

Current Chronicle: New York
[Jacques de Menasce obituary]
Musical Quarterly XLVI/3 (July 1960)

Jacques de Menasce was so much more than a composer and pianist that the loss occasioned by his death in Switzerland last January can be felt fully only by those who were privileged to know him well. He was as much an ornament to the world of men as to the world of music. In both, his role and his influence were far wider than would be indicated by the extent of his work or by the frequency with which it has achieved performance up to now. He accomplished much, if one measures by quality rather than quantity, but he will be remembered not only for what he did, but for what he was. To write that he was a rare personality, a being of an unusual and immeasurable kind, a personage in the grand manner, and the almost ideal representative at the same time of the great qualities of a disappearing civilization, is only to suggest the surface outlines of a great artist and a noble spirit.

Menasce had *style.* But beyond that, he had wisdom as well as intellect; he possessed wit, charm, kindness, and tolerance. Profound, honest, and humane, his conversation was memorable; he was one of the few in whom the art of discourse still lived. The justness of his judgment, the breadth of his culture, the liveliness of his opinions—and with this all, the charity of his conclusions—made his society valued by a large and diversified circle throughout the world. His friends ranged from artists like Berg and Bartók to the dozens of less celebrated musicians and colleagues in whom he sensed talent and whom he helped in more ways than can be described.

He was a discriminating judge of music, of letters, of art, and of people, and he was completely without pedantry. By the power of his perceptions, his imagination, and his judgment he exercised on the music of our time a beneficent influence far wider than one would suppose from the restricted sphere of his physical activity. He was an artist in an absolute sense, and in a way that is rare. Fortunately situated in life so as to be able to cultivate his gifts, he was unfortunate only in the delicacy of his health during the latter part of his life. Yet even in health, he would not, probably, have been a producer in quantity; he would still have worked for himself and for those values to which he could give his lasting belief. This is not selfishness; it is an aristocratic ideal of perfection involving not only talent but grace, to show what man can accomplish; and thus it is of benefit to all men. It is a true form of enlightenment.

Menasce was born in Bad Ischl, Austria, August 19, 1905. Educated in Vienna, he studied piano from the age of seven. He worked later with Emil von Sauer, and studied composition with Paul Pisk and Josef Marx. He had close and friendly relations with Alban Berg, under whose encouragement he composed his first piano concerto, and also with Béla Bartók. But Menasce's musical style, while absorbing much, was never directly influenced by anyone; it remained always his own.

Upon graduation from the *Gymnasium,* Menasce traveled widely, partly in connection with his family's many interests. While in Egypt and in England he acquired a considerable reputation as a polo player, in addition to his already established reputation as a pianist. Menasce was at home everywhere; he spoke English and French as well as German with perfect fluency—indeed with an elegance and precision to be envied by most monolinguists —and managed more than passably in several others. He was also at home at all levels of society, with a kind of vertical cosmopolitanism which enabled him to grace Bohemia as well as the polo field.

The war found him in Switzerland, whence he came to the United States in 1941. The impression he made on musical life here was immediate and enlivening. His activity in New York made him seem not a distinguished visitor from abroad, but a valued colleague and collaborator whose presence was as natural as it was stimulating. His occasional concert appearances, mostly as a performer of chamber music, left an unforgettable impression of pianism of the utmost intelligence and refinement put to the service of music of the most distinguished kind. Readers of *The Musical Quarterly* will remember also his contributions as a writer on music, and will recall his essays on Frank Martin and Henri Sauguet; one should also note his remarkable essay on Berg and Bartók in *Modern Music,* and his fine pieces on Richard Strauss and Stravinsky in *The Juilliard Review.* For *High Fidelity* he wrote a penetrating essay on Bernard Shaw as a music critic, itself one of the most perceptive essays on criticism to appear in any American journal devoted to music. Menasce not only had original and brilliant ideas, but expressed them in a style that made him a man of letters of the first rank.

Menasce's music was, or is, like his writing and his conversation and his manner of living, graced by originality, impeccability of taste, distinction of style, elevation of tone. It has warmth, wit, and power. Except for the Second Piano Concerto, it is not music for the large audience. Menasce in fact wrote little for orchestra. His finest music is to be found in works like the Sonata for Viola and Piano, in the songs, and in his delightful piano music. The Second Piano Concerto stands alone among Menasce's compositions; it is big, driving, almost "romantic"; it is a pianist's concerto as well as a composer's, and it should be a part of the standard contemporary repertory. The recording, made by the composer with the Vienna State Opera Orchestra under Edmond Appia, is the best reminder left us of Menasce's playing.

To paraphrase a sensitive appreciation written by Appia, "Some composers mature only by writing abundantly; others feel that a work should not be an experiment . . . but a realization: that it should express fully everything that the composer has achieved in his experience. It is thus that Menasce thought about his work, and why he wrote relatively little. He would not write a note without testing it against everything he knew . . ." Menasce's discipline and craftsmanship were remarkable. He exhibited to the highest degree that complete control which is perhaps the basic need in the composition of our century.

In the past few years Menasce spent most of his time in Gstaad. His health became more and more precarious and his intention of dividing his time between Switzerland and the United States could not be realized. But insofar as he could, he continued to compose. During the last year, he completed an exquisite set of four songs for tenor and string orchestra, and some incidental music for a play of Jill Weldon. None of this music has yet been heard here, but it is to be hoped that these last pieces, as well as a good representation of Menasce's other music, will not only be heard but recorded.

Of Jacques de Menasce it can truly be said that none who knew him can ever forget him, nor will they meet his like again. For those who did not have this privilege, the music remains as his living and enduring image.

Current Chronicle: New York
[Discussion of contemporary music]
Musical Quarterly XLVII/2 (April 1961)

Note: The paragraphs that follow may be arranged in any order the reader desires.

If one imagines an ear completely unfamiliar with the sounds or the conventions of Western music, one can suppose that it would find the continuity or logic of a Mozart symphony difficult, perhaps even impossible, to perceive. One would suppose also that a dozen or more works of Mozart would probably sound very much alike, and that it would be difficult to distinguish among them. Certainly one would not expect such an ear to make refined judgments about the music. Most Western musicians experience this difficulty in adjusting to the conventions of, for example, classical Chinese music; and it is considered no cause for shame or alarm that they do. But we are alarmed when we are unable to come to grips with music composed in the West, even when we are forewarned that this music seeks to break definitely and permanently with traditional Western forms. techniques, conventions, and attitudes.

An afternoon of "New Music from Europe," presented on February 5 at the New School by New School Concerts and the Fromm Music Foundation, brought this problem into focus for 1961. The concert resembled in its atmosphere a meeting of a political splinter-group, except that it attracted a full house, about equally divided between well-known professional musicians and very young men and women. How the very young hear this music, I do not know, although I suspect it is not much clearer to them than it is to their elders, whose attitude in this case generally could be described as one of open-minded uncertainty. There is no ready frame of reference, and although one is told (in somewhat cryptic program notes, as well as in the general literature of the advanced music groups) what principles are employed, and what one should hear, the question remains whether we can properly appreciate or value the embodiment in sound of radical ideas and theories to which we may or may not be, *a priori,* sympathetic.

I will cite, bearing on this point, the apparent disagreement, or uncertainty, among American proponents of advanced music about the quality of both the works and the performances. Since much of the realization of the music (or the *directions for music,* as will appear later) is left to the performers, the quality of performance is of the greatest importance. It appeared to me that the two percussionists (imported from France for the occasion) were admirable virtuosos; but some, who should know better than I the requirements of the scores, assured me that they were barely adequate. I will admit at once, also, that I cannot find a criterion for the music itself, which seemed to me to be "interesting" (for more reasons than one), but difficult to differentiate, except as one piece used different instruments from another, and except as certain combinations of timbre appealed more than others to my no doubt tradition-bound ears.

We are dealing here with a music that may, as M. André Hodeir tells us (in his remarkable book, *Since Debussy*), already be dated, or that may represent only the initial groping stages of an evolution towards new musical syntheses. Whether or not either hypothesis is true, this music attempts not so much to continue or re-define tradition as to break with it decisively: it postulates an absolute denial of harmonic continuity, thematic construction, rhythmic regularity, and fixed formal relationship. In this perspective, the figure of Webern can be made out only in the middle or far distance. Essentially, the new style is based on a polyphony of fluctuating tempos (within which symmetric rhythm is avoided), dynamic, accent, and timbre. By the nature of these concepts, which involve the manipulation of "sound objects" rather than of functional tone relations, percussion instruments are necessarily prominent; it is as percussion instruments that both piano and harp are used, and it is perhaps intended that the flute and the voice be employed primarily as sources of percussive sound. Only these instruments were in evidence at the New School concert. It should be mentioned that no electronic sounds were utilized.

The remaining, and perhaps most significant, element of the new style is discontinuity or chance. The key word now in the forefront of fashion (at least, as of February 1961) is "aleatory," defined in the Oxford Universal Dictionary as "dependent on the throw of a die; hence, dependent on uncertain contingencies." Essentially, the concept of aleatory music involves leaving to chance the order of performance of composed or "determinate" portions of a work, or the admission of improvised or "free" passages among the determinate ones. Thus it is a central tenet of aleatory music that it should not sound the same in successive performances. Among the landmarks of this style are Karlheinz Stockhausen's *Klavierstück XI,* Boulez's Third Piano Sonata and his *Improvisations sur Mallarmé.*[1] John Cage has also written music in which chance is a factor, and was probably, in fact, the first to do so. But with Cage, chance is unsystematized. With Boulez and his followers, it is part of a concept of total organization.

Whether the path chosen by this group is the only path towards the future is, I think, seriously open to doubt, and I do not intend to be humorous when I say that perhaps twelve tones are not enough. It seems inconsistent, at the least, to wish to overthrow traditional ideas of rhythmic organization in favor of complete fluidity or elasticity, but to accept at the same time the rigorous and artificial limitations of the tempered scale, which was, after all, evolved in the interest of harmony. A keen musical mind, that of Percy Grainger, anticipated this problem more than fifty years ago.[2] Grainger not only experimented with the ideas of fluid rhythmic polyphony, but also with what he called "gliding tones," that is, the complete range of microtonal intervals. Curiously enough, he also, before the members of the current *avant garde* were born, discovered the delights of the marimba and other percussion instruments, both tuned and untuned, that are now presented in ensemble performances with such an air of pleased daring. What is tragic is that these young composers have probably never heard of Grainger, such being the nature of the closed circles of our musical life, and since he was not an "insider," and never in his life used the word "aleatory," they would probably dismiss his ideas with contempt.

In any case, how a theory works can be determined ultimately only by the music itself and how it sounds, if indeed this is to remain a criterion for judgment. What was heard at

---

[1]Mallarmé himself is said to have planned a work to be called *Le Livre,* the text of which would be "alterable" at each reading.

[2]See R. F. Goldman, *Percy Grainger's Free Music,* in *The Juilliard Review,* Vol. II, No. 3, Fall 1955. [In this volume, pp. 5-11]

the New School concert, in addition to works by Stockhausen, Boulez, and Berio, all well-known composers, at least by name and reputation, were compositions by Paolo Castaldi (b. Italy, 1930), Roman Haubenstock-Ramati (b. Poland, 1919), Gilbert Amy (b. France, 1936) and the father of them all, Olivier Messiaen, now a patriarch of fifty-two. The pieces by Messiaen and Boulez were "old music." Boulez's First Piano Sonata, composed in 1946, is Messiaenic in more ways than one. The two works by Messiaen, *Mode de valeurs et d'intensité* and *Ile de feu 2,* date from 1949-50. In both the Boulez and the Messiaen, the central preoccupation is with rhythm. In the program provided by the New School, Messiaen is quoted as follows:

> I tried to separate the study of duration from the study of sound. I tried to liberate rhythm not only from the measure but also from metric and symmetry. I tried to recover the secrets of ancient Hindu rhythmics, the most evolved in musical history, and to revive them. Finally, I utilized the permutations of duration, that is, a great number of possible directions in time.

The difficulty is that little, if any, of this is audible, and that the piano, of all instruments, is probably the most refractory to this kind of rhythmic treatment. The two Messiaen works and the Boulez Sonata hit the ear as impressive masses of agitated sound; all of them require immense technical agility and strength. In none of them does a contrapuntal texture emerge with any clarity; the effect resides in what seems to be more an expression of crude power than of delicate calculation. The *Ile de feu 2* even gives something of an impression of rhapsodic romanticism, in the manner of middle-period Bartók.

Messiaen apparently has now come to rest in the contemplation and re-creation of bird-calls. The later works of Boulez are worlds removed from the First Piano Sonata, and it is difficult to hear or see much of a relation between this old-fashioned piece of fourteen years ago and a work like the *Improvisations sur Mallarmé.* Nevertheless, even for the First Piano Sonata and the two piano pieces of Messiaen, the ear will have to become much more sensitive in order to be able to discern the rhythmic refinements that we are told exist in this music (and that, to some extent, are apparent on visual analysis). In all of these pieces the polyphony of rhythm cancels itself out, and one is led to feel that surely, for this kind of music, the piano is an obsolete instrument. There are, also, and especially with the piano and the tempered scale, practical limits to dissonance. Major sevenths, minor seconds and ninths, augmented fourths and their combinations and agglomerations eventually become quite as conventional as thirds and sixths, and have perhaps even less flexibility. The vertical combinations lose not only any structural significance (this is, of course, intentional) but, much more important, tend to become tedious in the extreme.

A more fruitful path would appear to be the reorganization of the scale itself, and the employment of smaller intervals. This would provide additional resources, of which one very much feels the need. Except for the activity of Harry Partch, whose work should be better known, there appears to be at present little consistent interest in this kind of exploration. It is surprising, and striking, it seems to me, that composers of "mobile" or discontinuous music continue to employ instruments of absolutely fixed pitch, such as the piano and the vibra-marimbaphone, and that Boulez, for example, continues this practice in the much-discussed Third Piano Sonata, which we have not yet heard.

The instrument of fixed pitch is a remnant of conventionality that any truly advanced composer would do well to discard. Why be half-hearted about striking out on new paths? Surely the genius of the age can discover newer sounds than any we have yet heard, including those electronically produced on tape. Or is it imagination itself, and not merely technique, that has proved deficient?

The artist and the technician do not always meet in the composer, and it is interesting that students of engineering, philosophy, mathematics, or musicology contribute so many compositions that appear to be demonstrations rather than expressions. We have reversed not only the old ideas of continuity and form, but also the process of commentary, elaboration, and criticism. Where once the composer composed, and the critic or romancer told us what the composer "meant," we now have the composer first telling us what he is going to do, or has done, so that in most cases it is hardly necessary to listen to the music, since this is only likely to upset our satisfying ideas about it and leave us with a sense of disappointment. This is certainly true of Haubenstock-Ramati's *Liaisons,* for vibra-marimbaphone solo, in which, according to the program, "the distribution of the various sections follows two general basic criteria from which the performer may depart: this results in a combination of primary and secondary paths which cross each other reciprocally. This formal idea is comparable, in the visual arts, to a mobile." The music, unfortunately, seemed singularly uneventful and immobile, and the sound of the vibra-marimbaphone excessively pretty. The whole effect was almost that of a conventional piece descriptive of fountains, or reflections on the water. And, as we know, this has been done with less fuss.

The concept of mobility crops up in the works of Castaldi and Amy as well as in Stockhausen's *Zyklus* (1959), for one percussion player. The Stockhausen work

> . . . combines a "free" performance with a determinate one. The performer chooses the order of succession of the 16 pages upon which the work is distributed. Once this succession has been determined, the performer may freely exploit

the relationships between the groups, as well as those within each group. With reference to a predetermined time-coordinate, he may act upon the density and simultaneity of the groups, and move to the "free" and determinate groups at the same time.

In his *Invention I* (1959-60), for flute, piano, and vibra-marimbaphone, Amy

. . . has attempted to find and articulate continuously mobile relationships between the instrumental terms, particularly those involving similitude and fusion on the one hand, and antagonism and contrast on the other. An extremely diversified disposal of dynamic and instrumental elements characterizes the piece, which also alternates "free" and determinate structures.

Castaldi's *Frase* (1960), for

. . . two performers, a pianist and a percussion player, each of whom has several instruments to play . . . is distributed on nine large sheets: on each of these a particular individualization takes place, defined by the intrinsic characteristics of the sound material. The sheets are not numbered; the order is left to the performers. Thus every performance will present the work in a different aspect which is, at the same time, never arbitrary or uncontrolled.

For most of the audience, and certainly for myself, it was difficult to determine which parts of any of the works were improvised and which were "determinate." Perhaps, of course, this is not relevant. But the concepts of form, or their absence, are still too elusive for all but the tiniest minority of *aficionados* who, presumably, have some criteria for passing judgments on these works. For the rest of us, they remain a species of mystification to be accepted or rejected simply as continuums of sound, depending on whether they strike us as pleasant or unpleasant, significant or insignificant, and perhaps even as serious or frivolous.

Seriousness and frivolity appear as questions in the work of Luciano Berio with which the program closed. This composition, entitled *Circles,* a setting of three poems of e. e. cummings for voice, harp, and two percussion players, is an example of "action music": that is, it must be seen as well as heard. In spirit, it is a return to the Dada of the twenties, though in technique it is up to the minute, as its description indicates:

The use of the harp and the percussion instruments is intended to extend or induce sound qualities of the vocal part; for this reason the instrumental parts are occasionally not completely defined in conventional musical notation, but the general nature of the action is indicated. The specific result thus depends somewhat on the personal characteristics of each performer. The work itself is considered as a structure of actions which also determine the "theatrical" aspects of the performance.

Circles was the only work on this program that involved the use of the voice, and it illustrates the principle of discontinuity as applied to prosody and vocal writing. The words of the poem are wrenched apart (cummings, of course, has already begun this process for the composer) or banged together; the rhythms and intervals of the vocal line hit the consonants as violently as possible, so that the voice becomes part of the apparatus of tuneful percussion. Conventional "sense" in the setting of words is deliberately avoided. One wonders therefore why it is necessary to use a poem at all. cummings' poetry may be cute, and mildly discontinuous, but it makes sense of a sort, and does not respond to the discontinuity with which Berio endows it. The two sides of this coin do not match. Has it not yet occurred to anyone to serialize the alphabet?

That I found *Circles* very pretty in spots, and thoroughly amusing throughout, indicates, I am sure, only how completely I misunderstand it. But that cannot be helped, although I regret imputing an intention to entertain where probably none exists. The wonderful solemnity of the singer and the controlled athleticism of the two percussionists, being part of the "design" of the music, gave to the sound itself a slightly hysterical gaiety that may or may not be taken as an artistic triumph. But I would go to hear it again.

Berio's music, and all the rest, is a logical consequence of taking the position that Western music has (or already had, some twenty years ago) reached an absolute impasse. If one agrees that this is so, one must accept what is being done here and in Europe, as represented at this concert and in all of the experiments with tape, as an honest effort to create new music, not necessarily denying the past, but relegating it to the museum. Occasionally, listening to much of what is offered as contemporary music, one feels that there is ample justification for declaring that Western music is dead. But most of us are not quite ready to take so extreme a position. We have a few "conventional" composers among us who seem alive; not many, it is true, but even one should be enough to hold us back from writing, over the history of music as we have known it, the grim word *Finis*.

Current Chronicle: New York
[Review of Japanese electronic music performed at ISCM concert]
Musical Quarterly XLVII/3 (July 1961)

It can hardly come as a surprise to learn that the Japanese, with their genius for indiscriminate westernizing, are busy with electronic music. For our acquaintance with a sampling of recent Tokyo production we are indebted to the U. S. Section of the ISCM, which presented its first public event in several years last March at the New School.

If one were to judge by the four electronic compositions presented at this concert, one might conclude that the tape recorder and its accessory gadgets have done for the art of sound pretty much what the home movie camera has done for the visual arts. Perhaps one should be happy about the possibility that composition has become a game that anyone can play, provided he can afford the equipment. Certainly new possibilities of innocent amusement have been opened up. The only question that would seem proper to ask is whether the creations of happy tinkerers, playing with expensive toys, are of interest to any but those known, in nursery-school terms, as members of the peer-group. Schiller, one remembers, declared that art is a form of play; this is not, perhaps, precisely what he had in mind, but it is possibly also an illustration of a prophet being righter than he could have wished to be. The self-expression of the child, revealed through "artistic" play, does no one any harm, but it has a limited interest, confined as a rule to the child's parents, to psychologists, and to managers of progressive schools. The artistic play of adults, as in home movies, is seldom of interest to anyone. The social damage is done only when it is assumed that the products of play have a claim on the attention of any besides the players.

It is rather difficult to describe the four Japanese pieces, but one can begin by stating that all four were very long, and that among them they gave a fair representation of the conventional electronic techniques, using "natural" sounds, gimmicked sounds, and electronically produced sounds. Mr. Toru Takemitsu's *Relief Statique* presented the beeps and wind-machine effects that have become one of the commonplaces of the electronic tone-vocabulary. The same composer's *Ai* presented two human voices, male and female, in a lengthy series of transformations of the syllable *Ai,* high and low, loud and soft, harsh and gentle, legato and staccato, simultaneous and separate, calm and excited, in slow tempo and in fast. One's impression is that Mr. Takemitsu must have had great fun in a serious sort of way. One should not begrudge him this fun; and of course one is aware that all fun and amusement is a serious matter to those involved: one can't take one's own fun frivolously or one loses the point, but the spectator's stake in the game is entirely another matter. Mr. Toshiro Mayuzumi's *Campanology* is another case in point. For this work the composer traveled over Japan recording the sounds of a hundred bells: old bells, new bells, large bells, small bells; out of these he assembled a tape that made its point in the first thirty seconds and then rambled on for a good many minutes. The point is that bells produce pretty sounds, and that with variable-speed tape one can make them do glissandos in either direction. This is hardly of staggering artistic significance, and again one is forced to conclude that it must have been fun splicing all the bell tones and running them backwards or at different speeds. How happy Edgar Allen Poe would have been, with this electronic tintinnabulation!

The final piece, *The Black Convent,* composed by Mr. Shinichi Matsushita, a mathematics professor at Osaka University, was by far the most ambitious, and the lengthiest. I could not decide whether the speaker who introduced it described it as being an example of serialism or surrealism, but perhaps this is a happy confusion which aptly characterizes the work. A poem was recited, in the manner of the conventional narration with music, but here the background was provided by the carefully assembled and converted sounds made possible by the electronic studio. For all one knows, every sound may have been calculated with a slide-rule; the effect, however, was rather haphazard. Here again, one feels that what the composer was doing is a private affair: private in a sense somewhat new to art, since one has the feeling that any attempt at communication is secondary to the sheer joy of playing with sounds, and that, as with all play, the primary benefit accrues to the player. This perhaps may be said about much of the so-called "experimental art" of our century: if the experiments are in the exploration of a limited area of self-indulgence, they acquire public status only because of the public's willingness, even eagerness, to assume an interest in private concerns.

Whatever the Japanese electronic music may be worth, it provided more to think about than did Hans Werner Henze's dreary Woodwind Quintet, composed in 1952 in a style that Henze has long since abandoned, or than John Huggler's Quartet for Flute and String Trio. One may ask why the ISCM thought these pieces worth presenting, especially in view of the U. S. Section's rather difficult recent history and the necessity for it to re-make its place in the musical scene with activities of some significance. Webern's Pieces for Violin and Piano, Opus 7, also presented at the concert, serve only to show that not every note left by Webern need be considered immortal. And surely, in any case, the ISCM at this late date hardly needs to assume the responsibility for the Webern repertory.

The redeeming piece on the program was Elliott Carter's Eight Etudes and a Fantasy, for woodwind quartet, composed in 1950. This work has been heard previously in New York, and is available in a recording, but it is one of those pieces that one is happy to hear again. It is full of life, intelligence, and wit, and serves to bolster Carter's position as the most interesting composer active in America today. It also serves to remind us that music by genuine composers, conceived for live players, still has possibilities.

Current Chronicle: New York

[Wallingford Riegger obituary]
Musical Quarterly XLVII/3 (July 1961)

The death of Wallingford Riegger on April 2, 1961, at the age of seventy-five, occurred just a few days after the announcement of his selection as winner of the Brandeis University award for 1961. Recognition came late to Riegger, but the closing years of his life at least brought him his just share of awards and honors. Beginning in 1948, when his Third Symphony won the New York Critics Circle Award, his music was heard with increasing frequency, and began to make its way with the public. One can be grateful that so striking, original, and independent a figure on the American musical scene was able for a decade to enjoy a modest celebrity and some small degree of security.

Riegger's career is instructive in many ways. He typified the independent worker who belonged to no school, either literal or figurative; his work was carried on without grants, fellowships, or prizes; he followed no fashion or doctrine, and he supported himself by time-consuming but useful musical labors in editing, arranging, and teaching. He continued to write, and was not discouraged, in a day when the American composer was not pampered, and when performances, commissions, or subsidies were few indeed.

One of the most admirable aspects of Riegger's character and work was the manner in which he went his own way, asking no favors, and following his artistic and moral conscience. His music at all times carries a sense of conviction that is one of its basic strengths. Whether he composed with twelve notes or diatonically, he had a personal stamp that was unmistakable. He never composed with great facility, although he possessed a technique adequate to any need. He re-wrote and polished constantly, trying always to achieve the greatest conciseness and logic in each composition. One feels confident, looking back over his completed work, that a number of his scores—the Third Symphony, *Dichotomy,* the *Music for Brass Choir*, the string quartets, and at least a half-dozen others—should remain in the repertory for many years to come.

Riegger was a remarkable teacher, whose abilities should have attracted a far greater number of pupils than ever found their way to him. He loved and understood the music of the past as well as that of the present and, like Schoenberg, was able to convey penetrating insights into music of all periods through reference to the classics that he knew so well. He believed in discipline rather than in inspiration or experiment without rationale, and his criticisms were invariably apt and illuminating. He was too honest and too devoted to a high ideal of music and of craftsmanship to be free with praise. His encouragement was therefore the more meaningful and valuable. He was broadminded enough to look with interest and sympathy on all of the idioms of the 20th century, but all forms of expression were, in his view, the continuation of traditional forms and values.

Riegger's qualities of honesty, kindness, and humor will not be forgotten by those who knew him. He was a serious and devoted person, humble towards his art and unassuming in his relations with his colleagues. Like all serious people, he was able to laugh at himself. He viewed life with passion and accepted its difficulties with patience. He had conviction and faith, and at heart an unquenchable optimism about art and about people. In the best sense of an old-fashioned phrase, he was a man of character.

In any history of American music, Riegger's name must have an honored place. From the *Study in Sonority*, Opus 7, of 1927, to the Duo for Piano and Orchestra, Opus 75, of 1960, Riegger produced a body of work that for originality, craftsmanship, vigor, and sheer musical quality is not surpassed by any native composer of his generation. Neither musicians nor the public have yet done his music full justice. Although his seventy-fifth birthday brought a number of warm and gratifying tributes from his colleagues, Reigger's music is still not as often performed as it should be, especially in New York, and there are still too few recordings available. Some of his finest scores have never been recorded: *Dichotomy*, the First String Quartet, and the *Music for Brass Choir*, among others. These gaps in the recorded repertory should be repaired. Performances, live or recorded, are the best memorials to a composer, the best reminder of his work and his importance, and Wallingford Riegger surely deserves our most affectionate and admiring remembrance.

Current Chronicle: New York

[Review of Milton Babbitt's *Vision and Prayer*, Elliott Carter's Double Concerto, and Leon Kirchner's Concerto for violin, 'cello, ten winds, and percussion]
Musical Quarterly XLVIII/1 (January 1962)

The sessions of the Eighth Congress of the International Society for Musicology included one of the most brilliant concerts of recent years, presented at the Metropolitan Museum of Art through the generosity of the Fromm Foundation. The three works performed were Milton Babbitt's *Vision and Prayer*, for soprano with synthesized (electronic) accompaniment; Elliott Carter's Double Concerto for piano, harpsichord, and two chamber orchestras; and Leon Kirchner's Concerto for violin, 'cello, ten winds, and percussion. It is a curious sidelight on the status of music these days that this concert of contemporary music—so much more lively than most of those that have been given in recent years by societies specializing in modernism—should have been given by and for musicologists, and that the three composers represented should have been, respectively, professors at Princeton, Yale, and Harvard.

These three composers—with perhaps three or four others—represent America's best claim to musical vitality and distinction today. Strangely enough, the work that offered the least in the way of excitement was Babbitt's composition utilizing the electronic synthesizer and what superficially would appear to be the most "advanced" technique. This seems in many ways a peculiarly moral state of affairs, from which some generalizations may perhaps be drawn in the current discussions of conventional versus electronic music.

Both the Carter and the Kirchner are works of great vitality; this is the word that immediately suggests itself, and which one uses with a great sense of pleasure, especially in an age in which theoretical preoccupations seem to take precedence over those less *ordered* and more indefinable arrangements that give art its impact, and its advantage over limited systematic thought.

The problem that comes foremost is whether music is, or is to remain, an art of sound, rather than an art of calculation, systematization, or combination. It is universally recognized that music has at least all of these possible and diverse aspects, and several others as well. It is also recognized—although here our present situation is less clear, and there is more doubt—that music (at least Western music) has rested on a variety of conventions (tempered scale, meter, harmony, contrapuntal techniques) that have acquired meanings of a sort. (This is not to suggest that these conventions may not have served their purposes and now be outmoded; or that others eventually may not replace them, and convey the same—or different—esthetic meanings or communications.) But the burden of proof is up to those who are striking out with new systems and new techniques, electronic or otherwise, and it seems fair to say, despite the clamor to the contrary, that the proof is not yet clearly established.

The concert under discussion seems eloquent enough demonstration that the possibility is still the other way. Babbitt is a composer to be respected; and of all of those in this country now working with electronic systems he is, except perhaps for Varèse, the one who has so far produced (and seems most likely to produce in the future) the most interesting musical results. He is both serious and technically well-equipped. His *Vision and Prayer* (to a text by Dylan Thomas), although I think it a not entirely successful, convincing, or moving work, is nevertheless considerably more attractive and possibly viable than any of the electronic works heard last spring at the début of the Columbia-Princeton laboratory. What is amiss in Babbitt's piece is what is amiss in so much of current effort: 1) inconsistency (esthetically); 2) timidity; and 3) rigidity (technically). My terms may not be clear, and I will try to clarify them.

By inconsistency, I mean that the work hovers between two worlds and does not make up its mind to which it belongs. I have suggested in a previous brief review my impression that in music of this sort the human voice is obsolete. I feel that this is true on several counts: 1) the voice does not belong in a dehumanized performance; 2) the voice, if used, should be translated into electronic terms, i.e., it should be transformed, doubled in power, quadrupled in range, distorted—in other words, forced to become a completely "abstract" instrument; 3) it should not serve as the link between abstraction and "expression," especially when the material of the latter is a dead letter esthetically. A Dylan Thomas text is associated with a different world; its "meanings" are not reconcilable with this musical context. I was not altogether facetious when I suggested in a previous review that the solution here, if one must have "texts," is simply to serialize the alphabet.

By timidity, I mean that none of the explorations of electronic sound-possibilities seems to have been carried nearly far enough. Surely more interesting sounds must be possible! Granted that electronic music may be in its infancy, but I do not believe it is being breast-fed; it seems to be growing on formula. In any case, the question is not so much that of its relative youth; the musical application of electronic sound sources may be in the early stages, but surely, enough is already known about the production of noise so that a fantastically wide range of potential timbres, adjustments, and combinations should be possible. The sounds one hears in most electronic scores give one the same impression that one might derive from painting done in subtle shades of neon. Can it again be that it is imagination and not technique that is deficient? Are we forever to be limited to beeps, blips, sirens, percussive thuds, clanging metal, and, all else failing, the expensive imitation of a Hammond organ?

By technical rigidity I mean specifically doctrinaire serialism. We have had a variety of statements claiming that serialism is the only way to the future. Why? What is so magical about the idea of the series? So *necessary*? This challenge has not received a convincing answer. What we have developed is an academic formalism no better, or brighter, than that, say, of Saint-Saëns.[1]

The pieces by Carter and Kirchner seem to me to offer the best answer available at the moment to many of these questions. Neither is systematic or electronic. It seems improbable, on the other hand, that many people would seriously claim that they are not of our time. Of the two, Kirchner's is more conservative; but this is only a relative consideration. It has the strengths of his best work: powerful, almost "romantic" drive, independence of direction, and a fine sense of sound. Given the nature of the orchestra for which it is conceived, it is of a denser texture than his Second String Quartet (see *Current Chronicle* in *The Musical Quarterly,* January 1960)[†] and seems to occupy a point stylistically intermediate between the Quartet and earlier works such as the Piano Concerto. As do all of Kirchner's best works, the Concerto for violin, 'cello, ten winds, and percussion shows great individual character, and has an expressiveness bordering on the rhapsodic. Kirchner seems to be as far away as possible—for a serious composer—from ideas of pure abstraction. He appears to be a composer who is able, even when it is no longer fashionable, to laugh and to weep, show anger and joy. He is certainly not inhibited, and his music is unusual in this day and age for its power to communicate some of the essential things that have traditionally been associated with all forms of art, but which now are frowned upon as irrelevant curiosities. Kirchner's strength as a composer resides only partly in this power. The substance of his musical thought is solid; his technique and material are sufficiently original and of our times to make it impossible to dismiss him as a belated Romantic or a composer who in any sense looks backward.

Carter's Double Concerto continues the techniques developed in the First and Second String Quartets, but represents a further exploration, with additional resources of timbre, volume, contrast, and balance. It is a score of great difficulty to read, and is analogous, in some of its approaches to arithmetical calculation of counter-balancing and counter-operating time values, to Stockhausen's *Zeitmasse 5.* It is completely unlike the Stockhausen work, however, in that Carter seems to be able to hear, and to be interested in the actual embodiment of his ideas in sound, rather than in the mere theoretical demonstration that such calculations can form a basis on which to construct a more or less musical edifice. What comes out of Carter's preoccupation with his premises is interesting to listen to, so that one is not forced to limit one's praise to a grudging admiration of the constructive intelligence involved. Sound is by no means irrelevant to Carter, as it appears to be for a not inconsiderable number of our contemporaries. That is the first important thing about

---

[1] In connection with serialism I should like to refer the reader to Edward T. Cone's brilliant essay, *Music: A View from Delft* (*The Musical Quarterly,* October 1961).

[†] In this volume pp. 109-114.

Carter's new score. It is surprising, delightful, exciting, and original as a matter of sheer sound.

Whether or not Carter had in mind some kind of demonstration of the power of live sound, created on conventional instruments, I cannot say, nor is this necessarily relevant. Yet it is known that Carter has expressed himself as at best dubious about electronic music and that he has not himself seemed inclined to experiment with it. But I was most forcibly struck by the sense that Carter's Concerto for live performers, as sheer imaginative, beautiful, and original sound, made anything so far achieved by electronic music seem childish, silly, unoriginal, and limited.

I should add to the appeal of the sound itself the appeal of the liveness of the mere action of performance, the knowledge that imperfections are not only possible but almost unavoidable. The visual interest of musical performance is a question that has never been sufficiently discussed, or even admitted. Yet we all know that it exists, and that it enters into our attitudes and responses to staged or unstaged opera, to recordings and to the expressivity of conductors. It accounts for part of the uneasiness felt by so many people when watching a stage occupied only by four loudspeakers, even when these are accompanied by a soprano in evening dress. (The Columbia-Princeton electronic concert seemed to recognize this by fiddling with expressive lighting; will the next step be electronic choreography or abstract movies?)

The matter of imperfections in performance also raises interesting questions. Probably even the performer on the tape-recorder, being human, can err, but we are not invited to consider this possibility. The phonograph record, too, is immutable, except for needle-scratch and turntables that alter the pitch. But the hazard of live performance still provides something that is far more interesting than the suggestion that mechanical exactitude or perfection is possible. In the case of Carter's Concerto, about eighteen hours of rehearsal were needed to achieve what one of the players described as a performance *good enough for recording, but slightly risky for live performance*! I hope that some of my readers share my fascination with this comment and its implications.

Even aside from the matter of imperfections, there is of course the simple excitement of the live performance, the nuance and gesture of players who are themselves variable, and the intangibles of communication that exist in an assembly of live people. We accept, in our homes, the convention of the phonograph, another psychological phenomenon that merits serious study, but there is, I think, something grotesque about assembling formally for the purpose of listening to loudspeakers. Grotesque . . . and also rather frightening.

Carter discusses his Double Concerto in the following program-note, which is reproduced in full as a far more satisfactory description and analysis than anyone else could give:

My Double Concerto for Harpsichord and Piano, commissioned by the Fromm Foundation, is dedicated to Paul Fromm. Completed in August, 1961, it is an antiphonal work for two small orchestras each led by one of the soloists. The harpsichord is associated with an ensemble of flute, horn, trumpet, trombone, viola, contrabass and percussion (largely metallophones and lignophones) while the piano is joined by an ensemble of oboe, clarinet, bassoon, horn, 'cello and percussion (largely membranophones). In addition to being isolated in space and timbre, the antiphonal groups are partially separated musically by the fact that each emphasizes its own repertory of melodic and harmonic intervals, the harpsichord ensemble: minor seconds, minor thirds, perfect fourths, augmented fourths, minor sixths, minor sevenths and minor ninths; the piano ensemble: major seconds, major thirds, perfect fifths, major sixths, major sevenths and major ninths. Each of these intervals is associated, for the most part, with a certain metronomic speed with the result that the speeds and their interrelationships are also different for the two groups. Rhythmically the harpsichord ensemble is apt to specialize in derivations of the polyrhythm 4 against 7, while the piano ensemble in 5 against 3. These fields of specialization of the two groups are not carried out rigorously throughout the work but give way to the more important considerations which come from the fact that the two groups not only also have different repertories of musical characters, gestures, logic, expression and "behavioural" patterns, but that all of these are meant to be combined within each group and from group to group and result in recognizable overall patterns. The motion of the work is from comparative unity with slight character differences, to greater and greater diversity of material and character and a return to unity. The form is that of confrontations of diversified action-patterns and a presentation of their mutual interreactions, conflicts and resolutions, their growth and decay over various stretches of time.

The Concerto, although continuous, falls into seven large inter-connected sections. During the *Introduction,* the two groups in becoming progressively more differentiated, state each facet of their material with greater and greater definition. The *Cadenza for Harpsichord* presents in condensed form all the salient characteristics, rhythms and intervals of its ensemble. The *Allegro Scherzando* is primarily for the piano ensemble with brief interruptions and comments by the other group. An *Adagio,* largely for the winds of both groups accompanied by accelerating and retarding figurations by the two soloists and the percussion joined occasionally by the strings follows, and is concluded by an extended duet for the two soloists meeting at a stage in the piano's acceleration and the harpsichord's retardation only to separate as the piano proceeds toward its maximum speed while the harpsichord and its percussion toward their minimum speed simultaneously.

The *Presto* is for harpsichord and all the other instruments except the percussion and the piano, which latter constantly interrupts with fragments of the adagio. Twice this soloist breaks into a short *Cadenza* based on other elements of its material, and its second cadenza leads to an amplification of the questioning inflections of the *Presto* by all the instruments with the percussion dominating. After a brief pause, the work closes with an extended *Coda,* using the entire ensemble in a series of long-phased oscillations (that include many subsidiary short-phased ones) from one group to the other, during which previous ideas are recalled in new contexts. Reversing the general plan of the Introduction (although not the musical one), these fragments lose their definition bit by bit, become shorter, sometimes more condensed, sometimes more dispersed, gradually merging into the slow waves of percussion rolls that move according to the basic polyrhythmic structure of the whole work.

In addition to this note, Carter has made out a schema (presumably for publication with the score) detailing the arithmetical relations of rhythm and durations and tempos that are used in the course of the concerto. This schema is fascinating, but not essential from the standpoint of the listener. It will not, in fact, clarify anything for the listener or critic; it is directed to the performers exclusively, and remains in their province. It is, of course, interesting as an insight into Carter's methods, and will probably be studied by other composers. But it is to be hoped that those who study it will not be misled into thinking that Carter's methods, or his calculations, or his original approach to musical time, can be substituted for musical imagination. Carter himself has never made this mistake, and that is precisely the basis of his quality as a composer. One is tempted to add, as a composer of music.

Current Chronicle: United States
[Review of television première of Igor Stravinsky's *The Flood*]
Musical Quarterly XLVIII/4 (October 1962)

The much-advertised television première of the Stravinsky-Balanchine-Craft *The Flood,* on June 14, was perhaps one of the saddest hours in the history of art. Sad not because of any weakness in the Stravinsky score, but for almost every other aspect or implication of the production. When CBS chooses to speak with the voice of God, or perhaps when God is employed to speak through the facilities of CBS (it is hard to decide which), it is understandable (in either case) that His voice sounds weary, or that He finds script a poor substitute for Scripture. But there the matter is. What is so often the ailment of art in our time is not so much the difficulty of its language or the alienation of the spirit behind it, but its self-consciousness, its insufferable pretentiousness, and its falsification of its own premises.

This falsification involves not only the premises of art, but the position of "culture" as well as of communication in our society. *Don Giovanni* surely was not built up, *expected,* or inflated, as was *The Flood.* Possibly no work of art, even *Don Giovanni,* can survive this kind of treatment. No work of art can compete in a market place (which is what television is, when it is not simply a narcotic) with products that aim only at being marketed. The vocabularies of art and marketing ought to be somewhat different, and only the melancholy end-product of a generation of confusion, as represented by *The Flood,* could so mingle the two that there was little distinction to be made between the oily elocution for the sponsoring hair tonic and the greasy elocution in the music drama itself, to say nothing of its accompanying moments of "personalized" visits with genius, in the manner of a cross between the old Elbert Hubbard "Little Visits to the Homes of the Great" and an "exclusive" tour of the artist's inner life in the style of *Life* magazine.

The Flood brought home again the idea that we live in an age in which rhetoric, meaning, and language have destroyed themselves, in which the vocabulary of advertising has reduced values to bargains and popularization has reduced art from mystery to manipulation.

Communication (as opposed to "communications arts" and similar jargon) requires a minimum of two participants: two minds, two voices, two sets of ears or eyes. Art cannot be directed *at* people, cannot be addressed to a public artificially created for its consumption. This is what sponsors, systems, and practitioners of "communications arts" attempt to do. The results are not only perverted, but largely imaginary; and the imagined result is itself a perversion. The mind or the sensory apparatus that views a work of art, listens to music, reads poetry, is not to be defined as a *consumer.* But this is, essentially, the image of the art-loving public, presumed to exist, or hoped for, not only by the organizers and manipulators of art, but eventually, through contagion, by artists themselves.

"Consumer art," in which each miserable *pastiche,* pompous imitation, or elaborate repetition is touted beforehand in the wildest adjectival profusion, and which demands that three out of four commercial productions, whether motion pictures or television spectaculars, be hailed as "unforgettable masterpieces," depends precisely on this creation of a factitious enthusiasm, exactly as does the expansion of the market for patent medicines, cigarettes, electrical gadgets, and cosmetics. The concept of consumer art involves also, as does every other type of marketing, a kind of condescending explanation or cynical manipulation: "It drains all eight cavities" . . . "The filter makes the difference" . . . "The composer has used the five-finger system" . . .; the consumer is to be impressed, and to accept passively the voice of authority which tells him what is good and what is good for him. In this way, art loses whatever meaning it is possible for it to have: *it becomes pure product,* the bargain, not the value, the object, and not the subject of man's contemplation and feeling and energy.

The 20th century, in pursuit of an insane idea of making art a commodity of some commercial importance, has deliberately chosen to forget that art is a two-way communication; that a great deal of art is difficult, requiring sophistication and sensitivity on the part of the viewer, reader, or listener; and that no art has had real meaning for large numbers of people at a given time, or in a given place, unless that art has been rooted in a homogeneous body of myth, practice, tradition, and social custom. We believe that art has attained such meaning at various times and in various places, but we can see in each instance that art was not art alone: it was belief, and a believable part of life.

The Flood has nothing to do with belief, nor is it believable. It is merely, to use the cant term, "significant," yet it signifies nothing, except the ultimately vain attempt to sanctify the pretense that art can exist for itself alone, and as object, in a vacuum, not to be loved or believed, but merely to be admired or consumed. Our traditional symbols are exhausted, and the century has created no new ones that do not make one recoil. The weary end of art, or of a tradition of art, brings with it the borrowing and distorting and demeaning of *others'* symbols and aspirations and beliefs, and their combination into a commodity that must be good for everything and everybody precisely because it has borrowed everything from everybody. As the pitchmen might say: its seventeen dozen guaranteed ingredients, skilfully blended in our sanitary factory, and untouched by human hearts, are your assurance that the manufacturer has spared no effort or expense to make this the best and biggest art obtainable, or your money back.

The great TV production of *The Flood,* aside from its preliminary speeches (announcing the significance—presumably to be interpreted as the expense—of what was to follow), its shampoo commercials, and its guided tours with Stravinsky and Balanchine, included a Prologue, written by Jack Richardson, and declaimed as if it were another commercial. This Prologue, described by Paul Henry Lang as being "of junior high school quality" (he was being charitable), effectively set the tone for the remainder of the show. The libretto, by Mr. Craft, should have slowed down any composer less determined than Stravinsky.

Why a *pastiche,* assembled from Genesis, the York and Chester miracle plays, and some "additional original material"? Is the purpose to show off the librettist's erudition? Or merely to be different? Why could not a simple text, based on the King James version, have served? The answer is implicit in the questions: certain concepts of art preclude the possibility of being simple or even straightforward, and a greater value is attached to the obscure than to the direct. We must ransack the past, refer to medieval miracle plays, rather than remain with anything that still lives in our tradition, rather than attempt to re-interpret myth and symbol in a way having some meaning for our times. What we now have is *The Flood* not as morality, but as Art. As such it is meaningless.

The Flood (without shampoo commercials) is now available on a record (Columbia ML-5727), and, to quote Herbert Kupferberg, "is not quite the unmitigated disaster that it was on television" (New York Herald-Tribune, July 8, 1962). It gains from the absence not only of the commercials and Prologue, but also of the choreography and costuming, of the whole "visual aspect" of the production, which was a model of confused vulgarity. (One remembers with horror the extraordinary masks, in what can only be described as Graeco-Gothic-Melanesian style.) Stravinsky's score may survive its TV introduction, and likely will; it is, as one would expect, well-made, and also, as one would expect, somewhat desiccated in sound. The question of its relevance to its subject is a difficult one; but perhaps even this question is itself irrelevant. Stravinsky's *expressive* intentions have always been elusive. Unfortunately, *The Flood* is not an abstract idea.

To conclude this melancholy appraisal, one must record a sense of distress that an artist of Stravinsky's genius and influence apparently did not wish, or was unable, to make something less dismal of the production. Mr. Jack Gould, the television critic of the New York Times, is one of the few journalists who raised this important point. To quote Mr. Gould: "If men of their [Stravinsky's and Balanchine's] reputation and position, however inadvertently, concur in cumbersome intrusions into the artistic realm or, more particularly, appear indifferent to how their works are treated, this is bound to have a negative effect on the development of standards . . . Can they then dissociate themselves from the consequences of their own example?" (New York Times, June 24, 1962).

I applaud Mr. Gould for taking to task *the artists who submit,* as well as the corporation executives who require them to do so. But the whole affair of *The Flood* is an example of the effect of "communications arts" on art and on communication, and may stand as a paradigm of what television's relations with art always must tend to be. We may wait another generation (perhaps forever) for a final divorce between art and one-way mass communication, for the dissolution of a marriage that is based on each one's strange and false idea of the compatibility of the other.

Current Chronicle: New York

[Discussion of concerts at opening of Philharmonic Hall in Lincoln Center, including reviews of Aaron Copland's *Connotations for Orchestra,* William Schuman's Eighth Symphony and William Bergsma's *In Celebration: Toccata for the Sixth Day*]
Musical Quarterly XLIX/1 (January 1963)

When Carnegie Hall was opened in 1891, the occasion was marked by a five-day music festival, from May 5 to 9, under the direction of Walter Damrosch, who conducted the New York Symphony Orchestra and the New York Oratorio Society. The first concert presented the Berlioz *Te Deum*; the succeeding concerts gave New York audiences a chance to see and hear Peter Ilyitch Tchaikovsky as conductor and composer. Tchaikovsky and the music were enthusiastically received, and not much was said about tuning the hall.

The opening week or two of concerts in the new Philharmonic Hall at Lincoln Center were more notable for arguments about acoustical matters than for any great contribution to the musical welfare of society. Sharing the spotlight with Mr. Bernstein were Mr. Abramovitz, the architect, Mr. Beranek, the acoustical expert, and most of the planners and entrepreneurs through whose efforts the new hall was created. The Hall itself was the hero (or the villain) of the occasion.

There were, however, some new pieces performed, all commissioned for ceremonial or other reasons. These new works were of varying interest, as might be expected. Aaron Copland's *Connotations for Orchestra* was performed at the opening concert by the Philharmonic, which celebrated the opening of its regular subscription series the following week with the première of William Schuman's Eighth Symphony. In between these two concerts, the Juilliard Orchestra presented William Bergsma's *In Celebration: Toccata for the Sixth Day,* and gave the first New York performance of Schuman's *A Song of Orpheus,* for cello and orchestra.

One observation may be made at the outset. The composers performed and commissioned were all Americans, and the ceremonies thus underlined that there has been some change since 1891. It is no longer necessary to import Tchaikovsky. Of course in the 20th century everything is also bigger and better, but not, of necessity, in better taste. Some of us may regret that neither Damrosch nor Tchaikovsky was televised; others may, pardonably, regret that Bernstein was.

All of the new American pieces were highly conservative, which is perhaps to be expected in connection with so thoroughly "official" a cultural occasion. It was rather surprising, nevertheless, to realize how fundamentally conservative Schuman's Eighth proves to be, not only in its evident concern with tonality and its handling of melodic ideas, but in its structural concepts and its implicit esthetic. It is a big, romantic work, not unlike a Tchaikovskyan symphony, having many of the same virtues and possibly a few of the same faults. The orchestral handling is, of course, assured and brilliant; the opening pages in particular are stunning in sound. These pages are, in all respects, the most impressive of the entire work.

The Symphony is in three lengthy movements, of which only the last is at a fast tempo. The first is marked Lento sostenuto—Pressante vigoroso—Lento; the second is Largo—Tempo più mosso—Largo; the third is Presto-Prestissimo. The texture of the first movement is fairly thick, as is that of the second; as a result the final movement seems oddly lighter and not entirely relevant or successful. As with all of Schuman's large works, there are pages of astonishing power and beauty. But one cannot say that interest is sustained at an equal level throughout.

Technically, the Eighth reveals little change from Schuman's other works of recent years. The basic harmonic trademark is still the major-minor triad in wide-open position; the melodies are still more notable as "tunes" than as themes or motifs; and the rhythmic bounce and restlessness, the energetic punctuation of brass and percussion are still stylistically characteristic. In the Eighth Symphony, one feels this latter element of the Schuman style to be more of an overlay than it has appeared to be previously.

Copland's new piece represents another kind of conservatism, in a way a paradoxical one, since *Connotations* is the composer's first completely twelve-tone work. Yet it stays within bounds, and represents the most conservative way of being "advanced." It also, despite its technical commitment to a method the composer has hitherto only approached (in the Piano Fantasy, for example), has a sound reminiscent of the earlier Copland of *Statements* or of the Piano Variations. *Connotations* is a harsh piece, completely without charm; but it also does not seem to have the honest strength and sheer power of Copland's earlier "severe" music. It almost seems a pity that Copland feels impelled at this stage, for whatever reason, to try on a new method (for it would be incorrect to describe it as a new style) that gives the impression of being uncongenial, even though it may seem important. The method itself is no longer new enough to arouse interest for its own sake. The interest must be in what the composer has found to bring to it, and in this case it is rather difficult to be certain what that is.

Bergsma's piece, despite its title, was the most unpretentious of the new commissioned works and, within its own terms, perhaps the most successful. It is frankly a bright and cheerful piece for a program-opener, and does not set out to overpower or amaze. It is rhythmically lively, neatly scored, and tightly constructed on a main motif of twelve notes:[†]

It is always pleasant to hear an allegro that is really an allegro. This is the real merit of Bergsma's piece. The single unfortunate thing about it is its title. But then, the opening week of Lincoln Center was, in its own modest way, a bit like The Creation.

Current Chronicle: New York
[Review of Jean Barraqué's *Séquences*]
Musical Quarterly XLIX/2 (April 1963)

Thanks to Gunther Schuller and his Carnegie Recital Hall series of Twentieth Century Innovations, we have finally been able to hear a work of Jean Barraqué, whose music, largely through the propaganda of André Hodeir, has been the subject of much questioning and many rumors. At least we know now that Barraqué is not a mythical figure invented by Hodeir; more, we know that he is really a composer. Hodeir is a fanatic and, as all who have read *Since Debussy* must know, exaggerates deliberately to make his points. But he has some points. Barraqué may not be the greatest thing since Beethoven, but he clearly is interesting and has something to say. One feels that he is composing music, not demonstrating theories, and this, in these times, is no mean beginning.

Séquences, the work performed by Schuller (with superb assistance from his instrumentalists and the soprano Jan DeGaetani), has been amply analyzed by Hodeir in *Since Debussy*, and all that one can say after one hearing of the work is that it is of extraordinary technical interest. But from the listener's point of view this is not the central issue; what matters is that the technique is employed in what immediately appears to be a lively, sensitive, and imaginative way. One senses the ordering, as in all good music, but is not obsessed by it; it is the means rather than the end. Analysis can demonstrate it; but more important, the *effect* justifies the analysis. We have wasted a lot of time in the past few years—and by "we" I mean all who follow new music, try to teach, write, or explain, or merely to under-

[†] The example is printed by permission of Galaxy Music Corporation.

stand—dissecting music already in an advanced state of decomposition. We have found out not what made it live, but merely the causes of its death.

A single hearing of so complex a work as *Séquences* is obviously insufficient for the purpose of attempting even a provisional assessment. But the lyricism announced by Hodeir is there; and the work has power, intensity, and contrast. Barraqué evidently loves *sound* and is able to calculate timbres with great aural delicacy and felicity. (This quality, too, has been sadly absent from much recent music.) The work is challengingly difficult for the performers and conductor, but nothing is written *against* the voice or is inappropriate to the instruments. The voice, as is usual these days, is treated "instrumentally"; that is, as a part of a mixed ensemble. At least that is what we have been told. But in *Séquences* this is no more notable than it usually is in Wagner (whose name, incidentally, is not mentioned once in Hodeir's book). Nor is the concept of orchestra-as-instrument so remote from Wagner, the now always denied shadow behind the genius of Debussy. Being as French as we please still cannot erase Bayreuth; the subconscious recognition of this by Barraqué is perhaps revealed in his use of texts by Nietzsche, who also *suffered* Wagner, for and against (but knew that he was doing so).

In choosing the poems by Nietzsche (freely translated by himself) Barraqué, according to Hodeir, "merely wished to pay tribute to patterns of thought and sensibility which he feels are very close to his own." When the work was originally undertaken, and most of it composed, in 1950, the texts were by Rimbaud and Eluard. The Nietzsche poems were substituted in the final version of 1955. There is some meaning in this, and it has to do with artistic seriousness and indifference to fashion. Curiously enough, Nietzsche in French sounds a little like Rimbaud's Nephew.

Part of the meaning is in the "instrumentalization" of the voice and consequently of the text. Barraqué follows the pattern of breaking the text apart, of using vowels and consonants purely as phonemes, splintering words and word-sense. Without a text before one, one is lost in such passages. But do we still pretend that this is not so in Wagner? We like to delude ourselves; but we have memorized the lines if we are interested at all, and hence we think we hear them. Like Wagner, Barraqué uses the clearest prosody, or even *Sprechstimme,* when he feels that the exactness of the word is of any importance. He is, in fact, very good and very wise in his handling of both voice and text; this immediately sets him down as a composer of both musical and intellectual sensibility and illustrates a possibility of combining meaning and abstraction that we have not recently seen demonstrated, except by Dallapiccola.

Also reminiscent of Dallapiccola, though only from the standpoint of sensibility, is Barraqué's use of percussion. (*Séquences* calls for soprano, piano, harp, violin, cello, celesta, glockenspiel, vibraphone, xylophone, and assorted percussion requiring three additional players.) The opening sections of *Séquences* are in this respect the most beautifully imagined sounds since the opening of the *Canti di prigionia.* They are a far cry from the cute nonsense of Berio or the mindless pounding of the red-blooded American school. What lovely sounds are still to be created in a day when many think that we have heard them all!

Séquences is a remarkably mature and powerful work for a composer to have conceived at twenty-two and completed at twenty-seven (Barraqué was born in 1928). It is to be hoped that some company will be enlightened enough to engage Schuller and his group to record it, as an expedient to permit those to hear it who will not otherwise have the opportunity.

Current Chronicle: New York
[Review of Leon Kirchner's Second Piano Concerto]
Musical Quarterly LI/2 (April 1965)

Leon Kirchner's Second Piano Concerto (heard for the first time in New York last December as played by the Philharmonic with Kirchner conducting and Leon Fleisher at the piano)[1] poses a number of interesting questions for the critic, as it doubtless does for most listeners on a first, or even a second, hearing. It provides a musical experience of a sort not common in these times, not the less real for being hard to define. It is perhaps simplest to say that the Concerto is a *moving* work: one that succeeds in communicating some mood or experience or order of feelings, as pieces of music were once assumed to do. In this sense, the Concerto invokes the esthetics of an earlier age and demands conditions of receptivity that once were taken for granted; it is therefore described by some, since we have no better vocabulary, as a "romantic" piece.

The idea of "romantic" today involves a concept of tradition as well as one of expressiveness. Kirchner himself is quite explicit about these concepts. "An artist must create a personal cosmos, a verdant world in continuity with tradition, further fulfilling man's 'awareness,' his 'degree of consciousness,' and bringing new subtilization, vision and beauty to

---

[1]Commissioned by Mr. Fleisher in connection with the Ford Foundation Program in Humanities and the Arts, and first performed by him with the Seattle Symphony Orchestra on October 28, 1963.

the elements of experience." Or again: "One of the essential characteristics of an art work is its uniqueness or singularity . . . and yet this work is rooted in tradition, it is dumb without its historical connectedness . . . We move into, and test, unknown paths; we are able to extend ourselves into the future because of the balance established in historical precedent."

The crucial word used by Kirchner is *continuity*. Tradition is in a sense even more binding when one revolts against it or pretends to break with it. And the defensive position of today's typical artist is often to identify himself with a *part* of tradition, isolated from its own past and future. This is exhumation, not continuity; history, not tradition. Revolution, such as we live with, may be defined as the attempt to convert the present, by violence of thought, into an immediate past. An artistic revolution, like a political one, ascribes all evil to this immediate past, and attempts to break or deny any idea of continuity with what it represented. Thus, in music, it is in high style to call upon the "tradition" of Machaut, of Heinrich Isaac, or of the folk tunes of faraway places and semi-cultures, but it is square to admit that the 20th century was preceded by the 19th. The arbiters of contemporary taste, today more than ever led by Stravinsky, have called upon every age of music except those of Beethoven and Wagner, two giants literally excluded from present-day canons both of esthetics and of technique.

Kirchner, however, along with a very small number of other unclassifiable composers, chooses as the part of tradition most meaningful to him precisely that last great age that is now so unfashionable: the tradition of music from Beethoven to Wagner, a tradition obscured by Mahler and Strauss, and sought seriously in the 20th century only by Schoenberg. It is the sheer genius of Beethoven and of Wagner that makes attempts at continuation in their paths a challenge of such enormous difficulty. The greatness of Beethoven is conceded, not always for intelligible reasons; that of Wagner is persistently denied. But for most of those who have turned their backs on Wagner, there is reason enough today to suspect that the cause is willful inattention, mixed with a desire to bury the magnificence of the music under the repulsiveness of the librettos. It is claimed too that Wagner's technical accomplishment, in apparently stretching tonal harmony to its practical limits, and in enormously increasing the time-span of musical structure, represents an end—a dead end—and that nothing great or useful can proceed from it. *Verklärte Nacht* was once thought to prove the opposite; but it, too, is now a museum piece, and Schoenberg himself, in at least one sense, turned away from it. Yet even in his later development, Schoenberg did represent the continuity of Wagnerian tradition in a way that no other major composer of the 20th century may be said to have done. And with all of his intellectuality, Schoenberg remained essentially a "romantic" composer.

It is as a composer in the tradition of Wagner, through Schoenberg, that Kirchner is best understood. Kirchner is not a serial composer, or a theorist of any kind. This is, most importantly, precisely what he did *not* learn from Schoenberg. He appears to have learned a view of music; and when I suggest that Kirchner's music (perhaps all along, but certainly in this new Concerto) is fundamentally Wagnerian, I do not intend the kind of disparagement or condemnation that might be assumed, in or out of context, by most of today's practitioners of music or of criticism.

This view of music is what we perhaps understand as "romantic." It assumes that music in some way has something to do with life, or the expression of life, and that it is not simply about itself. And it assumes that life is not confined to the intellect, but that life is varied enough in its manifestations to include instinct, emotion, and irrational sensation. If music, like painting today, is merely about itself, and has no meaning beyond itself, then, if we are honest, we must simply conclude that too much importance is attached to it.

Kirchner is reaching out in his music towards something that he clearly feels is important beyond a demonstration of technical capacity or theoretical possibility. His esthetic is old-fashioned and his technique in many respects is conservative. Yet this conservatism is today perhaps a stronger proof of maturity and independence, when it is manifested by a strong personality, than any stylish avant-gardism. Kirchner's music is not imitative, nor does it show an inability to cope with complexities. On the contrary, it shows an avoidance of precisely those terrible oversimplifications that underlie much of current serial and mathematical procedures in composition. Kirchner's music is just as "intellectual" as any being written, in the sense that it is "abstract," and that it is carefully constructed. What he demonstrates is merely that construction need not proceed according to a formula or a pre-established hypothesis. Construction need not be a demonstration of a method. Composition can still evolve according to its own necessities, even though these must perhaps be "felt" rather than defined.

Kirchner suggests that the listener to his music concentrate on "the organic growth of the work as a whole" rather than on "thematic recognition" or, presumably, on other elements of structure. One must grant that this is refreshing, even if evasive and perhaps elusive. The Piano Concerto is perfectly susceptible to analysis, though one may agree with the composer that conventional analytical procedures are more often than not useless and misleading. But since I have suggested certain technical and esthetic affinities, I should perhaps elaborate specific points. The Concerto is in two movements, played without pause; it is actually a single long movement of two related sections, using much of the same motivic material. The structure is essentially Wagnerian, as are the characteristic shapes of the motifs themselves, built chiefly on the intervals of sixths (major and minor) and minor seconds (major sevenths or minor ninths). Tonality is constantly suggested, but clarification is avoided, as in much of *Tristan* or *Parsifal*; Kirchner achieves a further extension of suspended tonality without employing a twelve-tone technique or becoming systematically anti-tonal. We even meet, as perhaps we never expected to meet in the 1960s, that ancient ambiguity, the diminished seventh chord.

Although Kirchner uses a variety of contrapuntal techniques and devices, the prevailing impression is chordal and harmonic, with the arabesques of melodic ornament that have always characterized his work. Many of the vertical sonorities are soft, without jaggedness or harshness, and this softness is carried out in the orchestration which, despite a large battery of percussion and the usual brass, is on the whole subdued and gentle, and without brittleness. Rhythmically, too, the effect is wayward and undulating, meditative and almost improvisational. The style of writing here is mannered; the measures are generally based on eighth-or sixteenth-note units in extremely slow pulses, and the fluctuation is constant. A random sampling (pages 8-11 of the score):

($\quad$ =76): 3/4 4/8 7/16 3/8 6/8 4/8 6/16 9/16 3/8 12/16 continuing to
($\quad$ =96): 4/8 12/16 5/8 7/16 9/16 7/16 5/8 8/16 3/4 5/8 etc.

Despite the appearance of this metrical arrangement there is little force in any downbeat; the subdivision is complex, but the effect is easy and flowing.

It is difficult to think of anyone else, here or abroad, writing this way today. Like most of Kirchner's earlier work, this Concerto is intensely individual, occasionally difficult to follow, always interesting, and charged with a sense of urgency and power. At this stage of his development his music can be seen in perspective as that of a man sure of his direction, unaffected by this week's fad or last week's novelty, but committed to a view of music as a wholly serious pursuit in which the arrangement of sounds in time may communicate something more than efficiency, logic, or impeccability of design. This view of music is in the mainstream of a tradition that many contemporaries find difficult to accept; but it is not lightly to be discarded. And perhaps the time has come when we can re-consider the questions raised by the words "romantic" and "romanticism" with clearer and more open minds.

Current Chronicle: New York

[Review of Luigi Dallapiccola's *Parole di San Paolo* and Igor Stravinsky's *Abraham and Isaac* and *Elegy for J.F.K.*]
Musical Quarterly LI/2 (April 1965)

Recent works of Dallapiccola and Stravinsky were heard for the first time in New York during the late fall of 1964. Dallapiccola's *Parole di San Paolo* (Corinthians XIII) and Stravinsky's *Abraham and Isaac* (Genesis XXII) form an interesting contrast; and further food for thought is provided by Stravinsky's *Elegy for J.F.K.*, a setting of a *haiku* by Auden.

The Stravinsky works were heard at a special concert on December 6, with the composer and Robert Craft conducting; and the event seemed especially notable because of the air of depression that seemed to settle over the audience from the very first notes of the opening piece. This was the only work on the program not by Stravinsky, and, of all conceivable music, an interminable selection from Richard Strauss's *Le Bourgeois gentilhomme*. Whether the appalling cuteness of this music or the inept performance under Mr. Craft was the more dismaying part of the proceedings need not be discussed. But one may ask why it was played at all. Stravinsky has never had a good word to say for Strauss; and if the point, as some suspected, was merely to provide a comparison with *Pulcinella* (which concluded the program), this was hardly noble or even necessary. And it is really loading the dice to pick one of Strauss's least effective, original, or ingratiating scores.

However, the main business of the concert was new and old music of Stravinsky: the *Pastorale* of 1908, the *Berceuses du chat* (1915) and the *Pribaoutki* (1914), all minor but charming pieces, the *Pulcinella Suite* of 1920, a masterpiece of its kind, still fresh-sounding and full of wit, and the two new works. *Abraham and Isaac,* composed in 1962-63, is described as a "Sacred Ballad for Baritone and Orchestra," and is a setting of the Hebrew text of Genesis, Chapter 22. Stravinsky, it is said, has asked that it be sung only in Hebrew and never in any other language. This seems a reversion to his esthetic of latinizing Oedipus; but otherwise the two works have nothing in common except the technical mastery Stravinsky has never lacked. A first impression of *Abraham and Isaac* (the score is not yet accessible) is one of greyish monotony, but judgment should be reserved. It is said also that the performance in Berlin with Fischer-Dieskau as soloist had considerably more expressivity than the New York performance with Andrew Foldi and Mr. Craft. Nevertheless, it is difficult to imagine these notes, each one unquestionably placed on the page with logic and ingenuity, ever conveying a hint of drama or of passion. And this is the major issue with a text that demands some kind of moral and emotional commitment rather than a purely esthetic one. The Bible *is* literature; but the treatment of the Bible *as* literature nevertheless still involves considerable humbug.

What is·involved is by no means easy to argue, but some illumination is perhaps provided by considering both the new Dallapiccola work and Stravinsky's *Elegy for J.F.K.* Stravinsky says that "card-carrying 12-toners are practically extinct" (New York Times, December 6, 1964), but Dallapiccola nevertheless seems to be one. Whether or not this has any bearing on what Dallapiccola seems to have to express is not as important as the fact that Dallapiccola does seem to have something to express and that he uses a technique that, at least until a few years ago, and perhaps even now, despite Stravinsky's apparent scorn, would be considered contemporary even if not "advanced." The difference in tone between *Abraham and Isaac* and *Parole di San Paolo* is enormous. The latter is a brief piece, for mezzo-soprano and nine instrumentalists; but for all its brevity it conveys a sense of belief in its Latin text, the familiar and moving words of Saint Paul. This sense can be conveyed in twelve-tone music, or in any kind of music, and it is absurd to assume that novelty or familiarity of idiom has much to do with it. The sense of urgent meaning, of commitment, is present in Dallapiccola's vocal music, as it is in Weisgall's *Athaliah* or in a Bach cantata. It is absent in *Abraham and Isaac*; and more shockingly so in the *Elegy,* which is trivial, neutral, and to many, I think, offensive. Auden's *haiku,* to begin with, is no model of poetic grace, delicacy, or feeling. It is a finger-exercise; and that is also precisely what the music (for mezzo-soprano and three clarinets) seems to be. It is shocking that two artists whose achievements are so great should combine to give us an elegy in which there is much technique, much cleverness, perhaps even much novelty; what is missing is only a sense of involvement, or, more notably, of grief.

The next volume of "Conversations with Stravinsky" will undoubtedly contain the entire interview with Stravinsky that appeared in the New York Times on December 6, and from which I have quoted above. This interview should be read by anyone who is interested in the questions I have attempted to raise, and which seem to me to be infinitely more important than the "analyses" and explanations of new techniques with which we are deluged. Stravinsky explains in his conversation how and why he wrote the *Elegy,* and one therefore understands that the piece cannot be other than it is: a curious artifact from one of the advance glaciers of a new ice age. It is doubtless more "modern" in spirit and technique, and certainly more *chic,* than anything ever written by Dallapiccola or Kirchner, and yet the quality of human sensibility one feels in the music of these two composers is something of rather considerably more importance.

Current Chronicle: New York

[Review of Alberto Ginastera's opera *Don Rodrigo*]
Musical Quarterly LII/3 (July 1966)

The New York City Opera celebrated its move to the New York State Theater in Lincoln Center on February 22 by staging a splendid North American première of Alberto Ginastera's opera *Don Rodrigo*. The production was in every respect first-rate and brought well-deserved congratulations to the company under Julius Rudel's direction.

Don Rodrigo is a disappointment only because one had hoped that it would be better. Ginastera is an interesting composer, certainly the most gifted South American since Villa-Lobos, and decidedly in the mainstream of contemporary musical thought and practice. *Don Rodrigo* is full of interesting music, good vocal writing, and brilliant orchestral sonorities. There are effective scenes, and yet the over-all impression of the opera is an indifferent one. One can admire what Ginastera has done, but this does not mean that he has written the kind of opera one would look forward to hearing repeatedly, or that *Don Rodrigo* is likely to join the small company of 20th-century operatic masterpieces.

The fact seems to be that the notion of writing an opera, which exerts as powerful an appeal today as it always has, is somewhat paralyzing in this day and age. An opera is so big an undertaking, so important, the problem of achieving a satisfactory performance so discouraging, that the composer is burdened in advance with the notion that he must produce a masterpiece or nothing. And *Wozzeck* has been a bad example: it is a freak masterpiece, and the temptation to use it as a model is not always resisted. *Don Rodrigo*, like *Wozzeck*, is a carefully designed structure, with calculated symmetries, abstract musical patterns, and ingenious motivic variation. The score lends itself to the kind of analysis that proves how very well made it is. Such an analysis of *Don Rodrigo*, by Pola Suares Urtubey, was published in the Autumn 1965 issue of the magazine *Tempo*. This has every appearance of having been authorized by the composer, and probably written with his collaboration as an explanation of his *modus operandi* as well as of his aims. It is both interesting and characteristic as the forewarning of what one is supposed to listen for, and of how one is supposed to react. But it is questionable that this kind of analysis, however interesting, affects the listener to any great extent, or contributes to his involvement in the actions and emotions with which an opera must be concerned.

Most successful operas have been written by composers who have devoted all or a good part of their energies to precisely this form of art. There are of course exceptions; but one thinks of Verdi, Wagner, Rossini, Gluck, even of Meyerbeer, Puccini, and Massenet, as composers who learned to write viable operas through concentration on specific problems. The occasional opera composer looks at things differently. The difference is first apparent, perhaps, in the way he thinks about the libretto. It is not the choice or the quality of the libretto that is the question; it is really a manner of viewing it in relation to music and to the stage. As an example: the libretto of *Don Rodrigo* is certainly no worse, and may even be better in some ways, than the libretto of *La Forza del destino*, which it resembles at many points. Neither can be taken seriously as drama or as poetry; both are full of melodramatic platitudes, mock-heroism, and phony religion-cum-redemption. (In the last act of *Don Rodrigo,* when the hero and heroine meet at the monastery, one almost expected to hear *Pace, pace, mio Dio.*) But Verdi gets away with it, while the falseness is too apparent in *Don Rodrigo.* It is interesting to speculate why.

It is too easy to say that *La Forza del destino* is full of memorable tunes, and that is not, in any case, the answer. It is perhaps simply a question of the fittingness of an idiom, the suitability (and credibility) of a contemporary musical idiom applied to a peculiarly old-fashioned dramatic and poetic style. Verdi and Piave each spoke a language that was at least contemporary with the other's; Ginastera's music seems much too sophisticated, complex, and intellectualized for the solemn inanities of Alejandro Casona's libretto. It may be argued that *Wozzeck* too has a 19th-century libretto; but the present-day appeal of Büchner's play is precisely that it is so contemporary in feeling. One could hardly imagine Carl Maria von Weber setting it as an opera.

Don Rodrigo is in many ways more of a pageant than a drama, and perhaps that is another reason why the musical apparatus seems over-elaborate and inappropriate. The concern with musical and structural contrivance is possibly too conscious and evident, so that the listener or spectator, even without analytical guidance or intuition, may feel that two levels of art are in conflict: one that is essentially simple-minded, and one that obviously is not. The success of an opera is not necessarily determined by its admirable symphonic or schematic structure; often it is the accidental way in which a situation or a bit of poetic imagery may unexpectedly set the imagination of the composer in a musical direction that makes the difference. *La Forza del destino* is feeble in structure, but it lives, largely because it is full of musical surprises that make sense. This is true also, to take a much more recent work, of Prokofiev's *The Flaming Angel,* which, despite some odd meandering in both musical and dramatic construction, is both absorbing and convincing.

Ginastera's music is for the most part in what may be called a neutral 20th-century idiom. It uses serial techniques, tone-clusters, chords in fourths, and is on the whole fairly conservative, although perhaps not enough so for conservative opera audiences. The style is not far removed from Berg or Dallapiccola, although it seems less incisive than that of *Wozzeck* or *Il Prigioniero.* The appeal of *Don Rodrigo* to its first-night audience perhaps was in the idea of a contemporary opera that was attempting to be *grand* opera in the old style. For *Don Rodrigo* is that: it is big, noisy, full of pageantry, uncomplicated by "psychology," with a Coronation Scene, battles, prophecies, love, dishonor, redemption, and all the conventional works. Unfortunately, for all its virtues and for all the compositional skill it demonstrated, it somehow fails to be moving or to involve the listener in what is happening on the busy stage.

Reviews of Records

Musical Quarterly XXXVIII/4 (October 1952)

BERG: *Wozzeck.* Mack Harrell, Eileen Farrell, Frederick Jagel, and others; Chorus of the High School of Music and Art; Chorus of the Schola Cantorum, Hugh Ross, Director; N. Y. Phil-Sym. Orch; cond. Mitropoulos. 2 12″ LP. Columbia SL-118.

This splendid recording of *Wozzeck* is an accomplishment for which everyone, including the record-buying public, merits congratulations. Mitropoulos' concert performance of the season of 1950-51 is well remembered, and we are highly fortunate that it has been preserved.

About *Wozzeck* itself so much has been written and said that one supposes the time must again be ripe for minority opinions. Unfortunately, I am not able to offer one: I still feel that it is a powerful and magical work, as I did when I heard the performance by Stokowski in 1931. This may, of course, classify me as a delayed-reaction Wagnerian; the connection is much clearer to everyone than it was twenty years ago. Some of my more precocious students assure me that *Wozzeck* is movie music, although they concede that it is good movie music. Perhaps the time is coming when an observation like this (intended, I have no doubt, as a slur) will actually lose its meaning. In theory, at least, music for the operatic stage, for movies, or for television may come out to be quite the same thing. I permit myself a good deal of doubt on this point, but concede the possibility.

In any case, if we can see and understand something of the evolution of *Wozzeck,* we can also appreciate its anti-Wagnerism. The "symphonic necessity" of the music has received what I hold to be its most sensitive appreciation in the masterly article of Frederick Goldbeck (*The Musical Quarterly,* January 1951), to which I beg the reader to refer. For those not convinced by Mr. Goldbeck, there is the description by Willi Reich (*The Musical Quarterly* for January 1952, and now available as a pamphlet). I am not sure how relevant Reich's "Guide" really is; it seems to me that Berg himself, in his postscript to the "Guide," implies his own indifference to, if not, indeed, his distaste for the sort of thing it represents. Reich's "analysis" reminds me of a meticulous description of all the parts of an automobile engine, but neglects to mention that gasoline is used to make it go, or that there is some way of connecting it to the wheels. In general, I feel that this sort of mechanical description and classification is thoroughly anti-musical. It is made-to-order for the music appreciation trade, where little further damage can be done. But in the training of music students it is a deadly thing, for description so often becomes a substitute for listening, and an escape from the necessity of forming a musical taste. How often do students triumphantly emerge from "study" of a work with a pronouncement that is in essence: "This is a great work because it is in Sonata form!" But they are encouraged to consider this a revelation.

Berg, in the postscript mentioned above, seems to be making an effort to play down precisely what Reich emphasizes. But Berg goes off on a tack that is also amazing. After declaring that "no one, from the moment the curtain parts . . . pays any attention to the various fugues, inventions, suites, sonata movements, variations, and passacaglias about which so much has been written," he writes: "No one gives heed to anything but the vast social implications of the work . . ." Here indeed we have a suggestion of "analysis" that is as subjective as Reich's is supposed to be objective. "Vast social implications" is not the phrase that I should have chosen to apply to *Wozzeck*; it seems, at the least, an exaggeration, and at the most, a thoroughly dangerous remark, the implications of which lead to musical disaster.

Perhaps I admire *Wozzeck* for the wrong reasons. I am nevertheless aware that it makes a profound impression on me, and that I am grateful to have so fine a recording to renew the impression. Yet one further point comes to mind: is there a possibility that one, being very faithful to the literature on the subject, should not admire an opera on records at all? Where are curtain, actors, décor, lights, and gesture? Is one not, after all, accepting this opera without one's eyes, performing an anti-operatic act, and one even actually hostile to the composer? This problem, I admit, interests me a great deal, and has taken on additional charm from the moment I acknowledged to myself that I found *Wozzeck* completely satisfying in this recorded version and had no longer any desire to see it as well as hear it. (I have since been obliged to admit that I feel this way about other recorded operas and other concert performances.) The simplest answers, that *Wozzeck* is not an opera, or even that Opera Doesn't Exist, are hardly acceptable. I cannot argue that *Wozzeck* is not an opera. On the contrary it seems to me in every way one of the most ideally representative examples of what I think opera should be. What that is may possibly be of interest only to myself, and in any case does not affect the question of opera unstaged and unseen. The problem of opera in relation to radio and recordings is one that might be explored, with interesting results in esthetic speculation and theory.

Reviews of Records

Musical Quarterly XXXVIII/4 (October 1952)

SCHOENBERG: *Erwartung* (Monodrama, Opus 17). Dorothy Dow, soprano; N. Y. Phil.-
 Sym. Orch., cond. Mitropoulos. 12″ LP. Columbia ML 4524.

Whatever *Erwartung* is, it is certainly not entertaining, at least in the sense of being good
theater. Nor do I find it moving, or frightening, or in any way emotionally interesting. It
is a work to be studied with profit rather than loved with abandon, though both love and
study are better rewarded by *Wozzeck,* which is *Erwartung's* child, and which succeeds precisely where the parent fails.

The music in *Erwartung* is tantalizing. Such a mixture of the wonderful and the penny-
dreadful is not easy to find outside of Italian opera. What makes one wonder is what reason
or desire prompted Schoenberg to expend so much genius on so absurd an esthetic venture
as this "monodrama." It is perhaps nothing more than a prejudice on my part that I have
always felt Schoenberg to be at his worst when dealing with the voice. His odd taste in
texts (as here, and in the *Ode to Napoleon*) surely has something to do with it, but this
taste is in itself revealing. The choice of *Erwartung* (the text is by Marie Pappenheim)
marks him as emotionally a retarded child of his time, however in advance of his time his
musical technique may have seemed or may yet prove to be. If one takes "monodrama,"
or any literary-musical undertaking seriously, in its own postulated terms, one really has to
worry about text or libretto. Or should one (as I have not altogether facetiously suggested)
simply trust to foreign languages and gruesome diction to hide the bare unpleasant truths
of ineptitude and platitude? I do not know who may wish to take *Erwartung,* as a dramatic
scena, seriously; to me it seems rather like a parody of French prose-poetry from Aloysius
Bertrand on, a *Gaspard de la Nuit* on the Alexanderplatz. It is the sort of thing with which
Damia and other popular diseuses used to chill audiences at Parisian vaudeville houses. But,
needless to say, no one took these gory recitations very tragically.

Perhaps this is why I find it difficult to admit the artistic value of a work like *Erwartung.*
There is so much musical intensity and inventiveness wasted on a pseudo-drama that is not
even good Grand Guignol, that for all its pretensions towards symbolic or psychological
evocation is really a neurotic imitation of neurotic literature. Alas, too, that Schoenberg,
by his act of choice in using it, only confirms that he is not the man to resist the fully orchestrated emotional cliché. For this irritating and extraordinary music is full of clichés
that another generation will have no trouble in recognizing; that is, musical pictorializations
of verbal *trouvailles* like "Der Morgen kommt . . .," that are the same in essence as thousands of predecessors, even in twelve-tone.

When all this has been said, one can come back to the fact that *Erwartung* is an astonishing accomplishment, a *tour-de-force* (and *de-faiblesse*), that it illuminates a whole period as one of the great links in the chain from Wagner to *Wozzeck,* and that it is in many ways a work that sums up its creator's contradictions. It is consistent in its intellectual virtuosity and in what can be described only as its stubborn wrong-headedness. It is overwrought and unrelieved, at a constant and wearying pressure, lacking climax because of unremitting climaxes. It is always mixed and compounded in color and rhythm, the whole palette constantly on the brush, so that the ultimate effect, on the large scale, becomes grey and wandering and inexpressive. And the single voice, as a musical or dramatic character, does not survive very well; one longs, after a short while, for some other clear timbre, or at least for silence.

Reviews of Records
Musical Quarterly XXXIX/3 (July 1953)

BERLIOZ: *Funeral and Triumphal Symphony, Op. 15.* For large brass orchestra, string orch., and chorus. The Great Symphonic Brass Orch. and String Orch. of Cologne, Kölnischer Chor, cond. Fritz Straub; Helmut Schmitt, solo trombone. 12 ″ LP. Lyrichord LL 40.

To the list of sufferings endured by Berlioz the present recording may now be added. The *Funeral and Triumphal Symphony* has been a neglected work; its disinterment here is by no means triumphal. This is the more to be regretted in view of the fact that a renewal of interest in the symphony has been evident in the past few years, not only in France but in England and the United States as well. An acquaintance with the Symphony through this recording will, however, dishearten all but the most fanatical admirers of the composer, and persuade most listeners that the neglect of the work has not been undeserved. The recording demonstrates (if any demonstration is needed) that the LP is not an unmixed blessing.

The Symphony itself is Berlioz's Fourth. It was commissioned for the tenth anniversary of the Revolution of 1830, for performance during the ceremonies honoring the heroes of the Three Days, and dedicating the commemorative column on the Place de la Bastille. The composition and performance are described in some detail in Berlioz's *Memoirs.* We know also that the work made a powerful impression on the composer's contemporaries, notably Richard Wagner, who described it as "noble and grave from the first note to the last."

The Symphony is in any case not to be taken as in a class with [Beethoven's] *Battle of Victoria,* or with other pieces of similar character. The *Funeral and Triumphal Symphony* is a major work of Berlioz, and has additional interest as being the most imposing work ever conceived for performance by a wind band. (The string and choral parts were added as afterthoughts, and are marked *ad libitum.*) It is true, as Jacques Barzun observes, that we shall probably never hear the work as Berlioz meant it to sound; not only is it difficult to assemble 207 players, but the wind instruments themselves, and the techniques of playing them, have changed considerably since 1840. But we can at least make it sound like *music,* which Herr Straub and the "Great Symphonic Brass Orchestra of Cologne" emphatically do not. No one is apt to find nobility or gravity in this performance; it is a cruel disservice to the reputation of Berlioz that this "rendition" should be able, through its availability, to misrepresent to innocent ears an original work of genius.

Herr Straub's performance has the sensitivity and nuance of a player piano. The tempos are erratic; the attacks are rough; the tone is raucous. The 135 players, as advertised, sound actually like 35, all blowing their heads off. The trombone solo of the second movement, which is gentle and elegiac in character, is performed with brutality; there is no other word. The entire performance almost justifies French feelings of apprehension about the intentions of Germans.

There was a rumor, not long ago, that the *Funeral and Triumphal Symphony* was to be recorded by the band of the Garde Républicaine. Admirers of Berlioz, and all record collectors who believe in the principle of fair play for a work of art, will hope that in any case another recording of Berlioz's Fourth will at an early date replace this irresponsible travesty.

Reviews of Records
Musical Quarterly XL/1 (January 1954)

VILLA-LOBOS: *Nonetto,* for Flute, Oboe, Clarinet, Saxophone, Bassoon, Harp, Celesta, Battery, and Mixed Chorus; *Quatuor,* for Flute, Harp, Celesta, Alto Saxophone, and Women's Voices. The Roger Wagner Chorale and the Concert Arts Players, cond. Roger Wagner. 12″ LP. Capitol P-8191.

Brazil is indeed a fortunate country to have the only extant one-man history of music resident within its borders. Aside from the fact that, having Villa-Lobos, the country can dispense with all other music from Palestrina to Stravinsky, it must be conceded that Brazil can claim one of the few really interesting composers alive today. Villa-Lobos is impressive not only for his range and inconsistency, but equally for the strong mark of personality that he brings to all his varied materials, and that bursts out of all his disguises. Beside Villa-Lobos, the real Proteus of the 20th century, even Milhaud seems inhibited. Proteus (I quote from Sir William Smith's little Classical Dictionary) "at midday . . . rose from the sea, and slept in the shade of the rocks, with the monsters of the deep lying around him. Any one wishing to learn futurity from him was obliged to catch hold of him at that time: as soon as he was seized, he assumed every possible shape, in order to escape the necessity of prophesying, but whenever he saw that his endeavors were of no avail, he resumed his usual form, and told the truth."

The truth in these two works of Villa-Lobos (and they are two of the best that I know of this composer) sounds fairly improbable but quite authoritative. The *Nonetto* is sub-titled "Quick Impression of All Brazil," a country apparently settled by Stravinsky and the random survivors of an orchestral shipwreck some time after 1920. I have never seen a photo of Stravinsky coasting down the Amazon, complete with horn-rimmed spectacles and feathers, but it would rather suggest what the *Nonetto* sounds like. As a matter of fact, the piece is wonderfully original, lively and exciting; it is only Mr. Wagner's much too refined performance that emphasizes the properly civilized Stravinsky and minimizes the slightly mad extravagance of the instrument-infested jungle. The old recording by Hugh Ross, done for the 1940 Festival of Brazilian Music at the Museum of Modern Art, is incomparably better: it has gaiety, abandon, a bit of jungle and lots of honky-tonk; and I, for one, would rather have this than a few extra high frequencies or whatever it is that is supposed to make new recordings superior. Mr. Wagner's performance is timid and precise; it has about the same pungent flavor as vanilla ice-cream.

In the *Quatuor*, which actually should sound like ice-cream, with flute, harp, celesta, alto saxophone, and women's voices, the new recording comes off no better. Even when Villa-Lobos is replacing Saint-Saëns, as he is in this work, he has a lot of gusto. Ross got this marvelously well in the old recording; Wagner merely reminds one that The Swan must have a relative in Brazil.

Reviews of Records

Musical Quarterly XL/2 (April 1954)

DE MENASCE: *Concerto No. 2 for Piano and Orchestra; Divertimento on a Children's
    Song,* for Piano and Strings; *Petite Suite pour le Piano.* Jacques de Menasce, piano;
    Vienna State Opera Orchestra, cond. Edmund Appia. 12″ LP. Vanguard VRS-442.

It is a pleasure to greet this record, which represents Jacques de Menasce's début on LP
both as composer and as piano soloist. (One previous recording, of Barraud's pleasant
Sonatina for Violin and Piano, has represented him as pianist.) Little by little, the recording companies are repairing some notable omissions in their contemporary listings. De
Menasce and (until almost as recently) Peter Mennin and Wallingford Riegger come to
mind as three quite unaccountably neglected composers, the more strikingly so when one
studies the catalogues' relatively abundant entries of music by mediocrities and nonentities.
Perhaps, on the grounds that everything should be heard, and in the long run judged, one
should not cavil at the recording of so much that is uninteresting or even incompetent;
one may ask only that our better things be recorded too.

There is, of course, always also the question of how recorded, and by whom. One may be
grateful that in this case both performance and recording are superb. These works receive
what can hardly be other than definitive performances. De Menasce plays the piano beautifully and the Vienna State Opera Orchestra is in extraordinary form. Appia is a first-rate
conductor, and the collaboration leaves nothing to be desired. The quality of reproduction,
including the piano sound, is extraordinarily good.

De Menasce is a meticulous craftsman whose works have great verve in addition to fluency
and polish. A rare representative of a true 20th-century internationalism, de Menasce
brings a sensibility of the utmost refinement to the languages of our day, and creates a
musical idiom whose clarity and individuality are enriched by a variety of allusion. One
does not, residence or citizenship aside, think of de Menasce as a composer of a definable
nationality or school. He is neither an American, nor a French, nor a Viennese composer,
and yet he is all three. But one should regard him as being, in the best sense, a *professional*
composer, one with *métier,* tradition, and integrity, to which is added a rare quality of
discretion and taste. The Piano Concerto is apt to puzzle at first those whose pleasure it
is, in listening to music, to classify. One is at home in an idiom that appears to be, in general, dissonantly "Romantic"—driving, rich-sounding, emotionally energetic—but one does
not "place" it easily. It is interesting that the writer of the notes on the dust-jacket makes
a reference to Rachmaninoff; it was no doubt suggested to him by the brilliance of the

opening, the impressive sonority, the pianist's writing for the piano. How equally well he might have alluded to Bartók, to Ernest Bloch, or to a half dozen others, becomes clear when one hears the entire work. (One might note also a "Hebrew" theme in the last movement that curiously calls Gershwin to mind.) De Menasce's music is not without antecedents; it does not pretend to take the piano and the orchestra where they have never been; but it does, on the other hand, have an "originality" that is rather remarkable. This composer is not a neutral: he is a personality. Characteristic of the concerto are the combinations and contrasts of richness and sparseness in texture, of simple elegance and brilliant virtuosity in the presentation of ideas, of careful craftsmanship and apparent uninhibitedness in structure. These are as effective as they are sophisticated.

The concerto is a pianist's work as well as a composer's, and calls to mind the similar quality in Prokofiev's concertos that has made them successful with performers as well as with the public. The Second Concerto of de Menasce (it is interesting to note in passing that his First Concerto was written through the interest and encouragement of Alban Berg) should fare well in the same sense. It is certainly true that we have few enough concertos in our time that equally invite and deserve a relatively wide circulation.

The concerto is coupled with two smaller works: a Little Suite for Piano and a Divertimento for Piano and Strings. The latter, composed in 1940, one year after the concerto, is unpretentious and quite charming. It consists of eight character variations on the German children's song *Wer hat die schönsten Schäfchen,* all done with skill, humor, and warmth. The Little Suite (1951) contains five highly polished miniatures: *Rondino, Berceuse, Moment Musical, Romanza,* and *Toccatina.* They represent, on a small scale, essential aspects of de Menasce's more recent style, developing since the Violin Sonata of 1940. This involves a tendency to work in the minutest detail in a sharply dissonant counterpoint of rapid motion. Whereas in a sense de Menasce's technique is that of a "sixteenth-note composer," he does not generate mere busy-ness with many notes, nor does he arrive at musical conclusions merely by hastening. Each of his sixteenth notes is carefully calculated, precise, necessary, and telling. The most recent music, such as the Piano Suite or the striking song cycle *Outrenuit* (not yet heard in the United States), is remarkably transparent as to texture, with the greatest subtlety in weight, movement, and over-all design. Recordings of *Outrenuit* and of the Violin Sonata should be extremely welcome.

Reviews of Records

Musical Quarterly XL/3 (July 1954)

JOLIVET: *Concerto for Piano and Orchestra.* Lucette Descaves, piano; Orchestre du Théâtre des Champs-Elysées, cond. Ernest Bour. *Concerto for Trumpet, Piano and String Orchestra; Andante for String Orchestra.* Roger Del Motte, trumpet; Serge Baudo, piano; Orchestre du Théâtre des Champs-Elysées, cond. Ernest Bour. 12″ LP. Westminster WL 5239.

The name of Jolivet has been heard with increasing frequency as one of France's more interesting younger, or post-war, composers. A number of his major works (including the Piano Concerto now recorded, and the Concerto for Ondes Martinot) have been heard in America, and have drawn rather mixed reactions. Jolivet was born in 1905, studied with Varèse (among others), and became associated in 1936 with the group known as *La Jeune France* (Messiaen, Baudrier, Daniel-Lesur). His first significant works, a String Quartet and the Andante for String Orchestra, date from 1934. After the war, Jolivet became musical director of the Comédie Française, and his style and outlook seem to have undergone marked change. One has the feeling that Jolivet now takes rather great pains to establish his status as a "controversial" composer.

The dust jacket of this LP quotes the following pronouncement of the composer: "From the technical standpoint my aim is to liberate myself totally from the tonal system; esthetically it is to give back to music its ancient and original character as the magic and incantational expression of human groups. Music should be a sonorous manifestation directly related to the universal cosmic system."

Statements like this are quite delightful and obviously most illuminating. I recall a *Hopi Dance* of Jolivet—the first music of his I had seen, probably around 1946—but I did not at the time know that magic was "the ancient and original character" that held it together, and I therefore was unable to appreciate it completely. I am afraid that this is to some extent true also of the Piano Concerto, which involves the same sort of neo-primitivism, though on a very much louder and more elaborated plane. Even the anthropological areas are extended; the anonymous author of the dust-jacket copy mentions that the three movements "ostensibly evoke . . . Africa, the Far East and Polynesia." The loudness stems in part from an excessively "colorful" orchestration: full symphony orchestra, plus saxophone, celesta, xylophone, vibraphone, chimes, *besides* three additional and separate batteries of quite mixed composition.

In addition to evoking exotic geography (Virgil Thomson is said to have described the three movements of the Concerto as "travel posters") the Concerto evokes at times *Le*

Chant du Rossignol, at times *Ibéria.* It is nowhere strikingly novel so far as music is concerned, nor is it impressive in structure. The influence of Varèse, it might be noted, is rather hard to discern. The work as a whole seems to be, in the words of my favorite advertising-copy writer, full of genuine artificial flavor.

The other works do not give me a happier impression of Jolivet. The Andante for String Orchestra is serious, clearly musical, but rather ponderous, while the Concerto for Trumpet is a *morceau de Shostakovitch à la française.* Recording and performances seem good, but the chief interest of the record will possibly be for the non-discriminating high-fidelity addict who will be delighted by the odd and abundant noises of the Piano Concerto.

Reviews of Records
Musical Quarterly XLIII/1 (January 1957)

WEISGALL: *The Stronger.* Adelaide Bishop, soprano; Columbia Chamber Orchestra,
     cond. Alfredo Antonini. 12″ LP. Columbia ML 5106.

The news provided by this record is that it brings a highly interesting and gifted dramatic composer to the attention of a larger public. Hugo Weisgall is not exactly a young composer; he has been around for some time, and his work has become familiar to increasing numbers of people, but one cannot say that he is well or widely known. His opera *The Tenor* has been heard in Baltimore, the composer's home, and in New York, where *The Stronger* has also been performed. A few other works, including songs, are heard occasionally, and it is expected that Weisgall's latest work, an opera based on Pirandello's *Six Characters in Search of an Author,* will be presented this season. These works for the stage represent the major part of Weisgall's composition to date.

The Stronger is a remarkable work. It is billed as an opera in one act, but is actually a dramatic scene of considerable length, for one singer (and, when staged, a silent character). The text is taken from Strindberg's monologue-play. As adapted by Richard Hart, the "libretto" is extremely effective, unpretentious and swift-moving. It is this theatrical effectiveness that immediately sets *The Stronger* apart from Schoenberg's *Erwartung,* which comes to mind inevitably as the most famous contemporary work of the same general type. *Erwartung* is, however, neither dramatically effective nor emotionally intelligible, and its libretto cannot be taken seriously at all. Schoenberg's enormous inventiveness is thus in the end unable to accomplish its presumed purpose. A work of this kind is a dangerous undertaking; it may go to pieces at any moment either through musical ineptitude or through some absurdity in text or situation. Weisgall has avoided all the pitfalls with extraordinary success. His music is continuously interesting and appropriate, and manages strikingly to sustain pace and dramatic force. It conveys admirably the varieties and shades of emotion that form the "plot" of the monologue, and comments on the action with sharpness and wit.

The Stronger has been staged both with and without "action" on the part of the singer or of the silent character. On the recording it succeeds perfectly without visual aid. Weisgall manages to portray his character musically. His line is plastic and expressive, and his prosody unimpeachable. The music is consistently dissonant, tense, and nervous; one never loses the sound of the major seventh or minor ninth, yet despite a fairly unrelieved degree of tension, the music moves. Climaxes are reached chiefly through linear motion in the vocal and orchestral parts; the harmonic scheme is elusive, and motivic repetitions or relations are by no means obvious. The orchestra of eight players (two clarinets doubling saxophones, one trumpet, four strings, and piano) is handled with great skill to produce differentiated textures. The colors are biting, mocking, always strong.

Successful projection of a work of this sort demands an interpreter of unusual gifts, a singing actress able to hold the stage (or the ear) without interruption for about twenty minutes. Weisgall has been fortunate in the collaboration of Adelaide Bishop. She does not sing every note exactly as written, but she is accurate enough, and she projects forcefully. Her diction is excellent; fortunately so, since Columbia does not provide a libretto or even a synopsis with the record.

Reviews of Records
Musical Quarterly XLIV/1 (January 1958)

HINDEMITH: *Symphony in B-flat for Concert Band*; SCHOENBERG: *Theme and Variations, Opus 43A*; STRAVINSKY: *Symphonies of Wind Instruments.* Eastman Symphonic Wind Ensemble, cond. Frederick Fennell. 12" LP. Mercury MG 50143.

This is the most ambitious recording made to date by Frederick Fennell and the Eastman Symphonic Wind Ensemble. Mr. Fennell is motivated by the laudable desire to show what has been and can be done in composition for large bodies of wind instruments; he avoids the use of the term "band," despite the fact that both the Schoenberg and the Hindemith were avowedly composed for band and scored according to the customs and prejudices attached, in this country, to that medium. Mr. Fennell and Mercury Records deserve thanks and congratulations for undertaking this kind of recording, which is, for many reasons, a considerable service. It is well known that there are hundreds of college or university bands interested in "serious" band music, and it may well be that there is even a public which will acquire an interest in this repertory when it is well played, as it is here.

The difficulty in the present instance is that the intention so far outstrips the achievement. All band people are grateful to Schoenberg and Hindemith for seriously undertaking to write works worthy of the attention of musicians. It is thus in a sense ungracious for a professional like myself, with some stake in the future of band music, to wish that they had written better ones. It is undeniably true that "original" band music is in principle better than the old repertory of transcribed chestnuts; but, alas, because a work is "original for band" doesn't always make it a happy experience. The cause of original band music was won quite some time ago—largely, I should like to add, through the efforts of my father—and we do not now, I think, have to defend original works simply because they are original, or even, I suppose, because they are by acknowledged contemporary masters of the first rank.

Writing for band is difficult not because the instruments in themselves are strange, but because the agglomeration of instruments is irrational and exasperating. The conventional band or wind ensemble is weak at top and bottom, and its middle-low register is cluttered by a frightful assortment of saxophones, bassoons, bass clarinets, euphoniums, and other instruments of thick timbre. The doublings are generally unsatisfactory, and no real solution can be found, in this medium, through solo writing in the style of chamber music. Both the Hindemith and the Schoenberg scores fail to resolve these difficulties. The Hindemith, indeed, sounds very much like a poorly done transcription; the virtues of "original" band music are by no means made apparent, and one is tempted to think that a good arrangement of either the E-flat Symphony or the *Symphonic Dances* might achieve a more satisfactory result. The B-flat Symphony, in any case, can hardly be counted as one of Hindemith's mightier efforts.

The further difficulty with band (or, to yield to Mr. Fennell, with wind ensemble) is that of idiom. It is perfectly understandable and proper that a "serious" composer write in a lighter and less sophisticated vein for what is still essentially a popular medium. But it is also possible that a composer may wish to write a completely serious, even a severe work for band. In such instances, the composer challenges comparably serious judgment, and invites a discussion of means and ends that is rather too large for a review of this type. But one may at least mention the question of suitability and point out again that it is at least not usual to write marches for string quartet.

The intentions of the Schoenberg and Hindemith scores are noble, but no amount of special pleading will ever make the Theme and Variations very interesting. It falls, as does the Hindemith, between the effort to be popular and obvious, and the intention to remain unsmiling and uncorrupted. Both works are singularly dead, and of much the same ailments. Mr. Fennell, be it added, does everything possible to breathe life into them, justifiably taking the tempos a little briskly, and generally keeping things moving.

As a footnote for music historians, it may be noted that my father first mentioned a band work to Schoenberg in 1933 or 1934, and received from the master a somewhat cryptic note dealing with band music in general, and its function for the masses. The Theme and Variations was undertaken a good deal later, and was first performed, for the masses in Central Park, under my direction in 1946, not in 1943, as stated on the record liner.

The Stravinsky Symphonies for Wind Instruments were not composed for band, or for wind ensemble, but for the wind section of a normal orchestra. It is to be feared that some moral may be drawn, for the work, in contrast to the other two, is warm and life-lit, a pleasure to hear, with beautiful ideas and beautiful sounds. And a fine performance by Mr. Fennell and the Ensemble.

Reviews of Records
Musical Quarterly XLIV/2 (April 1958)

STRAVINSKY: *Perséphone.* Claude Nollier, speaker; Nicolai Gedda, tenor; Orchestre de la Société des Concerts du Conservatoire; Chorale de l'Université de Paris; André Cluytens, cond. 12″ LP. Angel 35404.

Perséphone is a curious and in some respects a shocking work, even now, almost twenty-five years after its first hearing. It is by no means among the greatest of the master's pieces, although it is enjoying a belated recognition and is now being overpraised by any number of recent converts to contemporary music. For a variety of reasons *Perséphone* will probably remain fashionable for some time to come; but these reasons may well be precisely those that will eventually relegate the work to a minor status.

With *Perséphone,* Stravinsky for once got himself entangled in some contradictions of his own making. It is dangerous to issue a belligerent statement on the subject of words, music, emotion, and expression, especially if one is a composer about to write a work for a "narrator," to a text by a literary luminary who presumably writes to be taken seriously. The occasion of presenting *Perséphone* was an odd one for Stravinsky to choose for the issuance of his perhaps most famous pronunciamento, the familiar one demanding not words, but "syllables—beautiful, strong syllables." With *Oedipus,* Stravinsky was more consistent, and considerably more successful: he commanded a Latin text, with the sensible idea that few hearers could follow Cocteau-Latin literally. In *Oedipus,* moreover, the spoken passages are subsidiary; in *Perséphone* they are just about half the show, and there are, even in the United States, quite a few people who understand French after a fashion, and for whom, unfortunately, the beautiful strong syllables will jell into words. One would think that from the Latin of *Oedipus* the order of progress should have been, for the enhancement of syllabic absoluteness, to languages like Basque or Kwakiutl.

There is a further difficulty. If we admit that Gide's French text is handled as a succession of syllables, and that Stravinsky, in the choral sections, achieves what he wishes in the relation of words, music, expression, order, vitality, and autonomy, we are still left with the one instance in his works in which he succumbs to the dreary mannerisms of the narration-with-music. (Stravinsky's esthetic, it should be noted, is entirely defensible; but it needs to be pointed out that *Perséphone* does not jibe with it.) Since everything in the history of music, from Chartres I to Vienna II, is now in the Stravinsky realm, it cannot be said that this mannerism is un-Stravinskian, but it is a temptation to do so. From the sin of pomposity, Stravinsky has always been happily free—except in the sections of "elocution" in *Perséphone.* For elocution—with all its insipid and pretentious connotations—is what all these fashionable recitations really are, despite the fact that actresses, dancers, singers, *Sprecher,* and some musicians try to pretend that it is something else, something meaningful, significant, fearfully *expressive.* And one wants to ask: what is our syllabifier doing with this kind of nonsense?

Alas, it does not much matter who does it; it is invariably the same: pompous, mock-solemn, and in the inflated style. *Perséphone* is no exception. It is a real "vehicle" for a *diseuse,* and not even Stravinsky is going to be able to intimidate any genuine specimen of this species from making a field day for herself. I did not hear Ida Rubinstein mime, dance, and recite *Perséphone* in 1934, but I will place a bet that the performance was "expressive" enough to make one writhe. Claude Nollier, on the present recording, has a lovely voice, the best Comédie Française diction, and, to judge from a photograph, must be a pleasure to look at. But she, too, throbs a bit too much; and I should rather see than hear her. This is irrelevant, but I cannot imagine what Stravinsky's position can be towards this too, too solemn delivery, this forced elegance, this quivering portentousness.

Much of the music in the choral and instrumental sections of *Perséphone* is charming, fresh, and truly elegant. One is not surprised that all of it is skilful, and illuminated by Stravinsky's technical and inventive mastery, especially in matters of sonority. Like so many of Stravinsky's works since the twenties, *Perséphone* makes a style out of allusions to styles. Stravinsky does not attempt re-creation, and his allusions, with all the affection they show, for Verdi, or Rossini, or Tchaikovsky, almost always contain an element of mockery. How truly of the 20th century this is, and how it appeals to insecure and reticent souls! Perhaps this is the final secret even of the Webern-influenced works, although here the subject of the allusion is so sacrosanct that the mockery appears hardly credible and certainly not quite polite. And one wonders whether, in certain works of the twenties and thirties, such as *Perséphone*, Stravinsky is not occasionally mocking himself. There is no gesture that more surely confirms his status as a culture-hero. The singing part of Eumolpe is charming music, and one should ponder the lesson of how much more effective it is theatrically than the spoken part of Perséphone herself.

Reviews of Records
Musical Quarterly XLVI/1 (January 1960)

PROKOFIEV: *The Flaming Angel,* opera in five acts, Op. 37. Jane Rhodes, s; Xavier Depraz, bs; Irma Kolassi, Janine Collard, m-ss; Jean Giraudeau, t; chorus of Radio-diffusion-Télévision Française; Orchestre du Théâtre National de l'Opéra de Paris, cond. Charles Bruck. 3 LP. Westminster OPW 1304.

Most readers of *The Musical Quarterly* are probably familiar with the history, but not the music, of this extraordinarily fascinating work, which is not only one of Prokofiev's best, but is a central point for the consideration of Prokofiev's work as a whole.

The Flaming Angel was begun in 1919 and completed in 1927. Prokofiev worked on it in the United States and in Europe, while he was writing the Third Symphony (which uses some of the opera's thematic material), the Third Piano Concerto, and other major works. Nestyev tells us that much of the material for the opera had been conceived before the composer left Russia. It was not, however, until 1954 that a concert performance of the work was heard, over the Paris radio. The first stage performance took place the following year at the Venice Festival, and its success is a matter of record. It has not yet been heard in this country or in Russia. The present recording, recently released here, has been available for some time in Europe.

One wonders what delayed production of the piece for so long prior to the Venice Festival, and why, since then, it has not reached the American stage. Difficult though it is, there are companies and singers who can do it effectively. It has the reputation of being somewhat shocking, but it is less so than almost anything presented in the non-musical theater these days; and while it is possible that the Catholic Church might not entirely approve of it, the fact remains that it was Italy that gave the first stage performance.

The libretto of *The Flaming Angel,* by Prokofiev himself after a novel by the Russian poet Bryusov, is no sillier than most. In fact, it has a certain perverse charm. A great deal of nonsense has been written about it, including that in the brochure accompanying the records, where it is made to appear that the opera is involved with the dizziest kind of philosophical speculation and the most urgent varieties of religious truth. Actually, the story is a simple one of religious and erotic hysteria, with magicians and nuns for flavoring. By setting the story in the 16th century, one is able to have magicians instead of psychoanalysts; and magicians, besides being more interesting, and possibly just as effective, look infinitely better on the stage.

The opera centers on its heroine, Renata, who first encounters the Flaming Angel at the tender age of eight. She relates her history in an enormously long soliloquy at the beginning of Act I, and we learn that the Angel deserted her when she was seventeen (after she had attempted to seduce him), that she later identified the Angel with a certain Count Henri, and that he too has deserted her. She asks Ruprecht, who becomes her faithful follower, to help her find Henri, for which purpose magic is invoked. Henri is found, spurns Renata, who then tells Ruprecht that he must kill Henri. When Henri appears at a balcony as the Flaming Angel, Renata is overcome and tells Ruprecht that Henri must be spared. In a duel, it is then Ruprecht who is wounded. Renata goes off with Ruprecht, lives with him, tires of him, and finally goes off to a nunnery, where a scene of wild hysteria takes place, terminated only by the Inquisitor ordering Renata to the stake.

This is a bare outline of the "plot." But it is made clear that Renata is "possessed" and that she spreads ruin all around. She is accompanied by little demons, mysterious voices, and knockings; and lives in a world completely charged with sex symbols. Stage-wise, all this should be very effective, for in addition to the magicians, the mysterious voices, and the demons, we even have Faust and Mephistopheles, a few skeletons, and an Inquisitor. Since sex and magic are the best of all possible ingredients for an opera libretto, and for opera music, one can forget about philosophy and moral significance in all of this; one can even stop worrying about the logic or construction of the plot, provided that an atmosphere is created on the stage, and especially of course in the score. Everyone seems agreed that the Venice production was stunning, and it would appear that with imaginative staging, and above all with excellent singing, *The Flaming Angel* should be a smashing success even at the Metropolitan.

The music is Prokofiev at his best. I can think of no score in which his virtues are more consistently exhibited or his failings less obvious. The music has power, imagination, and variety. If many of the ideas are not of the highest originality or distinction, the whole score nevertheless moves and builds up. The development is conventional, and there are some half-dozen easily identified leitmotifs. These are on ordinary Wagnerian lines, and in fact the music seems astonishingly close to both Wagner and Strauss, rather than to Tchaikovsky or Rimsky-Korsakov, though there are echoes too of Debussy and Mussorgsky. Much of the familiar Prokofiev is present: the diatonic melodies, the bi-tonal harmony, the perverse and idiosyncratic twists, the completely glittering orchestration; but the score on the whole is rather more "romantic" than the earlier Prokofiev, and less "popular" than the later. Most important, the music has its own appropriateness, and succeeds in creating the required operatic illusion of urgency and meaning. The last few pages are unquestionably weak, both musically and dramatically, as if the action were inexplicably truncated, but even this rather curious abruptness detracts very little from the effectiveness of the opera as a whole.

Vocally the work is fiendishly difficult. The role of Renata encompasses about ninety minutes of singing, all of it fairly violent, while that of Ruprecht is hardly less taxing. All of the other roles are necessarily brief, but all make considerable vocal demands. The performances on this recording are splendid. The orchestral playing could be cleaner in spots, and the recording itself is not always well balanced. But these are minor shortcomings in a recording that we must be very pleased to have at all.

Reviews of Records

Musical Quarterly XLVI/3 (July 1960)

CHÁVEZ: *Sinfonia India* (Symphony No. 2); *Sinfonia de Antigona* (Symphony No. 1); *Sinfonia Romantica* (Symphony No. 4). Stadium Symphony Orchestra of New York, cond. Carlos Chávez. Everest LPBR-6029.

These three works of Chávez cover a period of twenty years, from the *Sinfonia de Antigona* of 1932-33 to the *Sinfonia Romantica* of 1952-53. The *Sinfonia India* (1935-36) and the *Antigona* are familiar; they have been previously recorded and have been heard in concert. The Fourth Symphony (*Sinfonia Romantica*) was a Louisville Orchestra commission, and is recorded for the first time.

Both the *India* and the *Antigona* made powerful impressions in the thirties, and it is pleasant to report that time has not made them seem less original, vivid, or striking. Nor does the *Sinfonia Romantica* show any falling off in strength or inventiveness. On the contrary, it is a better and more interesting work than the *Antigona,* which is the weakest of the three, and which does not fulfill the wonderful promise of its opening measures. The *Romantica* slackens off a bit in its slow movement, but holds the interest more consistently than the *Antigona.* The *Sinfonia India,* the most original and violent of the three, is wholly successful, and ranks as a minor masterpiece.

All three symphonies have great freshness of sound, boldness of design, and originality of idiom. Stravinsky of course (early Stravinsky) is in the background, but far enough in the background so as not to get in the way. The music is not neo-Stravinsky; it is pure Chávez, genuinely personal and forceful. The *Sinfonia India* represents perhaps the best kind of sophisticated primitivism we have in contemporary music, and can still serve as a lesson to all others who have tried it. Given native material of considerable interest to begin with, Chávez puts a strong and vigorous imagination to work on it. Out of this, even in the works using no Indian or Mexican melodies, Chávez has made a recognizable and personal style, in its way a very beautiful one.

The scoring in all of Chávez's orchestral works is stunning, and again quite original. One thinks of the use of percussion in the *Sinfonia India* (perhaps inspired by *Les Noces,* but so completely different!). Yet while this is obvious, and has been of marked influence on composers north of the border, Chávez's use of woodwind and brass is no less personal or effective. Chávez is one of the few composers whose thinking seems *completely* orchestral; there is not a single bar that is conceivable on a keyboard. He is also one of the few who cannot do with anything less than the full orchestral resources he employs; there is no waste of instruments or of instrumental color.

The performances are good; Chávez the conductor is probably the best interpreter of Chávez the composer.

Reviews of Records
Musical Quarterly XLVI/4 (October 1960)

ARIAS, ANTHEMS AND CHORALES OF THE AMERICAN MORAVIANS, 1760-1860, Vol. I. Ilona Kombrink, s.; Aurelio Estanislao, bar.; The Moravian Festival Chorus and Orchestra, cond. Thor Johnson. Columbia ML 5427 (mono); MS 6102 (stereo).

This record will come as a pleasant surprise to all those who have not known about or suspected the existence of a great treasury of art music composed by American Moravians of the communities around Bethlehem, Pennsylvania, and Salem, North Carolina, beginning with the latter part of the 18th century. The Moravian Music Foundation, which sponsored this recording, may justly be proud of its accomplishment in this presentation, for it brilliantly proves its point about "the unknown century of American classical music" by making available a selection of interesting and moving sacred works in exceptionally fine performances. Every history of American music mentions the musical culture of the Moravian communities, but the music itself has not been widely performed, or, for that matter, even generally available for study. This recording is therefore the more welcome as a real contribution to a knowledge of music in America. It is also most gratifying to note that a series of authorized editions of early Moravian music is now being published for the Foundation. According to Donald M. McCorkle, Director of the Foundation, more than ten thousand manuscripts are preserved in the archives of the Moravian Church. These include, says Dr. McCorkle, "many lost works by leading European composers" as well as the bulk of the work of the American Moravians themselves. And if the quality of this work is fairly represented by the selection on the present recording, the archives indeed are a musical repository of the greatest interest and importance.

The composers represented on this recording are Johannes Herbst (1735-1812), John Antes (1740-1811), John Frederik Peter (1746-1813), David Moritz Michael (1751-1827), and Edward William Leinbach (1823-1901). Unlike their contemporaries in New England at the end of the 18th century, these Moravian composers were all professionally trained and artistically skilled. They are not "primitives" like Billings or Law, *dilettanti* like Hopkinson, or merely second-rate talents like Reinagle or Hewitt. They are beyond question the first real composers to work on American soil. They are, however, not "American" in the sense that Billings was; but if Billings's importance lies in his energy, his somewhat crude power, his authentic "Americanism," the importance of the Moravians lies in the fact that they continued a high tradition of European art music in the New World. It is a tragedy for American music that their work was never known beyond the limits of the small communities in which they lived. Had their music been widely known, it is more than possible that the history of music in America would have been different, and that the development of American art music would have begun earlier and had a more solid foundation than that provided by MacDowell.

The arias, anthems, and chorales heard on this recording are all in the German Baroque tradition. In terms of European composition of the late 18th and early 19th centuries, they look backward, and reflect the conservatism of a provincial society. But as musical expression, they suffer very little by comparison with their models. They are extraordinarily interesting, not only from the standpoint of antiquarianism, or from the bias of national or local pride, but as genuinely moving and deeply felt expressions of a culture that was musical as well as religious. The performances under Thor Johnson are beautiful, and the recording, from a technical standpoint, is superb.

Reviews of Records
Musical Quarterly XLVII/1 (January 1961)

DALLAPICCOLA: *Five Fragments of Sappho*; *Two Anacreon Songs*; *Goethelieder*; *Christmas Concerto*; *Five Songs*. Elisabeth Soederstroem, soprano; Frederick Fuller, baritone. Instrumental ensembles cond. by Luigi Dallapiccola and Frederick Prausnitz. Epic LC 3706.

This is one of a series of recordings subsidized by the Fromm Foundation, and one more reason to be grateful to Mr. Fromm for his discriminating patronage. Mr. Fromm has definite tastes and is not afraid of them. By and large, his preferences are for advanced chromatic styles, including the twelve-tone but not confined to it. All of Mr. Fromm's composers are serious composers, sometimes relatively "difficult" ones; all are respected and respectable; none is popular.

The works of Dallapiccola on this recording are all in his twelve-tone manner, which, as is generally accepted now, is a most personal and possibly romantic adaptation of the conventional discipline. The works date from 1942 (the *Sappho Fragments*) to 1957 (the *Christmas Concerto*). It is difficult to think of any dodecaphonist with a more individual or persuasive voice. In Dallapiccola a lyric quality always dominates, most curiously and effectively emerging from literary and intellectual preoccupations that extend even to symbolic visual designs in his scores. There is no doubt that Dallapiccola's lyricism, or his passion, is not something that flows unchecked, something that is a natural or uninhibited expression dominating technique. It is a miracle of the most concentrated art, and art, moreover, of an awe-inspiring complexity and skill. Almost any score of Dallapiccola is a paradise for the devout dissectionist: all of them abound in such things as double canons in reverse, overlapping imitations, symbolic interval relationships or motivic designs, complex rhythmic polyphony, and even direct picture-making. Thus, one page of the *Christmas Concerto* has the notes arranged on the score to represent a Christmas tree. What amazes more than anything is that so natural a lyrical flow emerges from this deep preoccupation with abstractions, symbols, and devices. It is only in the greatest composers—Josquin, Bach, and a few others—that technique of this rarity survives translation from the page to performance. Here it not only survives; it takes on the quality of life itself. What Dallapiccola proves anew is that the great composer (and Dallapiccola is one) uses what techniques he needs. What he produces is something that speaks to us as high art.

Reviews of Records
Musical Quarterly XLVII/1 (January 1961)

VARÈSE: *Ionisation*; *Density 21.5*; *Intégrales*; *Octandre*; *Hyperprism*; *Poème Electronique*. Instrumentalists, cond. Robert Craft, Columbia MS 6146 (stereo).

Listening again to *Ionisation,* composed in 1931, one easily sees how Varèse came naturally to the *Poème Electronique* of 1958, composed directly on magnetic tape for the Brussels World's Fair. The two works are extraordinarily similar in concept, in imagination, and even in sonority. *Ionisation,* it will be recalled, is scored entirely for percussion: thirteen players, using an assortment of thirty-seven instruments, including two sirens. At the end of the piece, Varèse also brings in chimes, celesta, and piano. *Ionisation* is not often performed, and although it has been at least twice previously recorded, it is pleasant to have it again, along with a representative coupling of other works.

Varèse is surely one of the most neglected among major contemporary figures, and it is hard to doubt that he *is* a major figure. He is always spoken of with respect, and yet has somehow been viewed as being off to one side, not really part of the major movements as they have shifted in the contemporary scene. Perhaps the activity in electronic music now makes his position more central, and establishes more securely an appreciation of his stature. That this may be the accidental effect of a lag, of a delayed catching up with Varèse, only emphasizes his originality and assuredness.

Assuredness is perhaps what is most striking about all of the pieces here assembled. Like them or not, the listener is bound to feel that Varèse has always known exactly what he is about. This confidence must extend to the *Poème Electronique,* which Varèse, disdaining the term *musique concrete,* describes simply as "organized sound." One has the feeling that Varèse, above all others working in the medium of music composed on tape, has established his right to be heard, and that in the electronic medium he is always a *composer* and not an electrician or a finger-painter. One must admire also his discretion in choosing the term "organized sound," and letting the listener decide for himself whether organized sound is necessarily music. Music is certainly organized sound; it is not yet taken for granted that the proposition works in reverse. Varèse is possibly the best point of departure for a consideration of this.

The *Poème Electronique* holds one's interest. One wonders whether even Varèse has yet created sounds as novel or as exciting as the tape medium presumably can offer. Many of the sounds seem trivial in themselves, or lacking in diversity, and the inclusion of the distorted human voice seems simply incongruous, the only really disturbing element in the composition. But the *Poème* remains worth hearing.

Octandre, Hyperprism, and *Intégrales* are all original and striking works. They are consistent and they have force. They are highly controlled, strongly designed, and they have the feeling of life. They are in many ways stark, but they will hardly impress, as they once did, as being brutal. And if they do reflect our century, they reflect most of all its positiveness and not its doubts. Perhaps it is in this that their appeal can now be seen to reside. Varèse does not give the impression of retreating, which is characteristic of so much contemporary art. His music is virile, healthy, and above all individual.

Reviews of Records
Musical Quarterly XLVII/4 (October 1961)

BOULEZ: *Le Marteau sans Maître*. STOCKHAUSEN: *Zeitmasse*. Margery McKay, alto, and instrumentalists, cond. Robert Craft. Columbia ML 5275.

According to some enthusiasts, *Le Marteau sans Maître*, composed in 1955, is already a classic, and Boulez already an immortal. The fact of Boulez's influence and prestige is inescapable; the lasting weight of his music is yet to be determined. Since he is now only thirty-six years of age, there is every reason to suppose that *Le Marteau* will eventually appear to represent an early and experimental stage of his development. It is, in fact, in many ways a conservative work, and the newer pieces of the composer already indicate that it is not entirely representative of the main stream of his thought.

Le Marteau is a grandchild of *Pierrot Lunaire,* with a mixed marriage in the intervening generation. Whatever its merits, it is a work much discussed, and must be considered one of the important new pieces of the past decade. A short record review is not the place for an analysis or even a description. The interested reader may be referred to André Hodeir's discussion and analysis in *Since Debussy,* or to Robert Craft's in the exercise in literature that accompanies the disc. Both of these authorities are ardent, if not entirely comprehensible, and both represent aspects of the *mystique* of musical criticism today, which is often even more intricate than the music presumably under discussion. Discussion is taking precedence over listening, and it is not impossible that this situation represents a rough approximation of justice. However, the service performed by Columbia Records in allowing us to hear *Le Marteau* is a considerable one, and the opportunity should not be missed by any concerned with recent trends in composition.

Stockhausen's *Zeitmasse* is so beautiful to see on paper that it is almost an anticlimax to listen to it. It is a model of arithmetical calculation, draftsmanship, and visual design. It attacks problems that are incontestably interesting; the only question would seem to be whether the elaboration of these problems is of any interest to the ear. At this point, it still appears to me that we are dealing with what I have previously described as an aural *demonstration* of a theorem that has been tried or proved elsewhere, and that sound itself is, in fact, all but irrelevant.

I feel that *Le Marteau sans Maître* suffers from other defects, chiefly that it is indecisive stylistically and retrogressive esthetically. The human voice is perhaps obsolete in 20th-century music of this persuasion. For the moment, my suggestions that sound itself may be irrelevant and the voice obsolete will indicate to readers that I echo strongly Jacques

Barzun's arguments about the "abolitionist" character of much recent art. I feel that these pieces do indeed represent an "abolitionist" tendency, an unhappy alienation, perhaps even a passionate hatred of music, and that that is precisely why they are greeted with such marked enthusiasm in so many quarters, and especially among the very young. My own enthusiasm, as will have been perceived, is not overwhelming.

Reviews of Records
Musical Quarterly XLVIII/3 (July 1962)

BERIO: *Circles*; BUSSOTTI: *Frammento*; CAGE: *Aria with Fontana Mix.* Cathy Berberian, voice; Francis Pierre, harp; Jean Pierre Drouet, Boris de Vinogradov, percussion; Luciano Berio, piano; and magnetic tape. Time Records S/8003.

It is a commonplace now that the prose accompanying new music is often more interesting, not to say more "artistic," than the music itself. It is also harder to understand. On Berio's *Circles* (reviewed previously in *The Musical Quarterly,* April 1961), the annotator, Heinz-Klaus Metzger, contributes the following:

> In the mostly free, by the composer only suggested rhythmic articulation and in the elegant relaxation of the entire writing, the piece arrives at a flexibility which previously has been hardly, or at the most, rhapsodically, anticipated in the specific Milanese tradition . . . The liberality of its musical language provides this piece with a remarkable power to adapt also heterogeneous, even heteronomous stimulations.

Berio himself informs us (in a note provided for a concert in Los Angeles on April 16) that *Circles* is to be "listened to as theater and to be viewed as music . . . Thus when we enter the concert hall where the Maestro celebrates his ritual, it may seem that we opened the wrong door, that we intrude on a private action . . ." Also, "the silent complicity of the public covers the Maestro and the obviousness of his gestures with well known, sumptuous garments."

Who's kidding?

Having "viewed" *Circles* when it was presented in New York, I was interested in hearing it, untheatrically, as it came from my phonograph. It is difficult to reach any conclusion other than that Berio is half-right and half-wrong. Parts of *Circles* are quite pretty, musical and imaginative; but for considerable stretches little of purely musical interest seems to be happening, and here no doubt one should be watching Miss Berberian and the percussionists. Even so, much of the entire antic seems to be part of a private world, whose concerns are not necessarily those of other worlds, or of a public.

Music of this sort cannot be ignored. It raises far too many questions of importance in contemporary esthetics, and indeed in sociology. The relation of public and private art in our time is one of these questions that can be explored only in a book or lengthy essay. There is also, as a subsidiary theme, the question of the fundamental conception of the function of art, as it is espoused by a large group of composers and painters. But these questions must, at least for now, be left open.

Sylvano Bussotti is less known to American audiences than Berio, and it is commendable of Time Records to give us this opportunity of hearing what is presumably one of his representative works, or fragments. This *Frammento,* again according to Mr. Metzger, is derived from a cycle, of which the cardinal principle is "non-economy." We are further told, "when it is isolated from the context, its fragmentary character is no longer perceivable, and it becomes a fragment (*frammento*) all the more . . . The fragment again consists of fragments, and the totality of the fragmental universe results in its negation, that is, totality."

The temptation to set such words to music is very great, but Bussotti prefers the method of *collage,* both musically and verbally, taking "far-fetched texts . . . from various languages and books." What price macaroni? Or what inspiration from John Cage? *Aria with Fontana Mix* is truly intolerable, a scrap heap of taped sounds, with gurgles and grunts in what may be one or several languages. But one cannot decipher them, and why should one care? At one time, it might have been said that Cage had at least the merit of having restored a kind of gaiety to contemporary music (a quality it sadly lacks), but *Fontana Mix* is drably depressing. *Fontana Mix* and *Aria* are separate pieces, put together here for no better reason than not putting them together. Here again I yield to Mr. Metzger, who tells us that "The simultaneity of both pieces is established in the Piano Concert in which both theoretically are contained, in which they even practically could occur."

Practically anything can occur, no doubt, but how much better for all of us if more of what occurs were interesting.

Reviews of Records

Musical Quarterly XLIX/2 (April 1963)

MUSIC FOR FLUTE by Evangelisti, Berio, Matsudaira; MUSIC FOR FLUTE AND PIANO
    by Castiglioni, Messiaen, Maderna. Severino Gazzelloni, flute; Aloys Kontarsky, piano.
    Time Records S/8008.

Once upon a time, perhaps in one of the earlier style-periods of 1961, a well-known violinist acquired an extraordinarily beautiful and very expensive Stradivarius. For his first
concert appearance with this magnificent instrument, he commissioned several prominent
composers, possibly Franco Evangelisti, Bruno Maderna, and Luciano Berio among them,
to write new works. The works were written and learned and the concert took place. The
audience, well-trained and docile, showed no surprise when the violinist began the program
by striking the back of the Stradivarius in different places with a variety of small hammers
and mallets, made of differing materials; they were mildly surprised when, during one of
the new pieces, the violinist lifted his instrument to his mouth and, by blowing through
the sound-holes, alternately left and right, produced sounds reminiscent of a mouse sighing
softly. These explorations of new sound resources were understood by the audience as
"breakthroughs of conventional limitations," and accepted as one of the conditions of
modern concert-going. The first real shock of the concert was caused by the violinist taking
up his instrument, placing it between his shoulder and his chin, taking up a bow from the
stand beside him, and raising it with his right arm. Angry murmurs were heard, and a few
hisses. But these were instantly quieted when the violinist, holding the bow sideways with
absolute immobility, produced yet another new *Klangfarbe* by slowly (but in pre-determined
random speeds, calculated with the aid of an authentic Tibetan sun dial) *moving the violin!*
(There were no strings, of course.)

Gazzelloni's breathing is breath-taking; there is no other word for it. And he must have
few equals as a key tapper. But of course some credit must be given to the recording engineers, too. Even the dynamics of the key-tapping come across clearly. And the breathing
is *stereophonic!*

One should begin one's experience with this disc by playing the *Merles noirs* of Messiaen.
This is a perfectly conventional piece and a very agreeable one. It is bird song with piano;
birds in Paris have listened to a lot of Debussy and it has improved them. One wonders if
the birds in the Wienerwald are practicing Webern.

Evangelisti's piece, *Proporzioni,* for flute alone, should be saved for dessert. The liner notes
tell us that its "sounds give the hearer a fresh sense of the mystery of the vibrating air col-

umn and he becomes conscious of the mechanics of venting and over-blowing which had formerly been private concerns of the player . . . there are so many glissandos and pitchless flutters that the listener is at sea with regard to pitch . . ." One wonders if a slide-whistle might not do it better, and why, in so many little ventures, of younger Italian composers especially, there is such a compulsion to air various private concerns. This is beginning to assume the look of an obsession. But if action-painters can do it, one supposes that the composer too may try to market his privacy.

In between the Messiaen and the Evangelisti pieces, one may hear Maderna's *Honeyrêves* (flute and piano), Matsudaira's *Somaksah* (flute alone), Berio's *Sequenza* (flute alone), and Castiglioni's *Gymel* (flute and piano). Matsudaira's piece is pleasant and pretty; it allows Gazzelloni to play the flute conventionally (and, nonsense aside, he does play well). The Berio *Sequenza* is inconsequenzial, and the Maderna is not more than mildly interesting. The best piece of the lot is the *Gymel* of Castiglioni, which exploits piano sonorities in an interesting way and contrasts piano and flute effectively. Both instruments are there used musically and, one feels, without a great deal of worry about exploring new areas of what the instruments are not supposed to do, or can do less well than assorted pieces of hardware or plastic novelties.

Reviews of Records
Musical Quarterly XLIX/4 (October 1963)

BERLIOZ: *Béatrice et Bénédict.* Josephine Veasey, m-s; April Cantelo, s; Helen Watts, c; John Mitchinson, t; John Cameron, bar; John Shirley Quirk, bs; Eric Shilling, bs; St. Anthony Singers; London Symphony Orchestra, cond. Colin Davis. London, Editions de l'Oiseau-Lyre, SOL 256/7.

"A caprice written with the point of a needle"—so Berlioz described *Beatrice and Benedict.* But the phrase is hardly adequate to a work that must be considered among the greatest of comic operas. More than a century after its first production (Weimer, 1862) it is still not recognized for what it is: the most perfect example of its genre after Mozart. It is an unalloyed delight to the mind and to the ear, a work of refined intelligence as well as a product of the liveliest imagination, and it brings to the listener the rarest of enchantments, that of true high comedy unmarred by false tears or forced laughter.

Comedy is not popular in our times; perhaps it has never been, for it is usually more difficult and more disturbing even than tragedy. We go easily from farce to melodrama, neither of which disturbs while it entertains. But the enchantment of the truest comedy is dangerous, and that is perhaps why *Beatrice and Benedict* is not welcome on our stages. Perhaps it is better so; it is, like *The Tempest*, a work too easy to mistreat, and one may justifiably shudder at the thought of what a slick and expensive production, or an amateurish one, could be like. There are works that cannot be done foolishly or pretentiously; being comedy, they mock foolishness and pretence, and can only be done seriously, with the humor of seriousness.

Berlioz knew that his opera required "an extremely delicate" performance. This recording would have pleased him. It is sensitively paced and controlled by Colin Davis, and the singers, on the whole, are excellent. Josephine Veasey deserves special praise for her Beatrice, which is almost as well-nuanced a characterization as one could want, and more than adequate in terms of vocal resource. The role is extremely challenging, and one can think of few artists today capable of singing it with the subtlety that it demands. The opera, to a great extent, depends on the tone in which the role of Beatrice is conceived. There are few operas, or, for that matter, few spoken stage works, in which irony, passion, melancholy, and fantasy meet and merge so perfectly or so imperceptibly.

The great comedies of Mozart inevitably come to mind, although, so far as I know, the kinship of *Beatrice and Benedict* to these has not often been pointed out. But we are faced in this instance with the same kind of dramatic and human truth, the same vividness of intellectual and musical play, the same economy and understatement, the same depth of passion and of passionate concern for art as a realm of life and of life as a realm of art, and the same final and unequivocal communication through the power of music that never attempts to be another language or a symbol of anything that it is not. It is merely, like comedy, an embodiment of intellect.

Everything in *Beatrice and Benedict* is clear, direct, and telling. Most important, Shakespeare survives, as he does in few of the operas to which he is said to have contributed. This is one of the miracles of Berlioz's intelligence, for much of *Much Ado About Nothing*, in the way of plot, character, and detail, is sacrificed; Berlioz, in fact, took only what he wanted of the play, and changed much else. Yet *Beatrice and Benedict* amounts in many ways to more than *Much Ado.* The *essential* qualities of Shakespeare's wit and fancy, his sensibility and melancholy, his irony and warmth, appear in music that is among the most touching and most appropriate that Berlioz wrote. Its affinity to the spirit of Shakespearean comedy is astonishing. If we rightly praise Mendelssohn for the music to *A Midsummer Night's Dream*, how shall we praise Berlioz for the Scherzo with which *Beatrice and Benedict* concludes? Perhaps only by listening.

Beatrice and Benedict is, in the best sense, a sophisticated work. Some of its refinements, and some of its power, are not to be perceived at once. But the perfection of design, the elegance of proportion and distinction of line, cannot be mistaken. And one marvels again, hearing this last of his works, at Berlioz's musical inventiveness, aptness, and originality. The work abounds in the unexpected turn, the musical equivalent of the *mot juste*; the unexpected here is always right. It is not the forced-unexpected, but the natural-unexpected that changes the values of light and shadow, and illuminates meaning.

Opera on records always poses the fascinating esthetic question of the meaning of opera itself. For if one does not see, the stage is denied. Gesture and scene, and the excitement of the theater, are absent. One concentrates on the music and the words, and perhaps, at the same time, one wonders how the work would be staged, or how Berlioz might have envisioned it. But the music of course is its own action, and given the quality of the present recording, one wonders how much one *needs* the stage. In terms of the present recording, too, there will no doubt be some criticism because of the omission of the spoken dialogue. It is undeniable that, as Berlioz conceived it, the work is incomplete without it. But here again, one faces the conventions of art, which can only in the rarest instances (perhaps never) be satisfied without the cooperation or participation—perhaps even the intervention—of the listener, reader, or viewer. We must always supply something! For opera on records (which, like the automobile, is here to stay), we must supply the stage, the personages, the lights, the costumes, and the action; why not the dialogue? (Let us be totally honest while we are here, and admit in addition that in the majority of cases we cannot understand the words, or most of them, in opera whether live or recorded, in English or in Serbo-Croatian.) Imagined (or read) dialogue is possibly better than recorded declamation which, for good reasons I believe, usually seems unbearably stiff and artificial. For declamation, more than singing, requires eye and gesture; it is more truly *acting*. And acting, if it is really necessary to opera (I am not convinced that it is), is what a recording cannot give us. Will we all eventually, with reasonable excuses, adopt the home video-tape reproducer that is now being perfected for the consumer of news, commercials, and art? And will we then be ready for the abolition of the *community,* the ceremony, the reality of human beings in concert (both figuratively and otherwise), and the effort of accepting or sharing experience except at second-hand? Perhaps, in the 20th century, this may appear an inevitable and even welcome end. Berlioz and Shakespeare would have had it otherwise. But that is another story.

Reviews of Records

Musical Quarterly LI/4 (October 1965)

WEBER: *Piano Sonatas: No. 3, in D minor, No. 4, in E minor,* Annie D'Arco, piano. Oiseau-Lyre SOL 271 (stereo).

This recording appears to be the only one currently available of the last two piano sonatas of Carl Maria von Weber, and, if the Schwann catalogue is accurate, there is no recording at all now available of the first two. Thereby hangs a tale indeed. How strange it is to contemplate the present low estate of Weber's reputation! Two generations ago, and per-haps even more recently, Weber was a great composer among Great Composers. Today, *Der Freischütz* remains, more or less, and the clarinet concertos are played by clarinet students; the *Invitation to the Dance* is performed at the ballet, but even the *Oberon, Euryanthe,* and *Preciosa* overtures are not heard as often as they once were.

The two piano concertos and even the *Konzertstück,* the sonatas, the variations, and other keyboard works of Weber are dead and buried. In a fairly long career of concertgoing I can recall only one performance of any of these: a brilliant reading of the Second Sonata, in A-flat, some years ago by Beveridge Webster. It is an entirely safe bet that not one of a thousand conservatory students has even looked at these works in the past thirty years. Yet they represent one of the great original styles in the history of piano literature—indeed in the history of music in general—and their interest is by no means exclusively historical. It is curious that they are so utterly out of fashion in an age that has recalled (and recorded!) almost everything that has been forgotten, but has chosen, inexplicably, to forget so many things that were better remembered.

The neglect of the Weber piano sonatas and the two concertos is a real loss from every standpoint, including even that of the technical formation of the piano student. Much that is inferior is in vogue, and one has the impression that the dustbin of history has been emptied out in search of novelty or "discovery," while at the same time the traditionally "established" works do not yield their places on conventionally acceptable programs. How delightful it would be to hear one of the Weber concertos at, let us say, a Philharmonic concert—with a suitably brilliant pianist—as a change from Tchaikovsky or Grieg or Rach-maninov, or even, to be heretical, from Schumann or Chopin or Beethoven! One might add, as a footnote, that there is only one recording of the Weber concertos, fortunately an adequate one, by Friedrich Wuehrer with the Pro Musica of Vienna under Hans Swarowsky (Vox PL 8140).

Weber had the good and bad luck to be born sixteen years later than Beethoven and eleven earlier than Schubert. It was his good fortune to be born at a time when music-making mattered, and when a musical language was highly evolved, sophisticated, and commonly understood. It was his misfortune to be overshadowed, in an age of activity, interest, and talent, by composers of genius more dominating than his own. But the musical language of Weber is his own, quite personal and different from Beethoven's or Schubert's, even when it most resembles theirs, as it inevitably does at times. Many of the characteristic sounds and textures of early 19th-century music originated with Weber, not with Schubert or Beethoven. This is as true of orchestral texture as it is of pianistic sonority, and it is especially true with respect to a distinctly new feeling for (and treatment of) the dominant and diminished seventh chords. This feeling, in Weber, is highly original even in early works, as is the consistent figuration of light appoggiaturas and flamboyantly luxuriant passing tones. No one before him exploited in the same way the evanescent false ninth or eleventh that was to haunt Romantic music in the 1830s and '40s. Neglected as he is today, Weber is nonetheless one of the major points of departure in the Romantic musical style.

The piano sonatas, which are among the finest of early Romantic works, and assuredly among the finest of Weber's compositions, may or may not, in the terms of modern criticism, actually be sonatas. They are certainly not like Beethoven's in depth or power or organic unity, but they certainly are *music.* They are marvelously exuberant, uninhibited and inventive, even if somewhat uneven. (But unevenness of this kind can be found also in many of Schubert's sonatas.) The slow movements of all four sonatas, especially that of the third, are naive, but they are nevertheless rather touching, and they have moments of incandescence. The slow movement of the third sonata is framed by fine opening and closing movements: a first movement full of drama and contrasting lyricism, a model of the *Sturm und Drang* style, and a scintillating rondo. The fourth sonata, in four movements, has weak spots, but the menuetto (properly a scherzo) and the rondo are brilliant. This last sonata was composed in 1822, and it is not surprising that one inclines to hear suggestions of Beethoven in the scherzo and of Schubert in the finale. But these suggestions are not totally to Weber's disadvantage; he has genius enough to be at home in exalted company. And pianistically he is unsurpassed.

Reviews of Records

Musical Quarterly LII/1 (January 1966)

NIELSEN: *Symphony No. 2, Op. 16 (The Four Temperaments); Little Suite for String Orchestra, Op. 1.* Tivoli Concert Hall Symphony Orch., cond. Carl Garaguly. Vox STPL 512.550 (stereo).

The first and perhaps the only useful thing to say about this recording is that both perform-ance and engineering are excellent. The Tivoli Orchestra is extraordinarily good, and con-ductor Carl Garaguly projects Nielsen's scores very convincingly.

But the recording suggests other lines of thought. The music of Carl Nielsen (1865-1931) is among the most recent of our re-discoveries. Perhaps one should not even say "*re*-dis-covery," for Nielsen has been almost totally neglected outside of his native Denmark. His name does not appear at all in Lang's *Music in Western Civilization* (1941) or, more surpris-ingly, even in so comparatively recent a work as Grout's *History of Western Music* (1960). It is perhaps less to the point to speculate on the reasons for the neglect of Nielsen's music, than to wonder why it is now being played by orchestras here and elsewhere.

We have a large appetite for anything different, provided, of course, that it is not too dif-ferent, and this appetite is notably whetted when there is either a "historic" or an "exotic" character, real or factitious, to add interest. The phenomenon exists in literature as well as in music. Obscure authors have sudden vogues, as if the supply of standard works were found to be either temporarily inadequate or too thoroughly explored and completely known. The minor writer, especially if he is from a small country outside of the main stream, is always an attractive discovery. But such artists are the victims as well as the bene-ficiaries of this process, for in many cases they are judged not on their merits, but on their relationships and "historical" or regional significance.

Beyond this there is the fact that the artist of a small country is a special kind of national property, often (though not necessarily) non-exportable. To be Denmark's greatest sym-phonist, or Bulgaria's greatest novelist, is not necessarily an advantage except at home; the condition immediately suggests its own limitation. That is not to suggest that much first-rate literature and music are not occasionally or even often to be found. But the bases of evaluation or comparison are likely to be peculiar ones, and one must ask, for example, in the case of Nielsen, whether he is interesting as a composer, or interesting only as a Danish composer.

The fact is that this Second Symphony, first performed in 1902, is not really distinguished music, nor is the *Little Suite,* dating from 1888. It is proper to remember that Nielsen's current reputation is based on later works, especially the Fourth and Fifth Symphonies. Yet *The Four Temperaments* is also with us, especially through its use by the Danish Ballet, and it is not an uncharacteristic work. The style is one of high post-Romanticism, with echoes of Brahms, Bruckner, Tchaikovsky, perhaps even Mahler and Strauss. There is nothing strikingly unusual in the music, nor anything that could be identified as "national." The symphony would, in fact, make a splendid vehicle for a musical guessing game. Who wrote it, when, and where? Only the date, within perhaps twenty years, would be easy.

The workmanship is skilful and the orchestration is colorful. But the impression remains, especially fter several hearings, that the symphony is neither very good music nor very interesting even as novelty or music history. Like so many other revived works of art, it is interesting primarily as *data*: one should hear it once so as to know what it is, just as one should, if one is to be thorough, hear a symphony by Gade, who was not only Nielsen's teacher, but his predecessor as *the* great Danish symphonist. One might read the enthusiastic praise of Gade in, for example, Naumann's history of music (1886), and compare this with the almost sneering references to the same composer in current histories. Our ancestors could not have been so frightfully wrong as we think them to have been when they took Gade seriously. If we claim that they were, we merely emphasize our own fallibility.

These are matters not only of taste and judgment, but of fashion as well. True, there have been lags in "appreciation," and works have been reconsidered and have outlived fashions. It is not easy to imagine that *The Four Temperaments* will become a fixture in the repertory, but it is possible. In an age of unsmiling music, and especially of pseudo-scientific solemnity, it is possible to understand a nostalgic taste for lush, overblown, "romantic" orchestral pieces, with which one can relax. But beyond that, there is, as we all know, a mania in our times for recovering and preserving everything. Or almost everything; we have not yet revived or "re-discovered" Gade or Raff or Anton Rubinstein. Or, at any rate, not yet.

Reviews of Records
Musical Quarterly LII/2 (April 1966)

ITALIAN CONCERTOS. The Academy of St. Martin-in-the-Fields, cond. Neville Marriner. Oiseau-Lyre SOL 277 (stereo).

Every once in a while one comes across a recording of which one can simply say that it is beautiful. Such a one is this disc, the more welcome and surprising as it comes unheralded and unaccompanied by fol-de-rol. I had not previously encountered The Academy of St. Martin in the Fields or its director Neville Marriner, but I should be happy to have them perform music for me any time. Their playing as heard on this recording is exquisite, a model for the modern Baroque ensemble or chamber orchestra. The selections themselves are, with one exception, unhackneyed; but they are not merely "novelties," or pieces played only because no one else has done them. Each is interesting, and several have not, to my knowledge, been previously recorded.

The familiar work is the D major Concerto Grosso, Op. 6, No. 1, of Corelli, here given a sumptuous performance by an admirable body of strings with exactly the right weight and manner of continuo support provided by John Churchill at the harpsichord. Despite the great vogue for the Baroque, decent continuo playing is still rare, and one cannot know how effective and important it is until one hears it done well. In the over-all ensemble, tempos, balances, phrasings, intonation, and style are impeccable.

Less often heard, though certainly not a "novelty," is the E minor Concerto Grosso, Op. 3, of Geminiani, a delightful work, beautifully performed. And quite unfamiliar to me is a concerto in C minor, for cello and strings (P. 434), by Vivaldi. This is a surprising and in many ways uncharacteristic piece, unusual in both construction and texture, sombre in color and elevated in tone. It is remarkable for lacking a brilliant movement; the finale, following two slow movements, an opening Andante poco mosso and a relatively brief Adagio, is an Allegro ma non molto, which Mr. Marriner takes at a most discreet and sensitive tempo, perfectly calculated to avoid the real risk of destroying the unity and intensity of the work as a whole. The concerto ranks as one of Vivaldi's most nobly eloquent and profoundly moving works. The solo cello part is admirably played by Kenneth Heath, and as with all of the other works on this recording, one could not wish for more refined ensemble playing.

The remainder of the disc gives us a little "concerto" for oboe and strings by Vincenzo Bellini, and an Etude for horn and strings by Cherubini. Both of these are gems in addition to being surprises. The Bellini has recently become known to oboists and wind-instrument historians, and is well worth having restored to circulation. There is little to it except humor and charm, but these are not qualities to be despised, especially in the wind-instrument repertory. The work apparently dates from Bellini's student days, and was originally scored for full orchestra. (The source is given as a manuscript in the library of the Conservatorio di Musica S. Pietro a Maiella, Naples.) The performance by Mr. Marriner, with Roger Lord as the excellent soloist, is therefore an adaptation, and it is also somewhat abridged. One feels confident, however, that Mr. Marriner's judgment is good, and that we have suffered no artistic loss. The "concerto" is really a polacca with variations, preceded by a brief and rather touching slow introduction. It is an inconsequential work, but a pleasant one, and again the performance is elegant and stylish.

The Cherubini is the second of two Etudes for horn and strings composed in 1802 (Berlin: Deutsche Staatsbibliothek). They have managed to elude attention, and are not mentioned in standard references or biographies of the composer (at least as far as I have been able to ascertain). There seems no reason to doubt their authenticity, although the writing for natural horn is indeed extraordinary for the period. The Etude here recorded, in F major, consists of a Largo and an Allegro moderato, neither of large proportions, but both containing solid music. The range of the solo horn part is from f to d″ using most of the chromatic notes in the middle and top registers, which were obviously produced by hand-stopping in Cherubini's time. Mr. Barry Tuckwell presumably performs the solo part on a modern instrument, which does not in the least diminish his claim to brilliant virtuosity. It is by any criterion a dazzling horn solo, with wide leaps, trills, and rapid passagework; and Mr. Tuckwell seems to take it all with resources to spare.

All in all, one could hardly wish for a more delightful recording. Mr. Marriner is clearly a musician of refinement, intelligence, and taste, and it is to be hoped that Oiseau-Lyre will allow him to make dozens of recordings for them. It may even be worth mentioning that among the minor virtues of this recording are the complete absence of misprints or misinformation on the liner (the notes on the works are both literate and calm) and the fact that no "credits" are given to the producer, the annotator, the page-turner, the electrician, or anyone except the players. (Despite this—or perhaps because of it—the sound is beautiful.) We may even be grateful that we are spared the personality build-up; there is not a word about the lives and hobbies of the performers, what they eat for breakfast, or the press-notices they received on their last tour of Patagonia. If other readers of *The Musical Quarterly* are as tired as I am of record jackets that combine the worst features of hardselling, confession-writing, and gossip-mongering, they will join me in hailing this recording for its modesty and seemliness, as well as for its other qualities.

Reviews of Records
Musical Quarterly LIII/1 (January 1967)

HUMMEL: *Septet in D minor, Op. 74*; *Quintet in E-flat, Op. 87.* Melos Ensemble of London. Oiseau-Lyre SOL 290 (stereo).

Hardly anyone has a good word to say for Johann Nepomuk Hummel, except for an occasional (and apparently grudging) acknowledgment of his talents as a pianist, or a brief mention of his historical importance as a link between Mozart and Chopin. He is hastily shoved off the scene in most current histories of music, and the "liner" of this recording opens, typically enough, by quoting a disparaging remark about him by Berlioz. Perhaps it is time that we took another good look at a composer so completely misjudged and dismissed by most of the 19th century that modern opinion about him has hardly had a chance to form. There is at the present time almost nothing of Hummel available in print, and I am sure that many musicians, like myself, have never heard a public performance of a work by Hummel in forty years of concertgoing. (I must except two minor works that I myself have performed in recent years.) I am therefore more than usually grateful, as others may also be, to those few artists and recording companies who have given us an opportunity to listen to a few of Hummel's works at home. For on the evidence of the present recording, and of the few others that have been temporarily available in recent years (none seems to stay "in print" for long), there appears to be reason to believe that Hummel is a considerably more interesting composer than his detractors or his eliminators would have us believe.

Hummel, as a perceptive anonymous annotator wrote on the liner of a short-lived recording of his G major String Quartet, Opus 30, was a composer of the second rank; but being of the second rank is not necessarily the same as being second-rate, and this is a distinction that might be heavily underlined. Being of the second rank at a time when Mozart, Haydn, Beethoven, Schubert, and Weber, among others, were active, is not doing too badly. Hummel lived and studied with Mozart for two years, and succeeded Haydn at Eszterháza. One could not say that he was contemptuously dismissed by his colleagues and contemporaries; that remained for the generation of Schumann and Berlioz, and is a curious phenomenon indeed. It is quite conceivable that they were wrong in their judgment because the esthetic of early Romanticism and the overwhelming weight of Beethoven blinded them to a number of musical and artistic virtues, or, in the case of Hummel, aroused conflicting feelings simply because Hummel had already indicated a direction that they were anxious to explore, and had done so without talking about it.

If one listens to these two superb pieces of chamber music, or to the two piano concertos recorded in the past few years, one sees that those who dismiss Hummel are quite simply wrong. Schumann and Berlioz were not infallible (Berlioz was not much interested in the piano, and Schumann noted that of all Hummel's work, only the F-sharp minor Piano Sonata was likely to survive); and it is rather wryly amusing to recognize that the Hummel Septet (written in 1816) must have been in Schumann's ear a good deal of the time. Schumann, one begins to suspect, may have learned a great deal from Hummel, including a style of writing for the piano. The points of similarity are very startling; but more startling still will be my suggestion, which I advance seriously, that both of the works on this recording are superior to the Schumann Quintet, or indeed to all but the very best of Schumann, Weber, or Mendelssohn.

There are still inadequate data for a more complete discussion of the interesting questions that now seem to me to arise in the case of Hummel. The Septet is the work of Hummel most often cited, and is presumably his masterpiece. But such works do not come from nowhere, and the other works available on recordings suggest that the level of Hummel's other major work cannot lie too far below that of the Septet, which is indeed extraordinarily beautiful and which shows the hand of a real master. This work did survive Hummel, as records of occasional performances through the 19th century show. Liszt performed it in Berlin in 1842, and it was played (for the last time?) in New York at the Aschenbroedl Club in 1894, with Victor Herbert taking the cello part. And one assumes that the piece was played for its musical interest, rather than merely as a vehicle for virtuoso display, which of course it also is.

The Septet is scored for piano, flute, oboe, horn, viola, cello, and bass, and is in four movements, beautifully proportioned. There is no problem of "form"; the proof is that one is not conscious of any manipulation; everything seems to be in the right place, and there is no padding. In this respect, one can surmise that Hummel did learn something of importance from Mozart, perhaps the one thing that composers of the next generation failed to learn. The musical ideas of the Septet are fresh and attractive; the harmony is again basically learned from Mozart, in the same sense as Chopin's was. (It is not only the pianistic figuration that forms the Mozart-Chopin link; it is also this very clear yet daring sense of harmony.) The Septet seems uncluttered by any sense of its own weightiness; this too comes from Mozart, and is "anti-Romantic" as an attitude or mode of expression. Mozart's seriousness is more profound than Schumann's, for example, because it doesn't insist on itself in obvious ways, and makes its points without grand gestures or rhetoric. The Hummel Septet has many Mozartean qualities; it sparkles with life, and is fundamentally serious as a work of art. What astonishes one on studying it is that Hummel's work in general is classified by historians as "superficial." Sometimes one wonders if they have looked or listened.

The Quintet (for piano and strings), Opus 87, dates from 1821, and is another fine work for a somewhat unusual combination, the fifth instrument being double bass instead of second violin. The Scherzo is perhaps weaker than that of the Septet, but the work as a whole can stand on its merits. It is extremely interesting harmonically, both in broad outline and in fine detail. Although it is nominally in E-flat major, much of it is in E-flat minor, and the first movement goes surprisingly into extended sections in A major and F-sharp major and minor. The short slow movement, a Largo, which leads directly into the finale, is especially lovely.

The performances by the Melos Ensemble of London are admirable, even though they are not faultless. But they have the virtues of movement, intelligence, and taste, and one has the feeling that the players enjoyed every moment of the music without trying to prove anything. I doubt that we will get a better performance unless Messrs. Heifetz, Piatigorsky & Company decide to include one of the pieces in their next year's repertory, which, incidentally, would be a splendid idea. The pianist with the Melos Ensemble, Lamar Crawson, has a flair for this type of music: his playing has both elegance and strength. Hummel's writing for the piano is a complete delight for the pianist; it is wonderfully in the fingers and never anything but right for the sonority of the instrument. Chopin's debt to Hummel is perhaps greater than is usually acknowledged, although Chopin himself was quite aware of it, and in fact insisted that his pupils learn the concertos of Hummel as the best preparation for playing his own works. But the piano style, it is clear, comes originally from Mozart, which detracts from no one's originality or mastery.

Reviews of Records
Musical Quarterly LIII/1 (January 1967)

MENDELSSOHN: *String Symphonies Nos. 9, 10, 12.* Academy of St. Martin-in-the Fields, cond. by Neville Marriner. Argo ZRG 5467 (stereo).

One should of course listen to these symphonies without knowing that they were composed by a boy of fourteen. But one does know, and it is therefore difficult not to judge the works from a special point of view. The symphonies need no indulgence; they are remarkable music. If one listens to them with the idea of detecting flaws or juvenile miscalculations, one may be disappointed; young Mendelssohn had a very sure hand. And as Hugh Ottaway points out on the record's liner: "This is music to be enjoyed, not puzzled over—enjoyed in its own right, not merely marvelled at as the work of a brilliant boy."

The symphonies, as most readers are aware, were written more or less as exercises under Zelter's tutelage, to be performed at home. They are not well known among musicians even today. If we are to judge by the three performed here by the excellent musicians of the Academy of St. Martin-in-the-Fields, it would be a benefaction to have them in general circulation. They are very little inferior, if at all, to much of the Mendelssohn that is known and performed, and they should be welcome additions to the string orchestra repertory.

No. 9, in C, is the longest of the three on this recording, a well-developed four-movement work, with neat contrasts of major and minor, much skillful and imaginative fugal writing, and beautiful voicing, with many *divisi* parts. The warmth and lyricism foreshadow the best of later Mendelssohn; throughout, the music sounds fresh and natural and spontaneous.

No. 10, in B minor, is in one movement: a charming piece with a brilliant prestissimo coda, marvelously light and effervescent. But the great beauty among the three symphonies is No. 12, in G minor, which is a small masterpiece for a composer of any age. It is in three movements. The first opens with a noble *grave* section in the Baroque manner; this has genuine grandeur, and leads into a vigorous and finely modelled fugue. The second movement, a 6/8 Andante, is as lovely as anything Mendelssohn ever wrote; the part-writing, with violas *divisi,* is superb. The last movement opens in the manner of a Baroque prelude and fughetta, the latter actually a transitional passage to the second subject, but comprising material again much used in the development. The structure of the movement is original and interesting, and Mendelssohn shows his extraordinary craftsmanship by providing it with a most remarkable ending. The whole shows the hand not only of a gifted composer, but of a thoroughly mature one.

I have previously expressed my admiration for the performances of Mr. Marriner's group, and can only say again that they are top-notch. These three early Mendelssohn symphonies are admirably done, with elegance, taste, and style.

Reviews of Records
Musical Quarterly LIII/2 (April 1967)

MESSIAEN: *La Nativité du Seigneur.* Simon Preston, organ. Argo ZRG 5447 (stereo).

About Messiaen's work in general I suspect that André Hodeir, in *Since Debussy,* is right. Yet there is an extraordinarily compelling quality in these nine long meditations, lasting about 55 minutes, that make up *La Nativité du Seigneur*—an early work, written in 1936, that perhaps represents Messiaen at his best. Hodeir views Messiaen as a great musician (and teacher) who has tragically failed as a composer. In view of what has happened to Messiaen in the past fifteen years, this appears to be true. The very qualities of early works such as *La Nativité* are technically limiting, and the pieces are, in fact, loaded with contradictions that Messiaen has not seemed to be able to resolve. These contradictions can work once or twice, as they do here and in other early works, where the "strange charm of impossibilities" is evident and quite powerful. One is, indeed, tempted to say that *La Nativité du Seigneur* is a masterpiece, and one of the great organ works of all time. It is certainly monumental and impressive, original and memorable, with or without the theoretical and mystical explanations the composer himself gives out. The organ repertory badly needed Messiaen—one might say that if he hadn't existed, it would have been necessary to invent him—for with Messiaen it is true that the organ has a new sound, and perhaps for the first time in many generations a claim on anyone's serious attention.

Messiaen's innovations are chiefly in rhythm and meter, although he also uses invented modes and harmonies derived from them. All this is well known, and more than adequately described by Messiaen himself. The preliminary note printed with the score of *La Nativité du Seigneur* is quite clear, and its expansion, written by Messiaen somewhat later, gives further insight into a mind at once mystical and theoretical, firmly Catholic, and rather reminiscent in some respects of the Huysmans of *La Cathédrale*. But the theoretician, at least in these early organ works, yields to the sensationalist who savors sound and color above everything; and one becomes aware that in this music time is not to be measured, but only contemplated or felt as another sensation similar to color or odor or timbre.

All of this is completely effective if one is willing or able to accept it. Many are not. But Messiaen carries complete conviction here, and the long pieces, many of them almost motionless and shapeless, like huge clouds reflecting light in a windless sky, get inside one if one listens quietly and not analytically. In some ways the pieces have the static and non-intellectual qualities of rock 'n' roll; but of rock 'n' roll as Franz Liszt might have written it. There is a real virtuosity of monotony, which is based on the repetition of melodic phrases of limited range, very much in essence like rock 'n' roll, and like it subject to inflection rather than variation. To this general stasis, the absence of pulse, invariability of mode, and continually oppressive richness of harmony and texture all contribute. And yet, as I have suggested, it is possible to remain fascinated for the entire duration of the nine meditations.

At least a part of the interest is provided by the organ itself, and Messiaen's remarkable handling of its resources. Messiaen's technique is, I think, completely ineffective for the piano, In such works as *Mode de valeurs et d'intensités* and *Ile de Feu 2,* of 1949-50, the sense is hard to perceive not only because the piano is incapable of gross contrasts of timbre, but also because it is percussive and its sound diminishes immediately, thus not permitting continued intensity. Nor is the piano, in works of this kind of polyrhythmic complication, sufficiently clear as to voicing. The registrations of Messiaen's organ works are carefully specified by the composer himself, and the sounds are not only sumptuous in themselves, but are differentiated with sufficient clarity so that voices can be isolated.

La Nativité is a work for virtuosos. One is not only reminded of Liszt, who appears here very formidably as Messiaen's spiritual and musical ancestor, but one is persuaded that music is possible on organs other than Baroque, and that a Romantic conception of the organ is not a sin against the spirit of the 20th century. These pieces of Messiaen, over the basic immobility, are wildly and uninhibitedly decorated, and exuberantly proclaim the joy and excitement of making noise. It is this, in the long run, that justifies the theorizing. Needless to say, to justify the making of noise, something else also is needed, and this is immensely skilful and imaginative performance. In the case of the present recording we have a superlative performance by the English organist Simon Preston, playing on the great organ of Westminster Abbey.

One must compare this record with the very much earlier one made by Messiaen himself for Ducretet-Thomson (catalogue nos. 2 and 3) on the organ of La Trinité in Paris. The differences are quite startling, beginning of course with the quality of sound itself. The old Messiaen recording is a little foggy, with much reverberation, but it should not be discounted simply because of its less advanced recording technique. Messiaen's performance, obviously, is authoritative; but it is also curious. And in a sense it must be heard in order to appreciate fully how superbly good Simon Preston's performance is. I have (and I think this is relevant) not heard "live" either the organ of La Trinité or that of Westminster Abbey. They are, on the evidence of the recordings, very strikingly different instruments, and the differences are possibly sharpened by the recording engineers. But the organist is invariably shaped by his instrument, perhaps to a greater extent than any other performing artist, and one must begin any comparison of performances with this idea in mind. There is less "focus" in Messiaen's performance partly because his instrument seems in general cloudier. Not that this effect of blur or remoteness is inappropriate; on the contrary, for this music it even adds to the somewhat dreamlike quality. And one cannot quarrel with Messiaen's own ideas of what is appropriate or "correct."

Preston plays more accurately (which is indeed an accomplishment) and in general takes the nine pieces not faster, but merely somewhat less slowly, than Messiaen. An exception is the eighth piece (*Les Mages*), which he unaccountably takes almost half again as slowly as Messiaen. This tempo does serve, however, to place in even stronger relief the breathtaking brilliance of the final toccata. Although in this pulseless and rhythmically over-lapped music it is difficult to establish a beat, one can generalize by calculating Preston's basic eighth note in slow sections as about 36 MM, and Messiaen's as about 30-32 MM. This is indeed leisurely, and difficult to maintain with complete steadiness. Messiaen wavers a bit more than Preston, which goes a long way towards accounting for some of the dismissals of his rhythmic experiments as being simply continuous rubato. Preston's ability to get Messiaen's *valeurs ajoutées* almost dead right is quite remarkable, and destroys the rubato argument completely. Messiaen's ideas and experiments in rhythm and meter do make sense if they are executed with absolute security and, above all, with absolutely *no* rubato. But it must be said that the sense is in detail, which is often beautiful as well as original; on the large scale of these pieces, or even of almost any one of them, the final result is the destruction of any sense of rhythm by placing it constantly in conflict with itself. It is out of this conflict that the sense of immobility and timelessness arises.

It is, in any case, the responsibility of the organist to make the detail clear, and this Preston does beautifully, aided by the remarkable neatness of the technicians who produced the tape. Preston may be considered a great organist on one evidence alone: he releases notes and evidently raises his fingers. It is extraordinarily clean playing. Preston is also very discreet and sensitive in his balancing of volumes among his three manuals and pedal; Messiaen calls for a dynamic range of *ppp* to *ffff*, but volume, absolute or relative, can never be specified exactly and is particularly tricky for the organ, and even more so for an organ recording. But Preston has calculated the volume relationships in a masterly way, and this helps greatly to clarify the complex contrapuntal rhythmic organization of Messiaen's music. The performance is altogether brilliant. Acquisition of this recording is strongly recommended to all who are interested in organ repertory or organ playing, as well as to all who are interested in a significant, though certainly curious, phase of 20th-century music.

Reviews of Records
Musical Quarterly LIV/1 (January 1968)

COWELL: Trio for violin, 'cello and piano (1965) SEMMLER: Trio for violin, 'cello and piano, Op. 40 (1964). The Philharmonia Trio: Charles Libove, violin, Alan Shulman, 'cello, Nina Lugovoy, piano. CRI 211.

Henry Cowell's last completed work is full of happiness, light, wit, and delight in making music. It is a joy to hear, and this excellent recording—excellent both as to sympathetic performance and good recorded sound—is a touching and vivid remembrance of a musician whose importance in our musical history and development will be more and more appreciated as years go by. In many ways, the Trio is a summation of Cowell; at the least, it conveys the essence of his quality as a composer. It is uninhibited, unforced, fresh and original.

Its qualities are the more remarkable when one considers Cowell's failing health during the period of its composition. Perhaps, consciously or otherwise, the Trio was conceived as a sort of retrospect. This at least seems possible, and may account for the indefinably moving quality of the work.

The Trio is of course not in orthodox style, either as to handling of the instruments or as to form and structure. It consists of nine short movements totalling about nineteen minutes. One is tempted to call the movements little studies, or perhaps even samples. In any case, they represent Cowell at his various, but in the long run unified, best. The movements recall idioms and experiments that interested the composer at different times, or perhaps more correctly, at all times. They are related motivically, and if each movement has the nature of a character piece, they are the characters in a narrative that Cowell has put together in a final and convincing order.

By and large, the Trio, like so much of Cowell's music, is in a diatonic idiom of mildly dissonant counterpoint that occasionally becomes sharper and more tense. But on the whole, it is relaxed and cheerful music. There are echoes of earlier Cowell pieces: a suggestion of the early dissonant woodwind quintet, of some of the hymns and fuguing tunes, even of *The Banshee* and other early piano pieces, especially in the use of harmonics and glissandi. But the separate movements and the apparently separate ideas add up to more than a sum of parts. The Trio is cumulatively impressive, unified by the mature thinking and technique of a composer who had discovered his world and was able to make it one through the strength of his creative personality.

The Trio is a fitting final work, and a major one. It has been suggested that it involves an esthetic derived from Cowell's studies of Oriental music. This, too, is possible; but it must be remembered that this entails no suggestion of imitation. What we sense is the absorption and integration of a time and form sense that has become Cowell's own.

The rate at which Cowell composed and the vast amount of music in apparently different styles that he left have tended to confuse those who must now try to evaluate his work. This Trio might be a good place to start, for it holds a clue to the underlying unity of Cowell's music, and demonstrates the quality that made Henry Cowell mean so much as a man and as a musician to so many of his contemporaries.

Cowell's Trio is played beautifully by the Philharmonia Trio, as is the Trio by Alexander Semmler, which is heard on the other side of the disc. The latter is an expertly written work, quite attractive in its ideas and working out. Both Trios were commissioned by the Hans J. Cohn Foundation of Woodstock, N. Y., and were first performed there in the summer of 1965 at one of the Sunday afternoon Maverick Concerts, of which Mr. Semmler is program director.

Reviews of Records
Musical Quarterly LIV/1 (January 1968)

THOMSON: *Sonata da Chiesa*; *Praises and Prayers*; Sonata for violin and piano. Betty
Allen, mezzo-soprano; Joseph Fuchs, violin; Lillian Fuchs, viola; Artur Balsam, piano;
ensemble cond. by Virgil Thomson. CRI 207 (mono only).

One adjective that can always be applied to the music of Virgil Thomson is *refreshing.*
Thomson's music is also, as everyone knows, highly personal and unrelated to the music
being written by anyone else. Whereas most of our music, good or bad, conservative or
radical, is academic and fairly predictable, Thomson is and remains unconcerned with
theorizing and well away from beaten paths. Experiment for its own sake does not seem
to interest him, and he does not appear to worry much about weight or importance. For
these concerns he substitutes several invaluable qualities: originality, absolute seriousness,
and a sense of high comedy. Originality is something for which many consciously strive;
Thomson simply does not have to. Seriousness is a quality to which many pretend, but
real seriousness about art is rarer than one thinks. And high comedy is a quality that is
almost totally absent in twentieth-century art.

Thomson is one of our more important composers, not because he has had influence on
others, or even because he has been in the mainstream of contemporary practice, but simply because he has unmistakable quality, evidenced in a variety of remarkable works over
a long span of years. Thomson's music is that of a man with a refined and distinguished
mind, able to reconcile means with ends, preserve proportion, and perceive new and interesting relations among assorted sounds and ideas. The music is never as simple as it seems;
it is always sophisticated and usually subtle. Complexity as such is never a factor, for it is
evident that Thomson is not interested in demonstrating how cleverly he can manipulate
ideas or material. It is the ideas and the material themselves that interest him. The music
never asks to be dissected in order to be appreciated, and one is almost never tempted to
analyze it. The idea that music should be delightful is one no longer widely held, but it is
one to which Thomson obviously subscribes.

The music on this recording is all delightful. The early *Sonata da Chiesa* (written in 1926)
is a masterpiece of comedy. Thomson describes it as his "bang-up graduation piece in the
dissonant neo-baroque style of the period." It is scored for E♭ clarinet, C trumpet, viola,
horn, and trombone, and its three movements consist of a Chorale, a Tango, and a Fugue.
The Chorale alternates with a somewhat drunkenly acid organum, interspersed with mel-
ismas on the viola. It is a wild dream of a religious service; perhaps only Ives, of all other
composers one can think of, could have imagined anything like it. The Tango, in alter-

nating 4/4 and 5/4, is equally original and disconcerting, while the final Fugue (a double one) is about as improbable, both structurally and instrumentally, as one can imagine. But it all comes off, not as satire or burlesque, but as genuine comedy. It is, incidentally, quite extraordinarily difficult for the players, and it should be said that the group directed here by Mr. Thomson does a superb job.

Joseph Fuchs in the Violin Sonata, and Betty Allen in *Praises and Prayers*, are also superb. The Violin Sonata, written in 1930, is typical of much of Thomson's work in that it seems to be simple, and is in fact unpretentious, but it is full of charm and naturalness as well as wit and subtlety. It has considerable substance and is by no means as simple as it seems. The effect is produced in part by the unexpected juxtapositions of elements that are often simple in themselves, but which take on new characters in the contexts that Thomson devises for them.

The song cycle, *Praises and Prayers,* was composed in 1963 for Miss Allen, and is the most recent of the three works heard on this recording. It is an eloquent and moving group, with a calm seriousness and beauty of line and color that only a master composer for the voice can hope to achieve. Thomson's songs make most others of recent vintage seem childish or laboriously manufactured. The intelligence Thomson brings to words is matched by his marvelous sense of what the voice can express. *Praises and Prayers* are songs of real intensity and gravity, and demonstrate Thomson's expressive range as well as his originality and daring. Miss Allen sings them magnificently and receives stylish collaboration from the composer at the piano.

All in all, this is a grand recording, and a bright one to have on a dull day.

Henry Cowell (1897-1965): A Memoir and an Appreciation

Perspectives of New Music IV/2 (Spring-Summer 1966)

I have before me, as I write, the attractively printed score of Henry Cowell's 15th Symphony. Like most of Henry's later works, it is full of apparent contradictions. It seems both of our time and remote from it. Compared to the music being written on the advanced frontiers, it is curiously innocent and removed; yet compared with the more academic writing of the sixties, it seems as fresh as spring flowers. One would hesitate to call it a great work, and yet it is hard to see how anyone could deny that it is an interesting one. Mr. Mellers might insist on his harsh judgment, and declare that it amounts to the exploitation of "gimmicks," but one more generously inclined would find in it manifestations of Henry's wide interests and enthusiasms, and of his ability to put together hymn-tunes, assorted orientalisms, curious sonorities, tone-clusters, and a strange assortment of "ideas" that somehow all manage to live together. What is perfectly clear on reading this symphony—or almost any other work of Henry's—is that no one else could have written it. It isn't "modern," it isn't old-hat, it isn't conventional or academic; it is simply Cowell. Of how many composers can one say the equivalent?

Being "simply Cowell" was harder than it may have seemed; it took imagination and daring, wit and gaiety, enthusiasm, energy and intelligence, and a comprehensive interest in everything musical from any time and any place. Richard French, writing in *The Musical Quarterly* in 1960, caught the flavor exactly. Henry, he said, "never recovered from the excitement of finding himself a composer." Henry did indeed compose as if he enjoyed it, and, even more unusually, as if he expected people to enjoy what he produced. He was resigned to being misunderstood often, but he did not expect to be. He was, as his wife, Sidney Robertson Cowell, wrote in a note to accompany his 7th Symphony, "dismayingly fertile," as he was indeed unpredictably varied. Again in Mrs. Cowell's words: "The many kinds of music he had always produced as necessarily as he breathes had led Cowell to be labelled neo-romantic, cerebral, neo-baroque, 'folkloristic,' granitic, dissonant, simple, and sentimental, or anything else suggested by a single piece at a given moment."

A delightfully candid comment! To think that music can and should be enjoyable as well as various, or as natural as breathing, is somehow often taken as indicating a lack of seriousness; and this is one of the unhappiest mistakes of our times. To be sure, there are other values, but these need not be incompatible or exclusive. Henry was in every way a serious person and a serious musician; he was also an enthusiast who enjoyed life immensely in all of its manifestations. In all of his music there is a feeling of life and of enjoyment, of a genuine impulse to mirror or re-create life. But as a rule, no one who enjoys life and phenomena completely is self-critical, and here Henry was no exception. The balance between inhibition and innocent prolixity is rare at any time. One learns not to expect every virtue and occasionally to take a chance. And this Henry was prepared at any time to do.

One of Henry's most endearing, and at the same time most exasperating, characteristics was that he liked music: almost every kind of music, including music he knew was bad. He was seldom against anything, and it was rare to hear him express disdain, anger, or impatience. He felt sincerely that anything that some one had made or done was worth looking at or hearing. One experienced something, perhaps even learned something; assimilation and evaluation came later. Henry was always interested and seldom bored. This too, in a sense, is an "un-modern" attitude; we cherish our doubts, our inalienable right to scorn and reject, and we guard our exclusivities. Henry scorned little, feared little, doubted little; the world at times may have laughed at him, misunderstood him, even persecuted him, but he refused to be "alienated." Far from retreating, he cultivated an unbounded curiosity, and toward whatever he found that aroused his interest, he went directly.

I recall going with Henry, twenty-five years ago, to a gathering of shape-note hymn-singers at White Top Mountain, high in the Appalachians where Tennessee, Virginia, and North Carolina meet. In those days it was a bumpy trip. We went in an ancient car, driving perilously, and found no accommodations; we slept in a barnloft and enjoyed all the discomforts of the backwoods. But within a few minutes of arrival, Henry was indistinguishable from the natives and participants, and that is the point. Henry went to enjoy the music, the people, and the environment, not to study them. He had no tape recorder, no camera, probably not even a pencil. Would anyone be bold enough to say that he had "discovered" less, or learned less, than if he had gone with a solemn and respectable ethnomusicological purpose and equipment? What Henry learned or experienced went into music and not into documents; it became part of himself rather than part of an archive.

This is wonderful enough at any time, but it is most wonderful today, in an academic age. Henry exemplified the important difference between learning things and studying them, or being taught them. He illustrated, and vividly, the advantages that a lack of formal schooling can give to someone with intellectual energy and a capacity for experience. He read widely and conversed brilliantly, but he did not read about the *shaku-hachi* or the nose-flute; he learned to play them. And one was never surprised—merely delighted—when Henry casually exhibited some new or unusual accomplishment, or spoke of some odd, but usually amusing and profitable adventure.

The notoriety of Henry as a smasher of pianos, and the oddness of some of his musical experiments, such as the use of the thunderstick, have tended to overshadow, at least among the unsophisticated, many of his real accomplishments. Henry occasionally contributed to this imbalance, for he took pleasure in humor and unexpectedness and was never solemn about himself. But one should remember that from his earliest appearances in Europe, in 1923, he aroused the interest and respect of musicians as diverse as Schnabel and Bartók, Schoenberg, Berg, and Webern. Oddly enough, Henry attended Schoenberg's lectures in 1923, and one wonders whether this may not have been an unsettling experience for Schoenberg; but one should remember that Schoenberg asked Henry to play for his master classes, and that Webern included Henry's *Sinfonietta* in his programs in Vienna. Many have forgotten, in recent years, that Henry was one of our first "contacts" with Schoenberg, Webern, Berg, and Bartók, and one of the first to talk about them here or endeavor to have their music performed. Yet Henry was self-confident enough to feel that he did not have to compose in the manner of any of them. He knew that they, along with Ives and Ruggles, Stravinsky and Slonimsky, Riegger and Seeger, Chávez and Varèse, were important, as well as interesting. Also interesting and also important, he felt, were Chinese opera, new notational systems, invented or unfamiliar instruments, the work of Theremin, and the folk or art music of any culture. And Henry's interest was never an idle or a passive one.

Henry got things done. Young musicians today may not appreciate, or at best may regard only as ancient history, the effect of Henry in the twenties and thirties. Yet the youngest as well as the oldest among us are immensely in his debt. Henry was one of those who made possible the relatively comfortable state of contemporary music in the United States today. In the twenties, modern music—anything consistently dissonant was usually called "ultra-modern"—was engaged in a constant struggle for serious notice of any kind. No benevolent foundations made things easy for composers; performances were rare and publication almost unknown. Henry arranged both, in days when it took resource and determination; and without his efforts we should all be poorer today. Paul Rosenfeld wrote in the early thirties:

> Wherever in his steady whirl he has set foot on earth, concerts have sprung up . . . and they have invariably included performances of the works of the leading American moderns. And he has got these revolutionary scores not only played, but printed and recorded as well. . . . In the last years, besides increasing in character, velocity, conspicuity, and scope, Cowell's business has actually increased in effectualness. Together with much that is sterile, he *has* performed, got into print, and pressed music of the sort that the present shies from and the future battens on; and half loaves are not to be despised in these hard times. . . . American culture is substantially indebted to his mental fluidity. His persistent and very practical championship of radical and unpopular work, too, has provided

steady encouragement to those with something individual in them to give. . . .
Indeed there is something almost saintlike in this activity. Cowell is after all quite
disinterested. He has always been, and he remains, a poor, man. What little money
he has derived from his concerts, his symposiums, his critical articles, has immediately been reinvested by him in new concerts, new symposiums, new musical pub-
lications and recordings. . . .[1]

Henry held a Guggenheim Fellowship in 1931-1932, which took him to Europe to study
Oriental music and comparative musicology with Hornbostel, but aside from this grant he
received no substantial funds for his own work, and made his own way. The New Music
Edition, which Henry founded in 1927, was managed on the proverbial shoestring. It
lasted for twenty-five remarkably productive years. In its first ten years, New Music published, among others, works of Schoenberg, Webern, Varèse, Ives, Ruggles, Chávez, Copland, Harris, Antheil, Riegger, and Brant. With proper respect to the Cos Cob Press, and
to other endeavors of the period, there was nothing comparable to New Music in imagination or effectiveness. And this continued to the end; in later years, works of Babbitt, Cage,
Carter, Hovhaness, and many others of interest and importance appeared in the series. For
many composers, New Music provided their first publication.

New Music was not a cooperative; the composers paid nothing for their publication. Henry
raised the necessary money by begging and persuading. Issues were often late; occasionally
one was missed, when money ran out; but New Music nevertheless kept going, as did the
New Music Recordings, simply through Henry's determination and energy. Times have
changed very much since 1927, because people have changed them, and Henry was one of
those who helped most conspicuously. That is why the *published* score of Henry's 15th
Symphony, written in 1960, has such special interest. For in a sense it was Henry's own
efforts that brought about the possibility of normal commercial publication and normal
expectancy of performance for himself and all of his colleagues. We need, perhaps, to be
reminded today that not long ago it was not so easy.

Henry, as Hugo Weisgall wrote in *The Musical Quarterly* of October 1959, "aside from
his life as a composer, has lived several other full lives as champion of new music, impresario,
performer, lecturer, critic, editor, teacher, and sponsor of the young." Each of these lives
was fruitful. Directly and indirectly, Henry's helpfulness was great. His interest was never
perfunctory, and his advice and action were never ordinary or predictable. He was of direct influence on those who studied with him, Cage and Harrison among others;

---

[1] Paul Rosenfeld: "Cowell," in *Discoveries of a Music Critic.* New York: Harcourt,
Brace and Co., 1936.

but his influence extended to many who in no sense could be called his pupils or his followers, or even in some cases, his admirers. He was always stimulating as a person and as a musician to composers and performers of widely diverse tastes and backgrounds. His critical writing was often brilliant, and little that was interesting escaped him. It is still illuminating to return to an article on Cage and Boulez that Henry wrote in 1951. Showing a new work to Henry, or preparing one with him for performance, usually produced something enlightening, and often something startling, by way of comment or advice. Henry was astonishingly keen; sometimes an apparently casual remark, often seeming even irrelevant, would later prove to have been directly to the point that the composer or performer himself had not perceived.

Of Henry as a composer no final critical word can be said for some time. The amount of work he left is as huge as it is varied. There is no apparent consistency among such works as *Synchrony,* the Concertos for Koto, the *Celtic Set,* and the piano pieces, to choose just a few. But the consistency is nonetheless there, a consistency that a lively and fertile imagination brought to bear on the variety of materials that caught its fancy. This is very real, and also very "personal." Weisgall quotes in his article an interview given by Henry in which he said simply, on the question of unified or "personal" style: "If a man has a distinctive personality of his own, I don't see how he can keep it out of his music. And if he hasn't, how can he put it in?" Anyone who knew Henry could answer for the distinctive personality: original, interesting, vital, amusing, enthusiastic, lively, and stimulating. In his best music, it is all there.

Henry would have heatedly denied what must seem evident to many: that his works of the twenties and thirties are more "advanced," and consequently more interesting to us today, than many of his later pieces—the "exotic" works seeking to reconcile the music of the West with that, for example, of Persia or Japan, or in many dozen pieces having their roots in an interpretation of the hymn-and-fuguing-tune style. To Henry, exploration or interpretation of any one musical resource could not be less interesting than the exploitation of any other; the modes and textures of the East seemed as important as the systematic development of dissonant counterpoint or serial technique in the West. His concern was the reconciliation and constant revivification of all music. His views here had explicit human and social implications as well as purely musical ones. He did not long for an international culture imposed by the West and was distressed by artistic colonialism. It is clear that visions of internationalism, whether human or musical, remain Utopian; and Henry was, in this one sense at least, isolated from the mainstream of musical, political, and "educational" interest in America and Europe. But his compositions may still be viewed with these considerations only remotely in mind. What is needed, for any judgment of Henry as a composer, is of course performance and recording of his major works that have been neglected: the *Sinfonietta* of 1925-1928, the Piano Concerto, *Synchrony,* and some of the brilliant exploratory chamber music once thought impossible to play. These remain significant achievements in American music.

Henry was a *mover,* and one of the enliveners of music in our time. All of us, whatever our musical tastes and practices, owe him a great deal. He helped two generations to see and think and hear, and he helped to create and build a foundation for "modern" music in America. This is not a small achievement; it is a gigantic one, and should not be forgotten.

John Philip Sousa

HiFi/Stereo Review XIX/1 (July 1967)

Not many years ago, if one asked casually anywhere in the world for the name of the most famous American composer, it is likely that the answer would have been John Philip Sousa. Of course, times have changed, and today the answer might very well be Aaron Copland or George Gershwin or Elliott Carter or Richard Rodgers instead. This is an interesting sidelight on the change of tone in American music: there is at least a chance today that the names of some "serious" composers might turn up in casual talk under almost any kind of circumstances. But, on the other hand, it is only in 1967, in our own time, that it is really possible to include Sousa quite seriously, without condescension or embarrassment, in a series devoted to "great" American composers.

Sousa obviously does not qualify as a "serious" composer any more than Johann Strauss does—rather less so, in fact. But it is on the level best represented by Strauss that Sousa has his secure and honorable place. Any music lover knows that Strauss was the best in his field, with sense enough not to wish or attempt to write symphonies, and that what he accomplished in his own limited musical world earned him the admiration of serious musicians as well as the affection of an enormous public. And so with Sousa. It is reported that Paul Hindemith once called Sousa the greatest American composer; whether the report is true or not, it is at least believable, and everyone can see why it might have been said. For, like Strauss, Sousa was not only the greatest in his own field, but was by and large quite satisfied to be what he was, and—again like Strauss—his name will always be associated with the undisputed mastery of a minor musical form which in a sense was his own creation. He was, so far as the march is concerned, an original as well as an important composer.

The marches of Sousa are part of the great heritage of the world's immortal music. Like the waltzes of Strauss, they elevate a minor form of the dance to the level of art, and they transcend with the completest success—and apparently with the greatest of ease—the merely functional or the exclusively national. For Sousa's marches, uniquely American as the Strauss waltzes are Viennese, are also international in appeal, and speak in all tongues. They are great American music, but they are also great music.

The march, like the waltz, is a kind of dance, as highly formal as the minuet. This is a fact too often forgotten, perhaps because the steps of the march are so simple, being, in effect, nothing more than walking in time to a regular beat. But the fundamental appeal of the march is nevertheless based on its character as dance. Beyond that, we judge the lasting musical values of any genre by the viability of the music in concert form, and here Sousa's marches, like Strauss's waltzes, speak for themselves. They are part of the concert repertoire, as well as of the marching repertoire, throughout the world.

John Philip Sousa was born on November 6, 1854, in Washington, DC, in the southeast section near the Navy Yard, then known as "Pipetown." His father, Antonio, who was born in Seville, Spain, of Portuguese parents, had lived briefly in England and arrived in Washington, via Brooklyn, in the 1840s. His mother, née Elizabeth Trinkhaus, was a native of Bavaria. Antonio Sousa played trombone in the Marine Band, although not, apparently, as a full-time occupation; he also worked occasionally as a cabinetmaker. According to John Philip's account, as given in his autobiography *Marching Along* (1928), Antonio was a kindly, intelligent, well-read man, fluent in several languages, but not a technically proficient musician. His mother was totally unmusical. But many musicians, especially from the Marine Band, were among the family's friends, and John Philip began the study of solfeggio at an early age with one of these, a Spanish orchestral player named Esputa. At the age of seven, young Sousa began the study of the violin with Esputa's son, who had organized a music school in the neighborhood. Sousa stated that he was "passionately fond of music" from earliest childhood and never entertained the idea of becoming · nything but a musician. He was also fascinated by military bands, of which there were many —good, bad, and indifferent—in Washington in those days. And so, while studying violin and "orchestration and sight-reading" at Esputa's school, he also found time to learn the trombone, baritone horn, and, apparently, the cornet and E-flat alto. His principal instrument, however, was and remained the violin.

By the time John Philip was thirteen, he was earning money as a musician, having organized a small "quadrille band" of which he was violinist and leader. Shortly afterward, he was offered a job playing baritone with a touring circus band, but to prevent the boy's running off with the group, his father had him enlisted, on June 9, 1868, as an "apprentice boy" in the Marine Band. Here John Philip's duties were fairly light—he passed out music, ran errands, and played the cymbals—and he had plenty of time for further study and for outside engagements as a performer. In his autobiography, Sousa notes that "the first time I heard really fine music (apart from the ordinary orchestra or band programmes) was when the Franko family of five wonderfully talented children came to Washington for a concert." This was in 1869, and Esputa insisted that every student in his school attend the concert. Sousa notes further that this "was the first time I had heard real violin playing."

Sousa was evidently what we would call a "quick study"; in any case, his musical progress was rapid. He joined the Washington Orchestral Union as a first violinist, and studied harmony and violin with its conductor, George Felix Benkert, a solid musician who introduced him to the sonatas of Mozart and Beethoven, and who encouraged him in his early efforts at composition. Benkert, from all accounts, must have been an excellent teacher as well as a fine pianist and competent conductor, and Sousa was fortunate to have found him. Sousa himself was well aware of this, and wrote of Benkert with great affection and admiration in later years. He never studied piano with Benkert; when he asked for some instruction on that instrument, he quotes Benkert as replying: "You seem to have a gift of knowing a composition by looking at it, and you may develop into a very original composer if you follow that line of procedure; whereas, if you become a good pianist you would probably want to compose on the instrument and, if you are not careful, your fingers will fall into pleasant places where somebody else's have fallen before."

Sousa composed a great deal of music while he was still in his teens. His first published work was a set of waltzes entitled *Moonlight on the Potomac*, brought out by J. F. Ellis in Washington in 1872. In the following year appeared a galop, *The Cuckoo*, and a march called *The Review*, the latter listed as Opus 5. These were published by the firm of Lee and Walker in Philadelphia, and Sousa's remuneration consisted of one hundred copies of each piece. Within the next few years Sousa wrote and published a considerable number of songs, salon pieces, and dance-tunes; by 1881, his catalog had reached Opus 135! After attaining that impressive total at the age of twenty-seven, he abandoned the practice of using opus numbers.

What is interesting in retrospect is that Sousa's early compositions did not include many marches. He seems to have been primarily interested in writing songs, for many of which he wrote his own verses. These songs range from the humorous to the sentimental, and it must be admitted that they are not distinguished. But it is typical of composers to love their least-favored works, and even in his later years Sousa was far more delighted when he heard one of his songs performed than he ever was to hear one of his marches. One wonders whether he ever heard a performance of the *Te Deum* he composed in about 1877, but of which no traces seem to have survived.

In any event, the *Te Deum* appears to be Sousa's only attempt at serious "art" composition. He seems to have been clearly aware that his real interests and talents were in commercial music for entertainment, and in the practical problems of earning a living as a performer. There is no evidence that at any time in his career he deeply cared for, or understood, the great music of the past or of his own time. But such an indifference is probably an asset to a popular composer; it prevents his becoming inhibited and precludes confusion about his musical aims. It must be remembered, too, that Washington in the 1870s was not exactly a cultural paradise, and that the opportunities for a serious musician, whether performer or composer, were pretty much limited to a choice between starvation and exile.

Sousa re-enlisted in the Marine Band on July 8, 1872, to serve for five years as a principal musician, playing trombone. But he soon saw that there was little professional future for him with the band, and he was lucky enough to secure an early discharge through the good offices of an assistant secretary of state. When free of his Marine Band obligation, he seized an opportunity to conduct the orchestra at Kernan's Theatre Comique, a local variety hall, from which he went on to Ford's Theater, where Offenbach operettas were being performed. His first important experience as conductor came when he was chosen to direct the road company of *Bohemians and Detectives,* a very popular show written by Milton Nobles, who was also the star. On his return to Washington, Sousa was engaged as conductor for a production known as *Matt Morgan's Living Pictures.* This was considered a rather immoral entertainment, for in it appeared, for the first time on an American stage, the "undraped female figure." Show business being show business, then as now, the production was of course billed as "artistic": the females posed in such edifying tableaux as *The Christian Martyr, Phryne before the Tribunal, The Destruction of Pompeii,* and other classics of the sort. The girls were nevertheless arrested in Pittsburgh, a city, in those days, apparently impervious to culture. And, as Sousa later related, the crowds grew bigger than ever as soon as the show, undraped female figures and all, went on again.

All of this was the direct method of learning the business. By 1876, Sousa had written and arranged a great deal of light theater music, and was beginning to look about for an operetta libretto for his own use. In that same year, he joined the orchestra conducted by Offenbach at the Philadelphia Centennial Exposition. This was an important experience for Sousa, for there can be no question but that the style of Offenbach made a real and lasting impression on the young violinist—perhaps the greatest single influence in the formation of Sousa's own style.

The Philadelphia Exposition also gave Sousa his first chance to hear Patrick Gilmore's famous band. Gilmore was the first great American band leader and a well-known entrepreneur and entertainer. His band was far superior to anything of its kind that had been heard up to that time. Gilmore had fine musicians, well trained and well directed, and he played a broad repertoire in generally excellent arrangements. Sousa was again attracted to the wind band as a performing medium, and when, a few years later, he started on his own sensational career as a bandmaster, the example of Gilmore was of considerable importance to him.

The preparation for his future success as composer and conductor was, however, still continuing. Remaining in Philadelphia after the close of the exposition, Sousa played in various theaters, did some proofreading for a music publisher, and acquired a few pupils. In 1878, he trained and directed a group of Philadelphia amateurs in a series of performances of Gilbert and Sullivan's *Pinafore.* Innumerable companies were touring the country with this extraordinarily successful operetta, and Sousa soon found himself conducting a professional group performing the piece in New York and elsewhere. It was *Pinafore* that made operetta or musical comedy "respectable" in the United States; an editorial in the Philadelphia *Public Ledger* went so far as to point out the innocence, cleanliness, and purity of the piece, in contrast to the vulgar and improper theatrical entertainments to which no decent person could possibly go.

The experience with Offenbach, followed by that with Gilbert and Sullivan, made Sousa all the more anxious to do an operetta of his own, and early in 1880 he started work on *Our Flirtation,* to a libretto by James B. Wilson. The music was written quickly, and Sousa's first operetta was produced that summer in Philadelphia. It was a moderate success, and Sousa took the company on tour following the Philadelphia run. It was while in St. Louis with *Our Flirtation* that he received the invitation that was to change his career once and for all: to return to Washington as leader of the Marine Band.

Sousa apparently had some hesitation about accepting this post. The Marine Band was then in terrible shape, and the pay was small. He had recently married, and had just seen his first operetta launched. But he found the appeal of bands and of band music irresistible, and, on October 1, 1880, he became the Marine Band's new leader. Having literally grown up with the band, and having acquired considerable and varied professional experience, he was completely aware of what had to be done and how to go about it. He proposed to create a band as good as Gilmore's or better; fortunately, he had a commandant who was in complete sympathy with his aims.

Sousa was then just short of his twenty-sixth birthday, and, like many young men, felt that a beard would make him appear older and give him a more convincing air of authority. He managed to grow a truly terrifying one which he kept, trimmed to various styles and sizes, for a good part of his life. But the beard of the early Marine Band period was far and away the most luxuriant. Whether it helped to establish his authority or not, it certainly helped to establish an image for its wearer; and the authority, in any case, was clearly proved by the very rapid reformation of the band in terms not only of repertoire and musical performance, but also of discipline, morale, and working conditions. Within a remarkably short time, Sousa accomplished a complete reorganization and made the Marine Band a top-notch performing group for the first time in its history.

During his first years with the Marine Band, Sousa continued to compose, and as might be expected, more marches began to appear among his compositions, although they were still outnumbered by songs and salon pieces. Two more operettas also appeared: *The Smugglers* in 1881, and *Désirée* in 1884. The first was a complete failure, but the second enjoyed a moderate success, and was notable for providing the vehicle for DeWolf Hopper's debut as a musical-comedy star. Sousa noted that *Désirée* was "not exactly a 'knockout'," but that "it was more or less kindly received as one of the pioneers in American comic operas."

By 1884 or thereabouts, Sousa was able to note with satisfaction that his marches were well received, being played frequently by bands other than his own. These early marches included *Across the Danube* (1879), written in commemoration of the Russian victory over the Turks, *Resumption* (1879), composed to celebrate the Treasury's return to specie payment, and *Our Flirtation,* taken from the operetta of the same name. Of these, *Our Flirtation* is the only one still played occasionally. Wilfrid Mellers, the English music historian, in his book *Music in a New Found Land*, professes to see a touch of Johann Strauss in the *Our Flirtation* march, but I should be inclined to think Offenbach a more likely influence. At any rate, it is one of the best of the early marches.

Across the Danube is one of the very few Sousa marches I have never seen or heard; there is no copyright entry for it in the Library of Congress, and it is quite possible that it was never published, although this would seem to make it unlikely that bands other than Sousa's played it, unless they did so from legally or illegally copied manuscripts. The *Revival* march, one of the very earliest (1876), is a curious but very jolly piece, using as its trio the hymn tune *In the Sweet Bye and Bye.* Whether or not this was composed for some special occasion is unknown, but Sousa occasionally followed the same procedure in later marches, using parts or the whole of well-known tunes—as, for example, *Onward Christian Soldiers* in *Power and Glory* (1922), or *Rule Brittania* in *Imperial Edward* (1902).

The connection between songs and marches in Sousa's work is always very clear. It is no longer generally remembered that many of the best marches came from operettas, in which they were, of course, sung. But still other marches were adapted from previously composed vocal pieces—*The Free Lunch Cadets* (1877), *We Are Coming* (1918), or *The White Plume* (1884), which derived from a choral piece entitled *We'll Follow Where the White Plume Waves,* to words by Edward M. Taber. For many of these pieces, as we have noted, Sousa wrote his own verses.

Sousa's first great "hit," a piece that is still familiar to anyone who has ever heard a band, was *The Gladiator*, composed in 1886. With this march and *The Rifle Regiment*, written in the same year, the authentic Sousa style became established. *The Gladiator* opens in a minor key, and is rather like a *pasodoble,* but it is full of original Sousa touches. It is a glorious march and well deserves its immense popularity, but it is surpassed, in my opinion, by *The Rifle Regiment,* which is much less familiar. There are of course good reasons for this, and these reasons bear on the basic nature and uses of the march itself. *The Rifle Regiment,* to begin with, is more difficult to play, a good bit more subtle, and cannot be done effectively by a band on the march. *The Gladiator,* on the other hand, is almost ideal for the marching band; it is straightforward, jaunty, and bold, and not technically impossible to play while parading. It is, however, difficult—as are nearly all of Sousa's marches—to play *well*!

The Gladiator was sold outright to a Philadelphia publisher for thirty-five dollars, and this remained the price the composer received for most of his famous marches until 1893. Several very lucky publishers thus secured at bargain rates such masterpieces of their kind as *Semper Fidelis* (1888), *The Thunderer* (1889), *The Washington Post* (1889), and *The High School Cadets* (1890). All of these were published in piano arrangements as well as band arrangements (and many of them in orchestra arrangements), and piano copies of *The High School Cadets,* for example, were ordered by dealers in lots of 20,000! (The piece, Sousa recalled, was often referred to as "The Ice-Cold Cadets.") The marches made Sousa's name a household word, but they did not make him rich. In 1890, a friend of Sousa's was able to report to him that he had heard no fewer than seventeen different bands playing *The Gladiator* during a single parade in Philadelphia.

The most famous of the early marches was unquestionably *The Washington Post,* named for the well-known newspaper and composed for a ceremony sponsored by that paper on June 15, 1889, "to encourage learning and literary expression in the public schools." The fiftieth anniversary edition of the newspaper recalled that the march "was an instantaneous hit, and soon all the bands in town were playing it." More important, perhaps, for the composer, it was selected by the Dancing Masters of America at their annual convention to introduce their new dance, the "two-step." When Sousa later went abroad, he found that the two-step itself was known as a "Washington Post."

The Washington Post soon was being played not only all over Europe, but also in places as remote as Borneo. Pirated editions rolled off the presses of a dozen countries, and when, at that time, a piece of American music was requested almost anywhere in the world, the chances were that the request would be answered with *The Washington Post.* Present-day march enthusiasts have forgotten that in the 1890s the march was not only a staple of the parade- and concert-band repertoire, but was also a ballroom dance and very often a topical song as well. Sousa thus arrived at precisely the right time to become a "hit" composer, for the circulation and popularity of his marches was vastly increased by the variety of their uses. At this time, it should be noted, when Sousa sold a march to a publisher, he was required to submit it in a version for piano and also to make arrangements for both band and orchestra. All this was included in the munificent purchase price!

By 1893, Sousa realized that he had given away a fortune, and in that year he reached an agreement with the John Church Company of Cincinnati and elsewhere for the publication of his works on a royalty basis. The first marches published by Church were *Manhattan Beach* and *The Liberty Bell*. *The Liberty Bell* brought Sousa a return of some $35,000 within a comparatively short time. (And, dear reader, remember that these were pre-1900 dollars, with no income tax!) This sum amounted to about twenty times what Sousa's annual salary had been as leader of the Marine Band before he realized, in 1892, that he was being grossly underpaid. One can hardly wonder that in that year he arrived at the decision that the time was ripe to launch his own independent "business" band, bearing his own name. He secured his release from the Marine Corps in July 1892, and on September 26 of the same year Sousa's new band gave its first concert, in Plainfield, New Jersey.

The forty-year history of the Sousa Band, from its founding in 1892 to the death of its conductor in 1932, needs little recounting. It was, as every reader knows, the most popular and successful band in history. It numbered among its members some of the greatest wind-instrument players of its time, and it created an enduring image of what a concert wind band ought to be. The band was never idle: it not only played in every part of the United States—lengthy engagements at fairs and expositions, and one-night stands at whistle-stops—but made four tours around the world. It was easily the best-known musical organization of its time. Sousa was fortunate to have as his manager in the early years of his band David Blakely, who had been manager of the Theodore Thomas Orchestra for a number of years, and who had also managed Patrick Gilmore's Band. Blakely had become acquainted with Sousa when he managed the Marine Band during the two tours that band had been permitted to make during the administration of President Benjamin Harrison. Blakely was also a music publisher, but in this field his judgment seems to have been less sure than it was in concert management. In *Marching Along*, Sousa recounts the following anecdote:

> I had understood from Mr. Blakely that he would undertake the publication of my compositions, since he had a large printing establishment in Chicago, so my first piece written after I went with Blakely was offered to him. This was the well-known *Belle of Chicago* March. Blakely rejected it and when I questioned his decision, he wrote me:

> > "My dear Sousa, a man usually makes one hit in his life. You have made two, *The Washington Post* and *The High School Cadets*. It is not reasonable to expect you to make another, so I am willing to let Coleman publish *The Belle of Chicago*."

Despite the fact that conducting his own band kept him as busy as any two ordinary men, Sousa was still anxious to make his mark as a composer of operettas. In 1895, a libretto was submitted to him by the manager of DeWolf Hopper's "Opera" Company, who reminded Sousa of Hopper's "happy recollection" of *Désirée*. The libretto, by Charles Klein, was that of *El Capitan*, and Sousa found it much to his liking. Klein was not, however, very apt at lyrics, and so Sousa, with the collaboration of a writer named Tom Frost, also provided these. Among the verses composed by Sousa were those for the show's most popular selections: *Sweetheart, I'm Waiting*; *A Typical Tune of Zanzibar*; and, needless to say, the two songs that were combined to form that everlasting favorite among all Sousa works, the march *El Capitan*.

The operetta opened in Boston on April 13, 1896, with DeWolf Hopper and his wife Edna Wallace Hopper in the leading roles. It enjoyed a moderate success, and was played on the usual touring circuit of those days; but it did not, as Sousa hoped, compete in popularity with the Gilbert and Sullivan operettas or with that greatest success among American operettas, Reginald De Koven's *Robin Hood*, which had appeared in 1890. *El Capitan* was revived a few years ago by Howard Shanet at Columbia University and proved amusing as a period piece. But its tunes, aside from the marches, simply are not in a class with those of Sullivan or of Victor Herbert, whose first operetta, *Prince Ananias*, was produced two years before *El Capitan*.

The careers of Sousa and Herbert overlapped almost exactly, both in time and in variety of activities. It is not generally remembered that Herbert assumed the leadership of the Twenty Second Regiment Band in 1892 (a post he held for seven years) or that he also wrote some of the finest marches of all time. Herbert is today remembered almost exclusively for the charming tunes from his operettas and Sousa only for his marches. Both might have wished it to be otherwise. At any rate, during the 1890s, both men wrote both marches and operettas, and established enduring places for themselves in American musical history. Herbert's early operettas included *The Serenade* (1896), *The Fortune Teller* (1898), and *Babes in Toyland* (1903), to mention only a few of the best-known. Sousa followed *El Capitan* with *The Bride Elect* (1897), *The Charlatan* (1898), and *Chris and the Wonderful Lamp* (1899).

All that remain from any of the Sousa operettas are the marches. It is a curious thing that, despite constant production of operettas, Sousa was never able to write a memorable tune that was not a march. On the other hand, it seemed impossible for him to write a march that was not memorable.

It should be noted that Sousa's marches do not all follow one pattern, as is often assumed and frequently stated, apparently by people who do not listen to them. It is true that all marches are in a two-to-a-bar rhythm, and consist for the most part of sixteen- or thirty-two-bar sections which are repeated. But within these patterns considerable variety is possible. The two-to-a-bar beat can be expressed as 2/4, 2/2 (*alla breve*), or 6/8 time, indicating that there are two quarter notes, two half notes, or two triplets to a measure. Sousa is truly the only great master of the 6/8 march, and this is the rhythm of many of his most effective ones: *Semper Fidelis, The Liberty Bell, King Cotton, The Washington Post*, and *Sabre and Spurs*, among others. The 6/8 march has a special swing, but in the hands of an untalented composer it can become a clumsy sort of trot. Sousa is certainly not the only composer to write delightful 6/8 marches (approximately half of all his marches are of the 6/8 type), but he is unquestionably the best and the most prolific.

The operetta marches, including *El Capitan, The Bride Elect, The Man Behind the Gun* (from *Chris and the Wonderful Lamp*), and *The Free Lance*, are unusual in that they combine the 6/8 and the 2/4. They are, in a sense, composites, but they all work beautifully, and the transition from one rhythm to another provides a mild musical shock that adds to their appeal. In each of these instances, Sousa took two separate numbers from the operetta and put them together for the concert version of the march. In *El Capitan* the opening strain is the song sung on his entrance by Don Medigua (who is also "El Capitan") in the first act. The words, by Sousa, are as follows:

	You see in me, my friends,
	A man of consummate bravery,
1st strain	My inmost nature tends
16 bars	To free the world from all slavery.
6/8	This thought then cherish,
	Though you perish
	Crush out Spanish knavery.
	Behold El Capitan.
2nd strain	Gaze on his misanthropic stare,
16 bars	Notice his penetrating glare;
6/8	Come match him, if you can,
	He is the champion beyond compare!

The second part of the march is taken from the Finale of Act II, and is in 2/4 time. The lyrics:

	Against the Spanish army	
	I must lead them, which is tough	
16 bars	(Chorus):	BOOM BOOM
2/4	I'll certainly get hurt,	BOOM BOOM

Unless I can desert,
                    BOOM BOOM
Although in this deception
I have dabbled quite enough
                    BOOM BOOM
I'll execute another little bluff
                    BOOM BOOM BOOM

(Chorus) break strain 4 bars	He'll lead them to the fray, They say they'll win the day, He'll lead them to the gory fray—
(Chorus) 16 bars 2/4	Unsheath the sword and the banners fly, When duty calls we will win or die; The trumpet note and the roll of drum Shall tell the foe the victors come. (twice)

The *El Capitan* March can thus be seen to consist of four sections (or strains) of equal length, sixteen bars each, with a four-bar introduction and a four-bar "break" or connecting section leading into the final chorus. Properly speaking, this is not a march with trio, but a song with chorus. Sousa used this four-strain form occasionally, as in *The High School Cadets* (which like many others has an eight-bar introduction), but his marches were more usually constructed of "A" and "B" sections, the "B" section being the Trio. Normally the "A" section consists of an introduction of four or eight bars, followed by two strains of sixteen bars each, and each repeated. In most marches Sousa then proceeds directly to the trio, the key of which is almost invariably an interval of a fourth higher. The trio will consist as a rule of a sixteen- or thirty-two-bar tune, repeated once or twice, with a "break strain" between the repetitions. In many marches, notably *The Stars and Stripes Forever*, the break strain is developed into a section of considerable importance, and is one of the highlights of the piece.

This most famous of all marches was composed in 1897, and according to the composer was what one refers to as an "inspiration." Sousa was in Europe when he heard the news of the sudden death of Blakely, his manager. He took the first available steamer back to New York, and tells this story in his autobiography:

> Here came one of the most vivid incidents of my career. As the vessel steamed out of the harbor I was pacing the deck, absorbed in thoughts of my manager's death and the many duties and decisions that awaited me in New York. Suddenly I began

to sense the rhythmic beat of a band playing within my brain. It kept on cease-lessly, playing, playing, playing. Throughout the whole tense voyage, that imagi-nary band continued to unfold the same themes, echoing and re-echoing the most distinct melody. I did not transfer a note of that music to paper while I was on the steamer, but when we reached shore, I set down the measures that my brain-band had been playing for me, and not a note of it has ever been changed. The composition is known the world over as *The Stars and Stripes Forever* and is prob-ably my most popular march.

Probably everyone who has ever heard a note of anything has heard *The Stars and Stripes*, and even knows how it goes. Some are also aware that Sousa himself wrote words for it. But there is no question that the best-known lyrics to the tune are not Sousa's ("Hurrah for the flag of the free! . . ."), but those of an unknown parodist ("Be kind to your web-footed friends . . .").

The Stars and Stripes Forever is one of the more characteristic Sousa marches. It consists of a four-bar introduction, two sixteen-bar strains, a twenty-four-bar break strain, and a thirty-two-bar trio, which is played three times. In this trio, the band plays softly the first time through, while on the repetition the piccolos play their famous counter melody, and for the grand finale the trombones thunder out still another counterpoint against the full force of the rest of the band. But of course the march is familiar to everyone, and needs no description. Sousa himself considered it his best, and the fact that it brought him (report-edly) over $300,000 in royalties must have added to his satisfaction.

Whether *The Stars and Stripes* is indeed Sousa's best march is a subject for debate among band buffs. Sousa composed about one hundred and forty marches, and not more than two dozen are now familiar to the public. This is a pity, for the quality of the marches is uniformly high, from *The Gladiator* and *The Rifle Regiment* of 1886, to *The Kansas Wild-cats* of 1931. The latter is, as a matter of fact, a rip-roaring, rowdy piece, with an intricate and technically challenging *obbligato* for the clarinets (in the second strain), and it is guar-anteed to send any audience home whistling and in good humor. There are, in all, perhaps twenty of the Sousa marches that I prefer to *The Stars and Stripes,* and this number would certainly include such magnificent examples as *The Fairest of the Fair* (1908), *Hands Across the Sea* (1899), *The Invincible Eagle* (1901), *The Gallant Seventh* (1922), and of course such beauties as *The Washington Post* and others of the early years.

One of the reasons for the general lack of familiarity with so many of the great marches is, as I have suggested above, that they are difficult. Many of them are too difficult to play on parade, and, in fact, most of them are too difficult to be played at all, as they were originally written, by the average high school band, which is now the average American idea of a band. They can, of course, be hacked at; but as every good bandmaster knows—and Sousa most definitely did!—one of the hardest things a band can be asked to do is to play a march well. None of Sousa's marches are simple-minded; they are forthright, which is not the same thing, but they are also full of ingenious touches, and many of them are extremely sophisticated within their self-imposed limits.

The characteristics of the Sousa march that are most immediately apparent are a strong and almost irresistible rhythmic propulsion and a wealth of jaunty and memorable tunes. But there is a good deal more: there is real invention and daring. Sousa's harmony is considerably more wide-ranging than that normally found in marches; he often makes surprising modulations and never confines himself to the simple chordal vocabulary of tonic, dominant, and sub-dominant that forms the basis of most other marches. He uses "color" chords effectively, and is very fond of excursions into the minor keys. All of these technical devices, even when they are not recognized as such by the people who whistle the tunes, contribute enormously to the effectiveness of the marches, and help to make them as interesting as they are.

Sousa also wrote good counterpoint, or, in the popular vocabulary, counter-melodies, but his sense of melodic movement was not confined to the obvious. The inner voicings in most of his marches are lively and interesting, and this is what is most often lacking in popular music in small forms. His bass lines are always solid and quite a bit more imaginative than the usual tonic-dominant oom-pah. But one of the most remarkable things about Sousa's style, almost unique in the march genre, is his telling use of rests. *The Rifle Regiment* and *Hands Across the Sea* are two fine examples of how effective a complete silence can be. Sousa may have admired and learned something from a famous earlier march, *The Washington Greys,* by Claudio Grafulla (d. 1880), who was bandmaster of the Seventh Regiment, N. Y. National Guard, during the Civil War and after. *The Washington Greys* is in a minor key and also uses rests with great effect; it is one of the few truly great pre-Sousa American marches. But if Sousa knew and admired it, which is probable, he soon surpassed it many times over.

Sousa had definite ideas as to what a march should be, and set them forth in *Marching Along:*

> . . . a march must be good. It must be as free from padding as a marble statue. Every line must be carved with unerring skill. Once padded, it ceases to be a march. There is no form of musical composition where the harmonic structure must be more clean-cut. The whole process is an exacting one. There must be a melody which appeals to the musical and unmusical alike. There must be no con-

fusion in counterpoints. The composer must, to be sure, follow accepted harmonization; but that is not enough. He must be gifted with the ability to pick and choose here and there, to throw off the domination of any one tendency. If he is a so-called purist in music, that tendency will rule his marches and will limit their appeal.

To go from Sousa's marches to his other compositions is a considerable letdown. The operettas and songs have been mentioned briefly, and that mention is sufficient. One should note that Sousa wrote ten operettas in all, and that he had hopes of one day writing a grand opera on an American subject. The last two of his operettas were *The Free Lance,* produced in 1906, with a ridiculous book by Harry B. Smith, the prolific operetta librettist who did *Robin Hood* for De Koven and a number of books for Victor Herbert; and *The Glass Blowers* (1909), with a book by Leonard Liebling. A study of the scores does not encourage one to think that either could be successfully revived: they are period pieces, but not yet quaint enough to be amusing.

Much the same must be said of the dozen suites and the variety of miscellaneous compositions that Sousa featured on his band programs. Many of these had a considerable vogue, and one or two are still occasionally heard. But such works as *The Chariot Race from Ben Hur* (described rather ambitiously as a "symphonic poem") or the "Scene Historical," *Sheridan's Ride,* are better thought about as belonging to the history of American popular taste than actually heard in concert. The suites, the best known and most popular of which was *The Last Days of Pompeii,* are essentially old-fashioned silent-movie music. Sousa himself thought highly of *The Last Days of Pompeii,* which he wrote in 1893, but which he deliberately withheld from publication until 1912. In an interview of about 1898, Sousa said that he considered it his best work and preferred it to anything else he had done. I have heard it performed as recently as a dozen years ago; it is almost unbelievably naïve, but its success in its time, and with the audiences for which it was performed, is quite understandable. It could conceivably be done today for a more sophisticated audience as a first-class specimen of musical "camp."

More interesting, at least from the standpoint of Americana, are the pieces that Sousa wrote for specific social or historical occasions, the grand march for the inauguration of President Garfield, for example, or *The Presidential Polonaise,* written at the request of President Chester A. Arthur for use at indoor ceremonies at the White House. *President Garfield's Inauguration March* was published in 1881 as Opus 131 (!), and clearly belongs to the days before processions down Pennsylvania Avenue were motorized. The *Polonaise,* too, evokes a picture of another day, and the idea of seeing it choreographed is one to dwell on.

Like most successful men, Sousa had immense energy. Tours with his band kept him on the road for a great part of each year, and must have been extremely taxing. Yet he found time and strength not only to compose constantly—the complete list of his musical works is quite lengthy—but also to write three novels, an autobiography, miscellaneous magazine articles, and an incredible amount of light verse, including lyrics for some of the operettas. The most successful of the novels is actually no more than a long short story. Entitled *The Fifth String*, it was published in 1902 by the Bobbs-Merrill Company, with illustrations by Howard Chandler Christy. The prose is a very deep purple, appropriate to the tale it unfolds of a great Italian violin virtuoso languishing for love of a haughty American society girl, and it is a bit hard to reconcile this with the style of the man who wrote *The Washington Post*. The meeting of hero and heroine will give an idea:

> During one of those sudden and inexplicable lulls that always occur in general drawing-room conversations, Diotti turned to Mrs. Llewellyn and whispered: "Who is the charming young woman just entering?"
>
> "The beauty in white?"
>
> "Yes, the beauty in white," softly echoing Mrs. Llewellyn's query. He leaned forward and with eager eyes gazed in admiration at the newcomer. He seemed hypnotized by the vision, which moved slowly from between the blue-tinted portières and stood for the instant, a perfect embodiment of radiant womanhood silhouetted against the silken drapery.
>
> "That is Miss Wallace, Miss Mildred Wallace, only child of one of New York's prominent bankers."
>
> "She is beautiful—a queen by divine right," cried he, and then with a mingling of impetuosity and importunity, entreated his hostess to present him.
>
> And thus they met.

A volume of Sousa's miscellaneous verse, excerpts from interviews, occasional jottings, anecdotes, letters, and magazine articles was published in 1910 by the Thomas Y. Crowell Company under the title *Through the Years with Sousa;* it gives an indispensable picture of the man, and must be read, along with the autobiography, to appreciate the flavor of Sousa as a person and as a personality. There is as yet no adult biography of Sousa; several books, written for children, or for the lightweight women's magazine trade, have appeared, but these, needless to say, are not entirely reliable. For that matter, Sousa's own *Marching Along* is not free of inconsistencies and inaccuracies. A good full-length book on Sousa, similar to Edward Waters' invaluable book on Victor Herbert, would be a welcome addition to American musical bibliography.

Paul Bierley of Columbus, Ohio, a long-time admirer of Sousa, has been working on such a book for many years,[†] and I am indebted to him for some information about early Sousa Band recordings. The earliest Sousa recordings, according to Mr. Bierley, were made in 1902 (Victor Nos. 242, 660, and 1193), and included the marches *Hail to the Spirit of Liberty* (composed in 1900, and, incidentally, one of the very best), *Semper Fidelis,* and *The Liberty Bell.* Other early recordings were made for the Edison and Monarch labels, but it is difficult to establish the dates with certainty. The majority, in any case, were made for Victor over the span of years from 1902 to 1931. There are not, however, as many as one would imagine, or would wish to have for documentary purposes. Most of the better-known marches were recorded at one time or another, but very few were re-recorded at later dates to take advantage of improved and improving recording techniques.

The recording business inevitably drew Sousa's attention once again to the economic problems of the composer, as it introduced a new element into the question of copyright protection. No composer at the time benefited in any way (except for publicity) through public performances for profit of his work. And since Sousa, as the most-performed composer in America, had a stake that was obviously very high, he took part in the discussions and activities that led, in February 1914, to the formation of The American Society of Composers, Authors, and Publishers (ASCAP). Sousa was one of the founders and charter members, along with Victor Herbert, and served as a director and vice-president from 1924 until his death. Thus, in a very real way, all American composers, lyricists, and music publishers remain in his debt.

Sousa remained active to the time of his death on March 6, 1932, in Reading, Pennsylvania, where he had gone to conduct a high school band. The Sousa Band stayed in business to the end, and its conductor continued to write new marches. Eleven of these were published in the years 1930 and 1931, and at least two of them, *The Harmonica Wizard* and *The Kansas Wildcats,* although seldom played and apparently not known even to most bandmasters, are especially attractive and can take their places with the best.

It is obvious that the memory of the Sousa Band itself is fading; the few recordings that exist do not do it justice, and there are each year fewer surviving players whose authentic recollections contribute to a real appreciation of the band's style. There are, of course, many thousands who can remember hearing the band, but for most of these it is a legend that they recall. The marches do live on, however, and keep the name of Sousa as well known and popular as ever. No one needs to campaign for their revival or to make a special case for their performance. In a somewhat unblushing statement, Sousa once declared that the only influence American composers could be said to have had on the international

---

[†] It has since been published as *John Philip Sousa: American Phenomenon* (New York: Appleton-Century-Crofts, 1973).

scene was shown in imitations of Stephen Foster's ballads or his own marches. In his lifetime this may even have had a grain of truth; in any case, Sousa understood quite well his originality as a specifically American composer, and was proud of it.

Sousa's own performance of his marches is now the subject of a somewhat confused verbal tradition. His tempos, however, as shown by most of the early recordings and verified by the recollections of his players, were on the whole rather slower than those generally taken by bandmasters today. This surely seems to be the only possible and proper style when one remembers the basic conception of the march as a form of dance. There is a good deal of evidence, however, to indicate that Sousa took slightly faster tempos as he grew older; but there is no evidence to justify the rather hectic speeds one often hears today. The content of the marches, with their genuine musical sophistication and occasional subtlety, also demands a speed at which one can hear distinctly; otherwise much is lost. And much *is* lost too much of the time. The published versions of the marches do not include many of the dynamic indications, accents, and other touches that made Sousa's own performances so distinctive. Sousa as a performer wanted to keep his own little bag of tricks to himself, and requested that completely and properly edited versions of his marches not be published until after his death. Since that time, some attempts have been made in this direction, but proper performance *à la* Sousa must depend today largely on the oral tradition, which is rapidly disappearing. And as the marches come into the public domain (fifty-six years after publication), many of them have been "simplified" for the use of high school bands, and in these versions they lost much of their character. These are counterfeits, but they are, alas, what is often heard and passed off as genuine Sousa.

The American march style, as established by Sousa, has not changed very much, and has certainly not improved since his time. There have been many fine marches written, of course, but in any list of the one hundred best American marches, if one wanted to make one, at least forty and possibly more would have to be by the March King himself. This is an impressive legacy of its kind; and it is, moreover, one that we can perhaps only now begin to estimate at its true value.

Wallingford Riegger
HiFi/Stereo Review XX/4 (April 1968)

The case of Wallingford Riegger, some seven years after his death on April 2, 1961, shortly before his seventy-sixth birthday, remains one of the most puzzling in the annals of music in America. His music, shamefully neglected during most of his lifetime, enjoyed a small critical and even public vogue during the Fifties, but is now once again much underrated and generally overlooked. And yet this is the music of a man highly esteemed by most of his professional colleagues and rightly regarded by many as one of the most original and important composers America has produced.

Riegger was never very notably in the public eye. He pursued his career quietly and independently, was never associated with publicity-minded groups or institutions, and was, as a person, unusually modest and unaggressive. Public recognition of a major sort did not come to him until 1948, late in his career, when his Third Symphony unanimously won the New York Critics Circle Award. And this symphony, composed when he was sixty-two years old, was also the first major orchestral commission he had ever received!

Nevertheless, Riegger was known, at least to musicians, as an important and striking composer as far back as the Twenties. When I was a student in those years, the name Riegger was one that was always mentioned among the members of the American avant-garde. The scandal produced by Stokowski's 1929 performance of Riegger's *Study in Sonority* was vivid. And the noise generated by the group known as the Pan-American Association of Composers (including Ives, Varèse, Cowell, Riegger, Slonimsky, Ruggles, and Chávez) was not inconsiderable, though of brief duration.

One wonders what happened. Perhaps an accident of timing, a chain of unavoidable circumstances. Riegger was no longer a young man in the Twenties, when American music had its first explosive thrust to maturity. The generation of Copland, Harris, and Gershwin (as well as rising younger men) was in the center of the stage. We know that both Varèse and Ruggles suffered eclipses similar to Riegger's over a period of years, and that both of them, like Riegger, "reappeared" at a later time, revalued and respected.

That they were too "radical" when their works were first heard is unquestionably true. Almost no one in America was ready for music of such dissonance, force, and novelty. But this is not the entire story. The composer Elliott Carter, in the *Bulletin* of the American Composers Alliance (1952), wrote:

Riegger has followed the dictates of his own personality and musical instinct unobtrusively for years, without caring whether he was or was not in step with the fashions of the time, or, apparently, whether he would become known or his music performed. . . . While Riegger has been quietly writing music, a host of aggressive, younger composers has appeared, most of them more impatient than he to gain acclaim. . . . So he was generally overlooked in favor of composers more determined and skilful about personal promotion. However, a number of still younger musicians, feeling the need for a change from points of view prevalent in the 1930s and 40s, have recently found him out and begun to take his music with the seriousness it deserves. . . .

My own article on Riegger, published in *The Musical Quarterly* for January 1950,[†] was, rather belatedly, the first large-scale critical appreciation of this composer to appear in any periodical, here or abroad. Even at that time, there was little critical material on which to draw—melancholy evidence of a lack of appreciation not only on the part of the public, but also on the part of those critics and journalists who are supposed to lead and enlighten the public. True, there had been honorable exceptions, notably Paul Rosenfeld and Alfred Frankenstein, and fellow composers John J. Becker, Henry Cowell, and Otto Luening, who had all on occasion called attention to the qualities of Riegger's work. But performances continued to be few and far between, and it was not until after 1950 that Riegger's music was taken up enthusiastically by many. But it is pleasant to record that for at least a decade Riegger enjoyed the knowledge that his music had made an impression.

Wallingford Riegger was a remarkable man, one for whom I have great admiration and affection both as a man and as a musician. He was, in the old-fashioned sense of the phrase, a man of character. He bore up under a life that was seldom easy with patience and with humor, regarded himself humbly and his art with humility, and was honest with himself and with others. He thought that "glamour" was rather funny. He had too much humor and sense of balance ever to strike a pose or to be impressed by a sense of his own importance. He had high principles and scruples, both morally and musically, and he never abandoned them. And he never looked for an easy way of doing things, an easy avenue to success, or a compromise that might produce some passing advantage.

It is one of the enduring peculiarities of American musical life that so many of its manifestations are tied to awards, festivals, anniversaries, dedications of buildings, and other nonessential activities that produce a flurry of promotional merchandising. And so Riegger

[†]In this volume pp. 15-32.

enjoyed brief fame when he received the award of the New York Critics Circle, and basked in congratulatory messages on the occasions of his seventieth and seventy-fifth birthdays, when, having survived, he more or less officially became a "grand old man" or even a "dean." His seventy-fifth birthday, in fact, brought forth exhilarating messages from people as diverse as William Schuman, Leopold Stokowski, Henry Cowell, Douglas Moore, and Leonard Bernstein. But there were, and are, still no recordings of *Dichotomy*, the wonderful Piano Quintet, and *Study in Sonority*, and a great deal of Riegger's other major work.[†] Riegger himself took all of the jollification with some amusement, and wondered what he was supposed to wear when being presented with a citation.

Wallingford Riegger was born on April 29, 1885, in Albany, Georgia, into a highly literate and musical family. His father, Constantin Riegger, owned a lumber mill, but was a musician at heart, and played the violin well. He was also active as a choir director. His mother, Ida Wallingford, was an accomplished pianist. There was always music, that of cultivated amateurs, in the home. When Wallingford was three, the lumber mill burned down, and his parents decided to return to Indianapolis, where both had been born. There, a few years later, Wallingford began to study the violin under the tutelage of one Beisenherz, an elderly gentleman who claimed to have been a pupil of Ludwig Spohr. Riegger said, later in life, that he practiced as little as possible, but he was obviously musical, and was amazed to learn, at the age of ten or thereabouts, that not everyone has perfect pitch. At this same time, he learned the rudiments of harmony, and played the piano by ear, no doubt with some instruction from his mother.

When the family moved to New York in 1900, it was decreed that Wallingford should learn the cello, so that the family could have its own string quartet. A younger brother, Harold, played the viola, and an uncle the violin. The family, as Riegger acknowledged, "was loaded with talent." In the course of time, Riegger recalled, "our volumes of Haydn, Mozart, and Beethoven became well worn, and I can truly say that these Sunday afternoon quartet rehearsals were among my most enjoyable musical experiences." Wallingford was supposed to go into his father's business (at that time plumbing supplies) upon graduation from high school, but he won a scholarship to Cornell University to study languages, and thus, as he put it, "staved off the evil hour." Music, however, proved to be a stronger interest, and he left Cornell after one year in order to enter the Institute of Musical Art as a cello student. Riegger's teacher there was Alvin Schroeder of the Kneisel Quartet. At the same time, he began studies in composition with Percy Goetschius. Riegger became a member of the Institute's first graduating class in 1907. He was then twenty-two years of age.

Of his studies with Goetschius, Riegger preserved a grateful memory, which may seem strange to some, since Goetschius was renowned as an arch-conservative even in the first

---

[†]To some degree, the picture is different now. Cf. the *Schwann Record & Tape Guide*.

decade of the century. But Riegger was aware of Goetschius' gifts as a teacher and disciplinarian, and in a letter to me dated September 11, 1949, he wrote:

> Goetschius, by the way—and this estimate, I think, is objective—was our greatest theoretician, and has not since been equalled. This in spite of his stopping with Wagner. . . .

A letter, amusing in retrospect, was sent to Riegger by Goetschius in June 1907, urging his former student and recent graduate to become a composer and to think of the cello as a means of livelihood. The letter concluded with the following exhortation:

> And let me warn you, most earnestly, to avoid the teachings of the ultra-modern school. If you will build your foundation on the principles of the *classic* ideals, you will (if diligent) one day attain the master's rank.

Riegger wrote a charming and instructive autobiographical sketch for the August 1939 issue of *The Magazine of Art,* in which he recalled many of the incidents of the next few years of his life and studies. In his own words:

> In 1907, not long after graduating from the Institute, I received a letter from Berlin from my old chum, Rudolph Reuter, who had enrolled at the *Hochschule.* In New York our favorite resort had been an ice-cream parlor on St. Anne's Avenue in the Bronx, where we used to annoy the proprietor's wife, a matter-of-fact woman who had no ear for harmonic niceties, by whistling "Merrily We Roll Along" in parallel fifths.
>
> To make a long story short, the next Fall saw me on the *Kronprinzessin Cäcilie,* leaving a Hoboken pier and familiar faces in the distance, en route to Berlin, then the Mecca of music students throughout the world.

Riegger goes on to describe his three years of study in Germany as "intensive, extensive, and expensive." He studied cello at first with Robert Hausmann, of the Joachim Quartet, and later with the celebrated Anton Hekking. In composition, he worked under Max Bruch and the American Edgar Stillman Kelley, then residing in Berlin. His daily schedule was

> . . . five hours' cello practice, two hours' piano and at least one hour at counterpoint. Besides this, I played cello in one orchestra, viola in another, belonged to smaller ensemble groups and attended one hundred and fifty orchestra concerts the first season alone, usually with small scores in my pocket. . . . Arthur Nikisch, who conducted the Berlin Philharmonic, was my idol, and has not, in my opinion, been equalled since. Richard Strauss conducted the Opera House orchestra, usually giving brilliant interpretations, but being at times indifferent and erratic (probably when a new opera was on his mind). . . .

As if this schedule were not enough, Riegger read the German classics, dipped into philosophy and the natural sciences, "did" the art galleries, museums, and cathedrals "with a vengeance, and got side-tracked on French poetry. . . ." He realized, after a time, that in order to become a composer, he would have to be more singleminded; but at the same time, he was much attracted to the idea of conducting. He made his debut as a conductor in 1910 with the Blüthner Orchestra, then the second-ranking organization in Berlin, in a program consisting of the Tchaikovsky Sixth, the Brahms Third, and the Saint-Saëns Cello Concerto, with Hekking as soloist. He conducted from memory, a procedure not too common at the time, and received a good press.

But funds from home were running out, and Riegger's student days were ending. He returned to the United States and took a position as cellist in the St. Paul Symphony Orchestra. Riegger described this as "a pioneer existence in more ways than one." But by playing hotel and movie-theater jobs on the side, he was able to make enough money to marry his high-school sweetheart, Rose Schramm, during the first year in St. Paul. Through the three years he remained in St. Paul, conducting became more and more his principal interest, and in April 1914 he managed to secure a post as assistant conductor in the Stadttheater of Würzburg in Bavaria. He spent the next several years in wartime Germany, conducting in Königsberg as well as Würzburg, and finally returning to Berlin to conduct the Blüthner Orchestra during the season of 1916-1917.

The Rieggers returned once again to the United States in March 1917, and Wallingford attempted to find a position as an orchestral conductor. As he wryly commented forty years later in an interview with Jay Harrison (New York *Herald Tribune,* April 7, 1957):

> I was perfectly willing to take over the New York Philharmonic or the Philadelphia. I was even willing to *move* to Philadelphia if it was absolutely necessary. The orchestra managers, however, didn't see it my way, and so I made a compromise—I accepted a job teaching cello at Drake University in Des Moines. And it was at Drake that I completed my first major composition.

This first major composition was a Trio in B Minor, for violin, cello, and piano, completed in 1920. It is a thoroughly conservative work, but written with obvious skill. As Eric Salzman commented when the Trio was finally recorded in 1960 (the recording is now out of print):

> It is an enormously competent and professional work in a thoroughly unoriginal style. There is a certain faded elegance in the Fauré-like contours, the old-fashioned gestures, and the attractive instrumental writing. He could prove that he knew how to draw.

The Trio won for Riegger the Paderewski Prize, and was published as Opus 1 by the Society for the Publication of American Music. It was not an inauspicious debut, and had Riegger continued to write in this traditional and conservative style, he might have enjoyed a modest but continuing success. He would, however, today be ranked with Edgar Stillman Kelley or Henry Holden Huss or Daniel Gregory Mason, names that the younger generation will recall with some difficulty.

Riegger's next few works were, in fact, quite respectable; they were successfully performed and generally admired. His setting of Keats' *La Belle Dame sans Merci*, Opus 4, composed in 1923, for four solo voices and chamber orchestra, received its first performance at the Berkshire Festival in September 1924, with the composer conducting, and won the Elizabeth Sprague Coolidge Prize for chamber music. It was the first work by an American composer to be so honored. A review in the Baltimore *Evening Sun* stated that "it proved a work of real imagination and not a little strength and received a reception so cordial as to amount to something akin to an ovation."

In view of the decisive step Riegger was about to take, this review is immensely significant. Few composers can resist anything "akin to an ovation," but it is striking evidence of Riegger's strength of character that that is exactly what he did. He came to the conclusion, out of inner conviction, and after three years of thought, that he was on the wrong track as a composer. From 1923 until 1926 he wrote nothing at all, devoting the time to a serious reconsideration of his musical position and beliefs. He had realized, even while in Berlin as a student, that he "had not resolved the conflict between the old and the new." Again, in his own words:

> In my childhood experiments at the keyboard I had invented whole-tone chords (literally invented, not having been exposed to any) and yet the home influence and all my training had been along orthodox lines. The *Hochschule* had made me a confirmed Brahmsite; I revelled in the works of the classic and for that matter the romantic period, and falsely construed them in the light of norms in my own creative undertakings—or to put it bluntly, I blushingly admit to having upheld at that time the good old academic tradition, so much so that at the first Berlin performance of Scriabin's *Poème de l'Extase* I hissed exactly in the same manner as did the Philadelphia box-holders twenty years later when Stokowski gave my own *Study in Sonority*.

The *Study in Sonority*, a crucial work in Riegger's career, was written in 1926-1927, and revealed the thoroughness with which Riegger had reconsidered. It is, even today, an "advanced" work, certainly one of powerful originality in idiom, texture, sonority, and logic.

As a first essay in a new style, it is absolutely realized; there is nothing tentative or hesitant about it, and it remains an extraordinary accomplishment. Shockingly, it has never been recorded.[†] But Stokowski did have the courage to present it to a Philadelphia subscription audience and, as Riegger noted, the audience, not surprisingly, was horrified and angry. Its strength was recognized, for the most part, only by fellow musicians, although even Olin Downes, not noted for his receptivity to modern music, recognized that the work was mature and sophisticated, with "some beautiful effects in the atonal manner," and added that Riegger "is obviously a musician with a keen ear for sonorous values, whose studies appear to have been very thorough." Henry Cowell, as might have been expected, hailed the work and also gave, in a review in the San Francisco *Argonaut* (October 18, 1930), a brief technical description:

> Wallingford Riegger's *Sonorities* for ten violins is a well written composition which explores many new possibilities of sonorous combinations of violins. Riegger establishes a new and self-invented dissonance as a tonic chord, from which the music proceeds, and to which it returns. He also establishes another dissonance as a dominant chord, which always resolves to the tonic. In this way he induces a logic which the ear can readily follow, though the material is very complex. Emotionally, the work soars like the choiring of angels in the altissimo register of ten fiddles.

As the reader will have learned from Cowell's review, the *Study in Sonority* was not written for full orchestra, but for ten violins (or any multiple of ten), itself a novel and imaginative conception. And Riegger did invent a sharply dissonant harmonic scheme that was both bold and logical. Virgil Thomson, commenting on a 1952 performance of the piece, stated that it "is dissonant in the grand way . . . the work of a master craftsman with a rich fancy. Atonal in harmony, elaborate in contrapuntal design, airy in texture, animated, atmospheric, and witty all at the same time. . . ."

The *Study in Sonority* announces, and almost completely reveals, the elements of Riegger's mature style. But his next work of major importance carried some of the characteristic elements somewhat further, and added one other technical procedure that Riegger used more or less consistently in his later work. *Dichotomy*, composed in 1931-1932, is based on two tone rows, the independence and opposition of which gives rise to the title. The tone rows are not orthodox Schoenbergian ones of twelve tones (Schoenberg's first avowedly twelve-tone works date from 1923), nor are they used in a manner reminiscent of Schoenberg. The rows in *Dichotomy* are of eleven and ten notes, respectively. The astonishing fact is that Riegger knew very little of Schoenberg's work or theories at that time. And although in later works he did use twelve-tone rows, and was, of course, an enthusiastic

---

[†]No longer true.

admirer of Schoenberg, Riegger's approach to atonality or dodecaphony remained entirely his own, and even his most strictly written twelve-tone works can never be mistaken for those of any rigid adherent of the Viennese school.

Both the *Study in Sonority* and *Dichotomy* reveal Riegger's fondness for melodies of highly profiled, almost jagged, contour, his rhythmic inventiveness and drive, his fondness for contrasting strains of pure unaccompanied melody with block harmonies of crushing dissonance. These harmonies are often built on seconds, and can, in some instances, be described as "tone clusters." But Riegger also retained a mastery of contrapuntal styles—fugue, canon, fugato—and of such traditional forms as the passacaglia, the sonata, and the theme and variations. Both of these works also reveal Riegger's wonderful sense of sonority and texture. *Dichotomy*, which was first performed in Berlin by Nicolas Slonimsky in 1932, was composed for chamber orchestra, and is utterly brilliant in sound. It retains, after thirty-five years, an astonishing freshness. It has never been widely performed in this country, and, like the *Study in Sonority*, is unfortunately not available in recorded form.[†]

Aside from Stokowski's performance of the *Study in Sonority*, Riegger had only one other major orchestral performance in the United States prior to 1948. That was when Erich Kleiber performed the *Rhapsody*, Opus 5, with the New York Philharmonic on October 29, 1931. The *Rhapsody*, a work for large orchestra, was written at about the same time as the *Study in Sonority*, and Riegger considered it, even much later in life, to be one of his best works. He described it as "atonal except for an impressionistic part in the middle . . . not twelve-tone." It was this piece that caused Paul Rosenfeld to write a brief article about Riegger, in *The New Republic*, which began:

> There would be little profit in leaving the field without attempting to make amends, to the full extent of our small powers, to an American composer stupidly neglected by the musical press. This composer is Wallingford Riegger, and the poor treatment he received at the hands of the professional critics incidental to the performance of his *Rhapsody* for orchestra . . . was characteristic. Some of the writers gave him space while others did not, but none gave him any of the applause his piece richly merited; and evidently for no better reason than the one that, with the exception of an episode in the middle of the *Rhapsody*, which was chromatic in scheme, the whole composition was atonal, or rather, free of diatonic tonality. Yet it was evidently the work of an excellent musician, magnificent in texture and consistent in idea, grateful to the ear and lucid in form.

Riegger had returned East in 1922, and had taught first at New York's Institute of Musical Art (later to merge with the Juilliard Foundation) and then at the Ithaca Conservatory.

[†]Two recordings are now (1979) available.

Shortly after winning the Coolidge Prize, he was awarded an honorary degree of Doctor of Music by the Cincinnati Conservatory, almost the last public recognition or award he received until 1948. In the late Twenties he returned to New York, where he enjoyed "Villaging" for a while, but also became acquainted with some of the pioneer figures in modern music in America, including Varèse, Ives, Cowell, and Ruggles. Realizing that he was "spiritually akin to them," he aligned himself with them, and, as he wrote:

> We had rejected the neo-classicism of a war-weary Paris, and had struck out for ourselves, each in his own way. We formed, of the remains of the International Composers Guild and the Pro-Musica Society, a new organization, the Pan-American Association of Composers (which included Latin-Americans) and gave numerous concerts here and abroad.

> It was undoubtedly the most anomalous chapter in American music, or in music anywhere. Here was a group of serious composers, literally making music history and yet without the slightest show of interest on the part of those newspaper pundits who are supposed to keep their readers informed. We gave, at no end of effort and sacrifice, concerts of our own and of Latin-American works, with a generous sprinkling of works by younger composers. In justice I must say that once we did obtain a review. It was of a program given at the New School for Social Research, and appeared in the New York *Post,* but unfortunately the day before the concert, which had been postponed at the last minute.

The review of the concert that did not take place is matched in Riegger's experience by the publication of his *Study in Sonority.* A major publisher undertook to bring out the work, evidently feeling that a composer who had won the Paderewski and Coolidge Prizes must be fairly safe, and that a piece for ten violins might be much used by violin teachers with large classes. The composer's royalty statement, the first year after publication, showed to Riegger's delight that *one* copy had been sold, and that he had earned ten cents. The following year's statement indicated, however, that the one copy had been returned, and the ten cents was deducted from future earnings.

Riegger's financial situation during most of these years necessitated his finding a means of livelihood, as composing was obviously not going to provide enough to eat. Fortunately, his thorough German training and his obviously meticulous craftsmanship in traditional media enabled him to find work in editing, arranging, proofreading, and other necessary, if time-consuming, professional chores. Riegger never minded hard work, nor did he feel that society was obligated to support him. Over the years, working for various publishers, he turned out some seven hundred choral arrangements alone, ranging in style from Palestrina motets to such evergreens as *Tea for Two* and *Shortnin' Bread,* arranged for almost every conceivable combination of voices. For these potboilers, he used a variety of pen names, including William Richards, Gerald Wilfring Gore, John H. McCurdy (a family name on his mother's side), George Northrup, Robert Sedgwick, Leonard Gregg, Edwin Farrell, and Edgar Long, some of them doubtless better known than Wallingford Riegger.

From 1933 through 1939, Riegger composed almost exclusively for modern dancers and their companies. He had written a score for Martha Graham in 1930, and had become an ardent admirer of her work. Other dancers for whom he composed included Doris Humphrey, Hanya Holm, Helen Tamiris, Charles Weidman, Anna Sokolow, and Eric Hawkins, practically a *Who's Who* of the American dance in those years. Most of these works involved themes of what is generally known as "social protest," a fundamental concern of the dance world at that time, with which Riegger was completely in sympathy. Despite his German background and training, Riegger was revolted by the Nazi regime, and ardently supported the Republicans in Spain. He became known for his outspokenly liberal views and was, of course, widely regarded as a dangerous Leftist, which obviously did not make things easier for him. He was, in the course of time, accused of being a Communist, or at least a sympathizer, and eventually, during the heyday of Joseph McCarthy, was called before the House Committee on Un-American Activities, which was investigating possible Communist influence at the Metropolitan Music School, of which Riegger was president-emeritus.

Murray Kempton, in the New York *Post* of April 10, 1957, commented as follows:

> Wallingford Riegger belongs among our few serious composers of substance, somewhere by himself with Roger Sessions. . . . He is a composer of monumental integrity; he went on in his grain during the most savage period of Soviet attacks on the bourgeois formalism of music like his. He was not so much resistant as absolutely inattentive to the aesthetic theories of Andrei Zhadanov; and this is the man the Un-American Activities Committee presents to us as submissive to Communist dictation.

> Wallingford Riegger, by the way, spit in the committee's eye with an elderly grace which would have suited Bach better in his relations with the Margrave of Brandenburg. "As an American," he said, "I fear the loss of my self-respect if I answered you." Riegger was standing on the First Amendment alone; the committee told him that he wasn't "being very smart." This means that he could expect to go to jail, and that is perhaps not very smart. It is, however, in the lonely, noble tradition of this old man's life.

Riegger's music for the dance is perhaps the least viable part of his work, though it served its purpose admirably, and at least one of the scores he did, the Finale of *New Dance,* achieved a certain popularity. Riegger arranged this Finale for a number of instrumental combinations. Two other dance scores, one composed for Doris Humphrey and the other for Martha Graham, were later reworked and used as movements of his Third and Fourth Symphonies, respectively. Riegger used to love to recount an anecdote connected with his composing for the dance. At one point, it appears, a prominent dancer came to him with a request for a new work—"something slow and noble, in three-quarter time, you know: one, two, THREE, um; one, two, THREE, um. . . ." Riegger wrote, as requested, a slow and noble piece, four quarters to the bar, and everyone was satisfied.

Riegger's last score for the dance was written in 1941, and he never returned to this type of composition. Shortly before the end of what may be called his "dance period," he began working on his first String Quartet and on an orchestral piece entitled *Consummation* (later re-written as *Music for Orchestra,* Opus 50). At about the same time, he produced several fine choral works and the lovely Canon and Fugue for Strings, Opus 33, one of his few works currently available on recordings. The most productive period in his career was under way; for the next twenty years, he continued to compose steadily, and although he could never be called a prolific or facile composer, he had reached the fairly impressive total of seventy-five opus numbers by the time of his death. Riegger as a rule composed slowly, revised extensively, edited his works with disciplined responsibility, and felt very strongly the need for absolute control and clarity of his ideas. At no time did he ever rely on the doctrinaire application of a system or method, nor was he ever attracted to casual music-making. Riegger felt strongly that the primary responsibility of the artist is to himself, and this responsibility he never shirked.

Throughout this final period of his creative life, Riegger's individuality of expression became, if anything, more accentuated, which is made more remarkable by the fact that he continued to write in several fairly well-differentiated styles. Riegger made a little catalog of his works in about 1950, in which he grouped his compositions as: Non-dissonant (mostly), Impressionist, Partly Dissonant, and Dissonant. The works labeled "Impressionist" are of course all early works, but Riegger never disavowed them. Although most of the works of his later years were atonal and dissonant, many being written in strict or free twelve-tone technique, others were more or less tonal and traditional. Thus, while the First String Quartet represents one of Riegger's most strict applications of the twelve-note idiom, the Canon and Fugue for Strings of about the same time is clearly tonal and neo-Baroque in character. Yet each piece bears the unmistakable Riegger stamp.

Riegger's achievement as a musical architect was that of combining, especially in his later works, an advanced harmonic and rhythmic idiom with traditional structures. He did this in a way unlike that of any other composer of this century. Basically, despite its wealth of invention and the depth of its technical vocabulary, Riegger's music is uncomplicated, almost always direct, and as concise as possible. Riegger strove for clarity and logic and never padded a work by so much as a single measure. He felt that the enlargement of the tonal vocabulary in the twentieth century was not a license to greater freedom for the composer, but on the contrary imposed on him an even greater need for discipline. In this sense his use of set forms acted as an integrating factor binding his work to a tradition from which, at first hearing, it may appear remote.

Riegger discarded two symphonies he wrote during the Forties (a measure of his self-criticism), and so did not actually write a symphony until 1946-1947, when he completed his Third on commission from the Alice M. Ditson Fund of Columbia University. As noted earlier, he was then past sixty years of age, outdoing even Brahms in waiting to be sure that he was "ready for a symphony." He was indeed ready; the Third Symphony is one of the finest works in the whole body of American music, and is still probably the single work of Riegger's that one would choose (if one were limited) to represent him most typically. The symphony demonstrates Riegger's application of twelve-tone techniques as well as his independence in their use. It is not written in a strict style, following the methods of Schoenberg or Webern, but uses a row as a basis of melodic and harmonic structure in three of the four movements, while modifying it or departing from it more or less at will. The reader interested in detailed technical analyses will be able to find several in various periodicals, but such analysis is less important for the layman than the general impression of power, order, and expressiveness that the symphony can hardly fail to convey. The melodic contours are full of contrast, the rhythmic vigor is extraordinary, and the scoring is full of imagination. Alfred Frankenstein described the symphony as "a work of great energy and impact . . . there is a grand, abrasive brutality about it . . . its orchestration rings clear and hard as hammer blows on steel, and at heart it is as romantic as anything of Mahler's." Henry Cowell (who, incidentally, was one of our finest music critics) also felt the strong Romantic impulse in this symphony and in other music of Riegger's, and noted that

> His real allegiance to music as a language of expression, rather than to "pure" music alone, is betrayed by his amused disregard of the idea, common among musicians, that any form must be followed slavishly to the bitter end. The enormous success of his Third Symphony was not due to its good construction, but to the fact that this well-constructed work had wide emotional appeal. . . .

Cowell mentions that the symphony was an enormous success. It was Riegger's first such success with the public, and, in fact, with many musicians who had previously had little opportunity to become familiar with Riegger's music. Its first performance at Columbia University's Fourth Annual Festival of Contemporary Music (May 16, 1948) was followed by several others in this country and a considerably larger number abroad. In 1951 it was recorded as a result of a Naumburg Award. This was, of course, also Riegger's first major recording.

A succession of stunning works followed the symphony, many of them commissioned as a result of Riegger's sudden celebrity. Among the most remarkable in the entire catalog of his works is the *Music for Brass Choir*, Opus 45, begun in 1948 and first performed under my direction on April 8, 1949. Like the *Study in Sonority*, which it in some ways resembles, it is a dazzlingly original conception not only in sonority and texture, but in musical content as well. The score calls for ten trumpets, eight horns, ten trombones, two tubas, and timpani. Such a massing of brass instruments had not been undertaken since the days of Giovanni Gabrieli, but needless to say, Riegger's music is rather different in style. There are twenty-six independent voices, only the horns being two to a part. The work opens with an unaccompanied melodic motif on the horn, followed by a six-note tone cluster on trombones, and the eight-minute work is built almost entirely on these elements. The tone clusters grow larger and thicker as the work progresses, climaxing in a twenty-six-note cluster that is one of the most remarkable sounds in all music. By a curious acoustical effect, this unheard-of dissonance is extremely gentle and mysterious to the ear. It is not only, as Henry Cowell pointed out, "a sound unprecedented in music . . . but an intensely exciting musical experience." And as Virgil Thomson put it, the whole work is "as impressive to the mind as it is invigorating to the ear."

The year 1948 also marked the completion of Riegger's Second String Quartet, Opus 43. This, unlike the first Quartet, does not use the twelve-tone idiom at all, but is freely atonal. It has the poise of an absolutely mature work, and is one of the most immediately accessible of Riegger's major compositions. From 1948 on, Riegger was able to compose more steadily, as he received a number of commissions for works and invitations to hold visiting professorships. The variety of work is interesting: aside from his Fourth Symphony (1957), two major symphonic works commissioned by the Louisville Orchestra, and several other orchestral works in various forms, Riegger wrote a number of fine songs, an assortment of chamber music, and even (on commission) a piece for solo accordion. Among the chamber works are several for winds and brass, and Riegger thus helped to provide some additional ensemble literature in this comparatively neglected area. Among these pieces are a Nonet for Brass, Opus 49 (1951); a Woodwind Quintet, Opus 51 (1952); a Concerto for Piano and Woodwind Quintet, Opus 53 (1952); and a Movement for Two Trumpets, Trombone, and Piano, Opus 66 (1957).

Music for Orchestra, Opus 50, was a revision, done in 1951, of a work entitled *Consummation*, Opus 31, completed in 1939 but never performed. At some point in the Forties Riegger told me that he did not consider it as successful as *Dichotomy*, adding, "It has never been done, so let sleeping dogs lie. . . ." The work, however, when revised, proved eminently successful. It is another of Riegger's freely atonal works, only seven minutes in . length. George Szell gave brilliant performances of the work with the Cleveland Orchestra in Cleveland and elsewhere in 1956, prompting Herbert Elwell to write:

> I was pleasantly surprised at the warm reception of his work here. Even persons who said they did not "understand" his music admitted that they intuitively sensed in it integrity and authenticity.

> I am coming more and more to the conclusion that it is Riegger who has been the real leader and pathfinder in contemporary American music and I was pleased that Cleveland at long last could make the acquaintance of this charming, unpretentious septuagenarian who is not only a master of his craft but in some ways a prophet and a seer. As one prominent Cleveland composer put it when listening to his work, "Here is the real thing."

Three major works of Riegger's last years are his Fourth Symphony, Opus 63 (1957); his Variations for Piano and Orchestra, Opus 54 (1953); and the Variations for Violin and Orchestra, Opus 71 (completed in 1959). The two latter were commissioned by the Louisville Orchestra, the Symphony by the Fromm Foundation. One can regret that commissions such as these did not come Riegger's way earlier in his career, but one must be grateful that they finally came. Other commissions came from the Stanley Quartet (Quintet for Piano and Strings, Opus 47, of 1951, a fine, strong work), from the University of Iowa (*Quintuple Jazz*, Opus 72, of 1959), from the Juilliard Musical Foundation (a setting, for voice and piano, of Dylan Thomas's poem "The Dying of the Light," of 1955), from conductor Thor Johnson (*Dance Rhythms*, Opus 58, of 1955), from the Koussevitzky Music Foundation (the Concerto for Piano and Woodwinds), and from the Conference on the Creative Arts sponsored by Boston University (*Festival Overture*, Opus 68, of 1957). These commissions gave Riegger, for the first time in his life, some leisure in which to compose, and enabled him to do less of the time-consuming hack-work he had been accustomed to performing.

No Riegger work had ever been done by the Boston Symphony until 1959, when both the *Study in Sonority* and the Fourth Symphony were presented. Riegger was among those American composers who apparently did not make an impression on Koussevitzky, and one wonders why. In any event, Boston was apparently ready for Riegger by 1959, for

Cyrus Durgin and other critics made up for lost time by going all out with enthusiastic praise. Of the *Study in Sonority*, Harold Rogers wrote in the *Christian Science Monitor* that "It is always a cause for rejoicing when an inventive mind goes exploring in the orchestra and pulls out something undreamed of." Durgin wrote of the Fourth Symphony:

> It is, upon first acquaintance, a work of much technical and orchestral stature, and of a great deal of expressive power. This is a Symphony which has both head and heart appeal, and whose texture ranges from free-flowing melody to grinding dissonance, with a good amount of mild and tonal harmony in between.

> Unless one is a qualified and licensed Prophet, prediction is but one man's guess. Yet I venture to think that this Symphony will wear well, and will emerge as a major score of American composition in the second half of the 20th Century. . . .

After Boston, one wonders what worlds are left to conquer. As far as I am aware, no Riegger work has yet been performed in Lincoln Center, either by resident or visiting organizations. Shortly after the premiere of his Third Symphony, Riegger observed to me, with his usual perfectly straight face, that he thought he was about to become the American composer most performed in Scandinavia. He estimated, however, that there were some 1,100 orchestras that had still never heard of him.

He was heard of, certainly, in Louisville. The two sets of Variations commissioned by the Louisville Orchestra are among the finest of Riegger's late works. Of the Variations for Piano and Orchestra, Theodore Strongin wrote (New York *Herald Tribune*, February 18, 1954):

> The *Variations*, twelve of them plus a theme and coda, are assorted in mood, but each does its job perfectly. Some dance, others throb with sentiment, still others are broad and noble in carriage. In none is the ear allowed to grow tired; the scoring is full of quick surprises and the rhythm makes every moment buoyant and free. . . . Everything is witty and neat, cool on the surface, warm and eloquent beneath. Because the work does not try too hard to be great, it becomes exactly that.

Riegger died as the result of a trivial accident, just a few days after the announcement of his selection as winner of the Brandeis Award for 1961. He tripped while walking near his home on a side street near Columbia University, and died after brain surgery a few days later at Columbia-Presbyterian Hospital. At his funeral, Carl Haverlin, President of Broadcast Music, Inc., spoke briefly and warmly:

. . . Wallingford Riegger, for those who knew him, will continue to be what he was to them—father or delightful companion or friend or teacher or composer. . . . His music, his bubbling good humor, his interest in puns, and words, his playing of little jokes upon his friends, his passion for all that seemed right to him, his thoughtfulness and generosity to others, many of them far more fortunate than he was—all these are still with us, impressed on printed page, on manuscript, on recordings or in the hearts and minds of those of us who were fortunate enough to know him. . . .

An X to the Left of the Writer

The American Scholar XXXVI/1 (Winter 1966-67)

There are times when it seems that one's mail consists entirely of questionnaires, most of them silly, and many of them impertinent. Letter writing, even in Business English, has apparently not for some time been considered a productive branch of Communications Arts; in any case, the Post Office clearly gives precedence in forwarding and delivery to bills, advertisements and solicitations of very slightly differentiated importunity. But the questionnaires are a class by themselves, and have not been given the study they deserve as the tribute of imitation paid by the American researcher to the American scholar.

Almost the first observation one makes is that the questionnaires are often accompanied by mimeographed or printed instructions of the most conspicuous rudeness. Those originating in state universities or schools of education are often equally notable for their idiocy and their peremptoriness. They normally demand immediate attention ("Return at once"—and with the recipient's five-cent stamp) and seldom bother to include a thank-you-in-advance for your time or your attention, whichever seems the more expendable. One is, however, occasionally reminded that one has been "selected" to receive the questionnaire, and that one is thus privileged to contribute one's mite to the successful completion of the sender's task. Candidates for doctorates are, as a general thing, especially offensive. Often, by the content of their covering form-letters (or, more properly, form-demands), as well as by the sheer beauty of their questions, they unknowingly reveal their immense lack of qualifications for scholarly work of any sort above the junior high school level, and betray the *tone* (as well as the expectations) of the institutions that harbor them.

The splendor of the language of the typical questionnaire is matched only by the solemnity of the purpose. When one is asked to specify the "major vocational commitments" of noted persons (example given: Beethoven—*Music*) or is asked to grade candidates for admission to dental schools on their Moral Attitudes (from "High Standards" as the most acceptable to "Licentious" as the least) or on Appearance ("Most Pleasing" to "Repulsive"), one cannot help feeling that humanity was never in history so well served or guarded against the possibility of mistakes. For this, a five-cent stamp seems a small contribution.

But occasionally the dreary procession of pointless or unanswerable questionnaires is enlivened by the arrival of one in which earnest nonsense is tempered by a faint melancholy fascination. Not long ago I received one of these, sent by a member of the psychology department of a large western university. The concern of this questionnaire was the "relative eminence," or "indices of eminence change," of writers born before 1870. One was asked to place "X marks to the left of the 25 writers" (but not to the left of the names of the writers) who have left works "most worthy to be called to the attention of our children and lay contemporaries" and to be preserved as a part of our heritage. *Et cetera,* Amen. One was not, mercifully, required to "rank order the names you have checked." Appended was a list of the names of 207 authors; recipients were invited to add names if they could think of any not included. But of course it is difficult to think when one is overcome by awe, and the questionnaire itself, being designed as a substitute for thinking, does not encourage one to go beyond its limits. The checklist serves up thought condensed, frozen and pre-sorted; one is seldom tempted to wonder why there are 207 names instead of 206 or 208, or how the names were "pre-selected." No one, to my knowledge, has spoken candidly about the essentially dictatorial nature of questionnaires, even of relatively polite or inoffensive ones. If one attempts to suggest that the answers sought are not simple, that not every question is resolved black or white, yes or no, or that there is no apparent reason for checking 25 items instead of 24 or 37 or 2 of the already arbitrary listing, one reveals oneself as a compromiser or perhaps even as a saboteur. One is reminded of the poor lady who, while tending an adding machine of some sort, reported to her supervisor that it made consistent errors, and who was thereupon summarily fired as a troublemaker.

O relative eminence! O measurement of altitude! We may not have read works of all of the 207 candidates, and we may not be sure what eminence is, but we can presume to rate them and it relatively. It is not important to know literature; what counts is reputation. Is an "eminent author" a thing similar in kind to an eminent general, or an eminent feature of a landscape? Is relative eminence a measure of current fashion, or did the author of the questionnaire believe that he intended something different? Or did he simply—what corruption! what lust for power and promotion!—wish to use us all to become himself an eminent authority on eminence?

It is of course a masquerade: simple inquisitiveness, aimlessly aroused, dressed in the fancy clothes of research and the exotic language of pseudo scholarship. One is sometimes tempted to find one's examples of precise prose and sweet reason among the unscholarly, especially in the thought and imagery of popular magazines and full-page advertisements. Nothing could speak more clearly, or briefly, of relative eminence than a caption in a travel magazine: *Greece is OUT—Egypt is IN!* No fuss, no questionnaires, no ambiguity. One knows what is meant and sees that it is so. And one immediately feels more easy when one sees that this firmness of touch can be applied not only to tourism but to literature. George Meredith is OUT—The Marquis de Sade is IN. (At least among those who *know.*) The eminence game is fun in all the arts: Carl Maria von Weber, Claude Lorraine, Thorvaldsen and Swinburne are OUT (low eminence ratings); Kleist, Magnasco, Carl Nielsen and totem poles are IN. But if one is to keep up, and to be *accurate,* one should look at one's ratings not less often than once a month. Things do move; and molehills have been known to become mountains.

When I was a child, we played *en famille* an "educational" parlor game called *Authors.* The authors immortalized on the playing cards of the set—identification of the authors' works was the winning trick of the game—were obviously selected for their eminence; they included, in addition to Dickens, Thackeray, Shakespeare, Sir Walter Scott and Milton, such eminent (or at least worthy of being called to the attention of our children) literary figures as Bulwer Lytton, Edmund Clarence Stedman, John Greenleaf Whittier, and General Lew Wallace. (But where were W. Harrison Ainsworth, Edna Lyall, and H. Rider Haggard?)

Were these authors selected or rejected by a committee or by tabulating the results of a questionnaire? I suspect not. Nor do I suppose that the company that published the game had hired an educational consultant, a child psychologist, or even an adult psychologist, to offer expert advice. In any event, the game reflected a conventional view of relative eminence in its time. But the point of the reminiscence perhaps lies elsewhere. My curiosity having been aroused, as I concluded that such a game could hardly be popular today, I decided to find out whether it was in fact still manufactured and distributed. I therefore made the effort of going out to inquire, with (or so it seems to me) results almost too appropriate to the undertaking. When I explained to a clerk that I was merely curious, and was seeking information, it became obvious that I was a nuisance, a nonconsumer, and possibly a dangerous nut. Since, on occasion, I can take a hint, and even make practical application of it, I decided that at the next place I visited I would say, with a proper air of importance, that I was *doing research.* And this, of course, works. No one can do enough to help serious people engaged on important labors of the mind.

One can only wish my eminence researcher luck. One is sure that he will find out, after a considerable expenditure in postage stamps, that Meredith has a low eminence rating, and Henry James a very high one. What will he do then? Is there any possibility that he will read—or, to be kind, that he will reread—Meredith to find out what's wrong with the poor fellow?

If he does, I should like to know, although I will never have faith in his methods. Of the peripheral "researcher" in literature, E. M. Forster wrote (in *Aspects of the Novel*) that "Everything he says may be accurate but all is useless because he is moving around books instead of through them; he either has not read them or cannot read them properly. Books have to be read (worse luck, for it takes a long time); it is the only way of discovering what they contain. A few savage tribes eat them, but reading is the only method of assimilation revealed to the west."

Eating them might add to our knowledge of taste. But an inquiry into "relative eminence" could have been completed in an hour or two in any large bookstore. The paperback presses provide up-to-the-minute answers by the evidence of what they have and what they keep in print. There is less of Meredith, for example, than of any English novelist ever considered "major"; he runs about even with Disraeli. (There is also, for those interested, very little of Balzac, at least in English.) But we all do know that there are many authors, great and small, who are in vogue, and whose every fugitive word is available in six or seven competing editions, with notes.

Meredith is an extreme example of an eminence diminished, perhaps justly. One expects that there are at least 25 writers (but why 25?) more worthy than he of "being called to the attention of our children," or preserved, or translated into Swahili. But this does not mean that he is not at all worthy (not of being classified, but of being read) or that his once immense reputation was not in some degree deserved. If we assume that our ancestors, who thought him a demigod of literature (see *The Encyclopaedia Britannica,* 14th edition), could have been so thoroughly mistaken, we merely emphasize our own fallibility, and accept fashion, or eminence by poll, as a judgment of something less constant than our own variability.

So much for "indices of eminence change." George Eliot was once much out of fashion, and is now again in favor, much helped by puffs from Professor Leavis. But some readers never forgot that she was worth reading. Meredith's reputation may never again be what it was, but "eminence" and fashion being what they are, this is clearly no guarantee against his being some day "rediscovered." He was, for all of his often fancy language, a serious writer, and he had to a refined degree an awareness of comedy and the uses of the comic spirit. And in the *Essay on Comedy* he did at least remind us that in scholarship as in literature, or indeed in any of the circumstances of our mortal careers, the final word should not be with the agelast, the one who never laughs.

The Wonderful World of Culture *Or: A Strictly Highbrow and Artistic Subject*
The American Scholar XXXV/3 (Summer 1966)

Some time ago I toyed with the idea of organizing a committee for the purpose of raising equestrian statues of American composers to form an avenue approaching Lincoln Center. While the encouragement I received was negligible, the idea recurs to me whenever I am forced to consider the consistently pedestrian nature of most pronouncements on the arts circulated in these United States. The *Summa Theologica*, or monument to America's current concern with the arts, appeared in the spring of 1965 under the imposing and characteristic title, *The Performing Arts: Problems and Prospects,* with the subtitle, *Rockefeller Panel Report on the future of theatre, dance, music in America.* This is, properly speaking, not a book; it is a publication: a model of the new style in Communications Arts that is destined to replace prose, and perhaps even exchange of ideas.

Although the volume is called a report, its tone is that of a Manifesto. But some readers may look at it in other ways: as a romance in the tradition of *Erewhon, Looking Backward, Brave New World,* or even *1984*; as an unconventional horror story somewhat deficient in suspense; as a contribution to the new folklore; or simply as a lexicon of misuse of the English language. Perhaps it is a combination of all of these. If, as has been said, the camel is a horse designed by a committee, there are grounds for suspecting that the writing of committee reports is on occasion entrusted to the camel.

One might begin with this possibility. "The performing arts" is itself a vulgarism so established that no one, apparently, any longer notices it. It is matched, in the language of this volume, by such delights as "the charitable dollar," "religious giving," and a variety of catachreses bewildering in their ingenuity and inelegance. But when writing of art and culture, or, more exactly, of "arts organizations" and "cultural standards," a certain imprecision and even incoherence are perhaps necessary. And perhaps the experts, "researchers," and members of the Sanhedrin who are the joint begetters of this work do in fact mean that the arts perform and that the dollar expresses emotion. When one considers, one sees that this is literally so: the arts, in partnership with the artistic dollar, are expected to perform miracles. It is the arts that will raise our "cultural standards" and that must "enhance the nation's cultural life." We are not permitted to conceive, in this mythology, that art *reflects* a culture or a way of life, or that culture, while it may have roots and traditions and embodiments, can hardly be said to have "standards." On the contrary; it is plain that in this folklore, art and culture are special varieties of consumer goods, foods that are "enriched," to be marketed in conventional ways, "with all the resources of advertising and public relations." The spectacular difference is that it is morally virtuous to sell these goods, *because they are good for the consumer.* One merely has to persuade more consumers that this is so.

They are also good for the manufacturers and distributors. According to the *National Economic Review* published by the New York *Times* on January 11, 1965, culture was a three billion dollar business in 1964, and will be worth seven billion by 1970. The *Review* notes that "Culture is the latest big business in the country . . . Interest in culture, say researchers in the field [*sic*!], has become the newest status symbol, and conspicuous esthetics may become the norm, to the surprise of no one."

And this, despite sanctimonious phrases about the beauty and the efficacy of art and culture, is what the *Report* is about. Its aesthetics are, at the mildest, as conspicuous as Lincoln Center. There is something touching in the *Report's* assumptions that art is a cure for most of our ills, including idleness (which, in the *Report,* is of course called *leisure*), that art "reminds us of our better nature," and so on, but these positions seem, in context, a bit strained. When it is possible to write cheerfully about "the sale of arts services" (by "arts organizations"), one is assuming either that the reader has accepted the premise that he is a consumer, or that the reader has no idea what one is talking about. The procedure is dishonest in either case.

As one would expect, the *Report* is concerned with "elemental matters" (elementary? fundamental?) such as "numbers of performing groups, types of facilities, character of services, and sources of financial support." It does admit that after all matters of "arts organization" are taken care of, "there must also be a sizable public, prepared through education . . ." and laments that it is impossible to determine "with statistical accuracy" whether such an audience exists today. That accuracy in these matters is never statistical is a concept foreign to the authors of nearly all reports; but no doubt we shall, eventually, as the folklore gains "increasing acceptance," be persuaded to accept as an Index of our Enhancement the accurate statistical reporting of such matters as the annual per capita consumption of Brahms in the United States, with breakdowns by sex, age, income, social status, and locality. The exhortation that inevitably follows is that we must do everything in our power, statistically speaking, to increase our individual and collective Brahms-ratings.

The *Report* is an almost flawless model of the twentieth century's most popular style. It is immensely *significant,* without ever being serious. Its most striking characteristic is its attempt to substitute for serious matters, such as art and culture, the factitious seriousness of "arts services," "arts organizations," and "cultural standards." The tone of the *Report* is earnest; but being earnest is not the same as being serious, any more than being nervous is the same as being sensitive. The significance of the *Report* resides precisely in this pretension of seriousness, in its confusion of the vocabularies of art and marketing, and in its substitution of statistical clichés and easy pieties for any real notions of the concerns of art. The *Report* is all the more important, or "significant," for these reasons. It defines for us the vocabulary of the art and culture trade, and lets us know, once and for all, the nature of the thinking that creates arts centers.

For those whose dream it is to dwell in marble halls, Lincoln Center may well represent "a pioneering experiment." We are to have arts centers, if the dream of the *Report* comes true, wherever the artistic dollar can put them. The *Report* handsomely concedes (p. 117) that when the arts centers are built, "of *equal importance* [italics mine]is the attention devoted to planning the artistic program for which the facilities will be used . . ." The horse —or the camel—is now lost somewhere behind the cart, but at least we know in which direction it has gone. The first televised production from the Los Angeles Music Center was a program featuring Dinah Shore, Bob Hope, Henry Mancini, a jazz organist, and a virtuoso of the *bossa nova,* a use of the facility that does show a certain kind of devoted attention. And Lincoln Center wishes to persuade us that an expensive arts center is needed to present plays by Arthur Miller and S. N. Behrman. This suggests that the artistic dollar, too, is subject to inflation.

"Equal importance" finds its parallel in the *Report's* doctrine of equal talent: "As talent is needed to create and perform a work of art, so equal talent—though of a different sort— is needed to create and govern the institutions that provide the settings for these arts." There are—or are there? —perhaps just a few concerned with the arts who will not accept this equation of the talent of a Beethoven with the talent of a Board member, however carefully auditioned the Board member may have been ("Board members should be as carefully screened as performers." p. 151).

In 1872 Nietzsche wrote: "Never has there been so much loose talk about art, and so little respect for it." He was born too soon. Nevertheless, in *The Birth of Tragedy* he said almost everything that can be said about the nature and fate of "the performing arts" in our day. Yet even he did not foresee the assumption that culture can be purchased or imposed, or imagine the mentality that could state as a matter of course that "for an arts institution to reach stardom requires time." He did foresee, with considerable loathing, the mentality that relates the pursuit of art to the collection of statistics and that suggests that "the performing arts have perforce been laggard in sharing in the research revolution." Nietzsche, moreover, knew exactly what this meant, which the authors of the *Report* quite evidently do not. In their charmingly innocent view, what this means is that "arts organizations" must study "their long-range goals in the community," acquire pertinent information about "audience composition and tastes," and "explore systematically what the continuing scientific revolution . . . can mean for the technological improvement of their artistic endeavors and for the strengthening of their economic sinews."

The notion of culture as something to be measured and consumed is a commonplace of the new folklore. It is defensible as a recognition of fact, the moment one redefines culture, or restores it to its original meaning in biology: "The artificial development of microscopic organisms in prepared media." This is the definition that the *Report* seems to accept; it conceals a real animosity toward people, who are conceived as organisms to be manipulated or developed. Art is in this way to serve the purpose of giving people, individually and collectively, a status rather than a function, and an image rather than an identity.

In a sentence remarkable for its grammatical slovenliness, art as the giver of image is delineated: "When the arts go abroad, as they are in increasing degree through cultural exchanges, they can disclose the vital and creative aspects of the countries originating them." This fine flower of thought for export is perhaps designed to show that we have rejected English as a means of communication, and substituted culture, or aspects. There are guilt and fear as well as bad grammar here. And the same guilt and fear underlie the statement that "a thriving development of the arts is essential to a well and safely balanced society." One wonders about safety, and whether no one has ever told the authors of the *Report* that art can be dangerous. (But not "the arts.") And when one comes on the thought that "increased leisure also creates a social imperative for the development of the arts," one can begin to worry as well as wonder.

On the other hand, there is reassurance in the *Report's* explicit statements. "The arts can be a major source of strength for the business community . . . Their availability certainly encourages new firms to locate in a city and helps attract tourists and conventions. They constitute a growing market and provide expanding avenues for employment. There are, therefore, compelling reasons why, in the interests of his community and, indeed, in his own self-interest, a businessman and his firm should be concerned with the cultural and artistic life of his community."

Has anyone heard this before?

> Some of you may feel that it's out of place here to talk on a strictly highbrow and artistic subject, but I want to come out flatfooted and ask you boys to O.K. the proposition of a Symphony Orchestra for Zenith . . . Culture has become as necessary an adornment and advertisement for a city today as pavements and bank-clearances. It's Culture, in theaters and art-galleries and so on, that brings thousands of visitors to New York every year and, to be frank, for all our splendid attainments we haven't yet got the Culture of a New York or Chicago or Boston—or at least we don't get the credit for it. The thing to do then as a live bunch of go-getters, is to *capitalize Culture;* to go right out and grab it.

Pictures and books are fine for those that have the time to study 'em, but they don't shoot out on the road and holler "This is what little old Zenith can put up in the way of Culture." That's precisely what a Symphony Orchestra does so . . . it goes right into Beantown and New York and Washington; it plays at the best theaters to the most cultured and moneyed people; it gives such class-advertising as a town can get in no other way; and the guy who is so short-sighted as to crab this orchestra proposition is passing up the chance to impress the glorious name of Zenith on some big New York millionaire that might—that might establish a branch factory here!

The paragraphs above are from *Babbitt,* by Sinclair Lewis, published in 1922.[1] The research revolution has not greatly refined thought or speech on strictly highbrow and artistic subjects. But it is no longer out of place to talk about them anywhere.

To be sure, the *Report* does allude, on every fourth or fifth page, to Excellence, a quality that it finds admirable, and of which we should have as much we can get. All of this concern for excellence would be considerably more convincing if the *Report* itself showed the slightest respect for the English language, or the slightest indication of concern with excellence in its use. The compilation and writing of the *Report* took two years, the labor of thirty members of the Panel, a "Special Studies Project Staff," forty-four "panel participants," thirty-one "others contributing to the study," a number of experts who prepared papers, and, obviously, a good deal of money. In view of this, one might think that the Fund might have been able to afford a copy editor, if not a writer or two, instead of another two or three "researchers" whose labors over the allotted time produced the staggering information that orchestral musicians, dancers, and actors are not overpaid, and that opera companies operate at a deficit. But the propriety of showing respect for art by showing respect for language obviously never occurred even to those members of the party who should know better. In the new folklore a "writer" is evidently anyone who owns a typewriter, just as a "researcher" is anyone empowered by a committee to go about asking people what time it is.

One wonders how the authors of this *Report* define excellence in art. Perhaps they think it is the same as "stardom." Matthew Arnold was a polite, well-educated man, who used words precisely, and who, despite his good manners, or perhaps because of them, was able, when writing of Culture, to use the words Philistine and Barbarian. We may need these words again, as we need a Matthew Arnold to remind us of what excellence really is, and where it dwells: "among high and steep rocks, . . . reached only by those who sweat blood to reach her." As an antidote to the Rockefeller's bathetic little manifesto on Culture and Organization, one might do worse than turn again to the literate decency of *Culture and Anarchy.*

---

[1] Copyright, 1922, by Harcourt, Brace & World, Inc.; copyright, 1950, by Sinclair Lewis. The excerpt above is reprinted by permission of Harcourt, Brace & World, Inc.

INDEX

Dorothy Klotzman holds B.S. and M.S. degrees in composition from the Juilliard School. As a graduate student there she was awarded a fellowship in the Literature and Materials of Music program and was an assistant to Richard Franko Goldman.

A professor in the Department of Music at Brooklyn College, she has served as its Chairman since 1971. Through the years she has won a variety of prizes and awards as a musician and educator, including, in 1972, the Harbison Award for gifted teaching (Danforth Foundation). She conducts the Brooklyn College Symphonic Band, which she organized in 1970. Under her direction it has premiered several important new works by American composers and has performed many of the finest and most difficult contemporary pieces for winds and percussion.

Dorothy Klotzman has made numerous appearances with The Goldman Band as a guest conductor and has also made a number of arrangements which the band performs regularly.

————————————————

The Institute for Studies in American Music at Brooklyn College, established in 1971, is a division of the Department of Music in the college's School of Performing Arts. The Institute contributes to the field of American-music studies by publishing a monograph series, bibliographies, and a periodical newsletter. In addition to serving as an information center, the Institute participates in conferences and symposia dealing with all areas of American music, including art music, popular music, and the music of oral tradition. It encourages and supports research by sponsoring fellowships for distinguished scholars and is currently supervising the series *Recent Researches in American Music,* published by A-R Editions, Inc. I.S.A.M. activities also include concerts held at Brooklyn College for students, faculty, and the public.